Microsoft® Expression

ILLUSTRATED

Introductory

D0077196

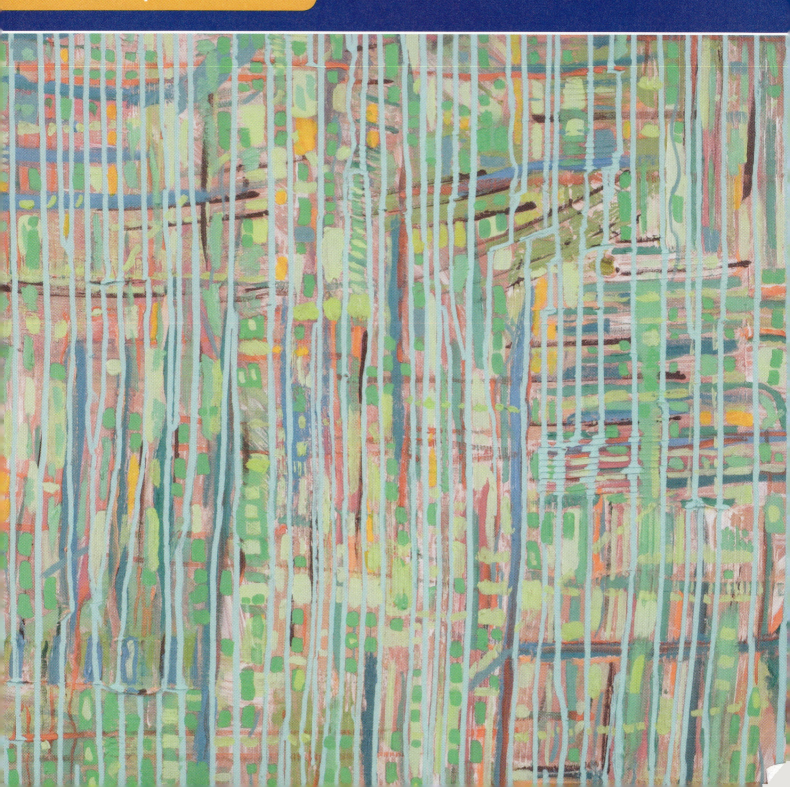

Microsoft® Expression® Web 3

ILLUSTRATED

Introductory

Julie Riley

COURSE TECHNOLOGY
CENGAGE Learning™

Australia • Brazil • Japan • Korea • Mexico • Singapore • Spain • United Kingdom • United States

COURSE TECHNOLOGY
CENGAGE Learning™

Microsoft Expression Web 3—Illustrated Introductory
Julie Riley

Executive Editor: Marjorie Hunt

Associate Acquisitions Editor: Brandi Shailer

Senior Product Manager: Christina Kling Garrett

Associate Product Manager: Michelle Camisa

Editorial Assistant: Kim Klasner

Director of Marketing: Cheryl Costantini

Senior Marketing Manager: Ryan DeGrote

Marketing Coordinator: Kristen Panciocco

Developmental Editor: MT Cozzola

Senior Content Project Manager: Cathie DiMassa

Proofreader: Harry Johnson

Indexer: Rich Carlson

QA Manuscript Reviewers: John Freitas, Jeff Schwartz, Susan Whalen

Cover Designer: GEX Publishing Services

Cover Artist: Mark Hunt

Composition: GEX Publishing Services

© 2011 Course Technology, Cengage Learning

ALL RIGHTS RESERVED. No part of this work covered by the copyright herein may be reproduced, transmitted, stored or used in any form or by any means graphic, electronic, or mechanical, including but not limited to photocopying, recording, scanning, digitizing, taping, Web distribution, information networks, or information storage and retrieval systems, except as permitted under Section 107 or 108 of the 1976 United States Copyright Act, without the prior written permission of the publisher.

For product information and technology assistance, contact us at
Cengage Learning Customer & Sales Support, 1-800-354-9706

For permission to use material from this text or product, submit all requests online at **www.cengage.com/permissions**
Further permissions questions can be emailed to
permissionrequest@cengage.com

ISBN-13: 978-0-538-75041-7
ISBN-10: 0-538-75041-3

Course Technology
20 Channel Center Street
Boston, MA 02210
USA

Cengage Learning is a leading provider of customized learning solutions with office locations around the globe, including Singapore, the United Kingdom, Australia, Mexico, Brazil, and Japan. Locate your local office at:
international.cengage.com/region

Cengage Learning products are represented in Canada by Nelson Education, Ltd.

To learn more about Course Technology, visit **www.cengage.com/coursetechnology**

To learn more about Cengage Learning, visit **www.cengage.com**

Purchase any of our products at your local college store or at our preferred online store
www.CengageBrain.com

Trademarks:
Some of the product names and company names used in this book have been used for identification purposes only and may be trademarks or registered trademarks of their respective manufacturers and sellers.

Microsoft and the Office logo are either registered trademarks or trademarks of Microsoft Corporation in the United States and/or other countries. Cengage Course Technology is an independent entity from Microsoft Corporation, and not affiliated with Microsoft in any manner.

Printed in the United States of America
1 2 3 4 5 6 15 14 13 12 11 10

Brief Contents

Preface x

Expression Web 3

Unit A: Getting Started with Microsoft Expression Web 3.0 ....Expression Web 1

Unit B: Creating a Web Site...Expression Web 23

Unit C: Adding Text and Links ....Expression Web 47

Unit D: Structuring and Styling Text ....Expression Web 71

Unit E: Working with Pictures ....Expression Web 97

Unit F: Enhancing a Design with CSS..Expression Web 121

Unit G: Designing Site Navigation ....Expression Web 147

Unit H: Testing and Publishing Your Web Site..Expression Web 171

Glossary ....Glossary 1

Index..Index 1

Contents

Preface x

Expression Web 3

Unit A: Getting Started with Microsoft Expression Web 3.0 ....**Expression Web 1**

Understanding Web Design Software ....Expression Web 2
    Understanding Web standards

Starting Microsoft Expression Web..Expression Web 4
    Starting Expression Web quickly

Exploring the Expression Web Workspace..Expression Web 6
    Thinking like a designer

Opening a Web Page and Previewing It in a Browser...Expression Web 8

Working with Views and Panels ....Expression Web 10

Viewing Web Page Elements and Visual Aids ....Expression Web 12
    Combining software programs for Web design

Getting Help..Expression Web 14

Printing and Closing a Page and Exiting Expression Web ....Expression Web 16
    Saving and closing files

Practice ....Expression Web 18

Unit B: Creating a Web Site..**Expression Web 23**

Researching and Planning a Web Site...Expression Web 24
    Organizing your site

Planning the Page Layout ....Expression Web 26
    Using basic page layouts
    Avoiding a dated design

Creating a Web Site ....Expression Web 28
    Using Expression Web templates to build a site

Creating a Web Page and Setting CSS Options..Expression Web 30

Adding a Title, Page Description, and Keywords...Expression Web 32

Importing Web Pages ....Expression Web 34
    Understanding Web site addresses

Managing Web Pages and Folders..Expression Web 36

Changing the Web Site View ....Expression Web 38

Practice ....Expression Web 40

Unit C: Adding Text and Links ....**Expression Web 47**

    Pasting Text into a Web Page .... Expression Web 48

    Typing Text and Inserting Symbols .... Expression Web 50

        Text-based navigation

    Checking Spelling and Using the Thesaurus .... Expression Web 52

        Checking the spelling in an entire Web site

    Creating an Internal Link .... Expression Web 54

        Maintaining your links

        Understanding absolute and relative URLs

    Creating an External Link .... Expression Web 56

        Ensuring accuracy of URLs

    Creating and Linking to a Bookmark .... Expression Web 58

    Creating an E-Mail Link .... Expression Web 60

        Writing good link text

        Avoiding spam generated by e-mail links

    Copying and Pasting Content Between Pages .... Expression Web 62

    Practice .... Expression Web 64

Unit D: Structuring and Styling Text ....**Expression Web 71**

    Structuring Content with HTML .... Expression Web 72

        Understanding screen readers

    Creating Paragraphs and Line Breaks.. Expression Web 74

    Creating Headings.. Expression Web 76

        Creating a visual hierarchy

        Introducing XHTML

    Creating Lists... Expression Web 78

        Using lists for site navigation

        Understanding browser defaults

    Understanding Cascading Style Sheets.. Expression Web 80

    Creating an Element-Based Style Rule .... Expression Web 82

    Modifying a Style Rule .... Expression Web 84

        Taking control of your styles

    Creating a Class-Based Style Rule... Expression Web 86

        Understanding the cascade in Cascading Style Sheets

        Working with CSS font measurement units

    Applying and Removing a Class-Based Style Rule............................ Expression Web 88

        Using multiple style sheets

    Practice .... Expression Web 90

Unit E: Working with Pictures..**Expression Web 97**

    Understanding Web Graphics..Expression Web 98

        Finding photographs for your site

    Inserting a Picture ....Expression Web 100

        Writing meaningful alternate text

    Resizing and Resampling a Picture ....Expression Web102

        Thinking in pixels

    Editing a Picture...Expression Web 104

        Using the Pictures toolbar

    Setting Wrapping Style and Margins ....Expression Web 106

    Setting Auto Thumbnail Options ....Expression Web 108

        Maintaining a consistent graphical style

    Creating a Thumbnail Picture..Expression Web 110

    Styling a Thumbnail Picture ....Expression Web 112

        Understanding automatically generated styles

    Practice ....Expression Web 114

Unit F: Enhancing a Design with CSS..**Expression Web 121**

    Understanding CSS Layouts...Expression Web 122

    Adding Background Images..Expression Web 124

    Setting a Background Color Using the Eyedropper ....Expression Web 126

    Setting a Background Color Using a Swatch..................................Expression Web 128

        Ensuring sufficient color contrast

    Adding a Border ....Expression Web 130

    Adding a Font Family..Expression Web 132

        Choosing fonts

    Styling Headings ....Expression Web 134

    Styling the Footer...Expression Web 136

        Understanding semantic div ids

    Setting Padding and Margins...Expression Web 138

    Practice ....Expression Web 140

Unit G: Designing Site Navigation ....**Expression Web 147**

    Understanding Effective Navigation ....Expression Web 148

        Architecting information

        Learning how your visitors think

    Creating an Interactive Button ....Expression Web 150

    Editing an Interactive Button ....Expression Web 152

    Creating a Navigation Bar...Expression Web 154

Adding a Navigation Bar to Site Pages ....Expression Web 156
    Choosing fonts for navigation buttons
Understanding Link Styles ....Expression Web 158
    Using more than one set of link styles on a site
Creating Link Styles ....Expression Web 160
    Rearranging your styles
Practice ....Expression Web 162

Unit H: Testing and Publishing Your Web Site..**Expression Web 171**
Verifying Hyperlinks ....Expression Web 172
Viewing and Editing Page Titles..Expression Web 174
Understanding Accessibility...Expression Web 176
    Being visible to search engines
Testing Accessibility ....Expression Web 178
Understanding Connection Types...Expression Web 180
    Choosing a hosting provider
Setting Up and Connecting to a Publishing Destination....................Expression Web 182
    Testing your pages using SuperPreview
Publishing a Web Site..Expression Web 184
    Excluding unfinished files from being published
Practice ....Expression Web 186

Glossary...**Glossary 1**
Index ....**Index 1**

Preface

Welcome to *Microsoft Expression Web 3—Illustrated Introductory*. If this is your first experience with the Illustrated series, you'll see that this book has a unique design: each skill is presented on two facing pages, with steps on the left and screens on the right. The layout makes it easy to learn a skill without having to read a lot of text and flip pages to see an illustration.

This book is an ideal learning tool for a wide range of learners—the "rookies" will find the clean design easy to follow and focused with only essential information presented, and the "hotshots" will appreciate being able to move quickly through the lessons to find the information they need without reading a lot of text. The design also makes this book a great reference after the course is over! See the illustration on the right to learn more about the pedagogical and design elements of a typical lesson.

Coverage

This text is organized into eight units. In these units, students learn how to use the Expression Web interface; plan and create a Web site and Web pages; add text and links; structure text with HTML and style text with Cascading Style Sheets; work with pictures; enhance a design with CSS; design site navigation; and test and publish a Web site.

New features covered in this edition are improved publishing functionality, making it faster and easier to publish multiple files and to multiple sites; support for SFTP (Secure File Transfer Protocol); and support for Internet Explorer 8.

Each two-page spread focuses on a single skill.

Introduction briefly explains why the lesson skill is important.

A case scenario motivates the the steps and puts learning in context.

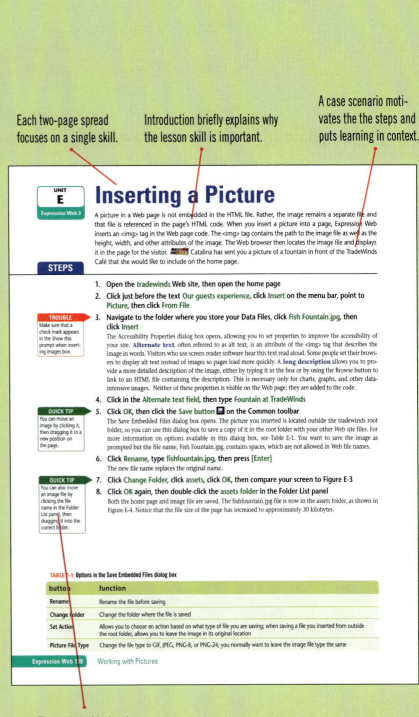

Tips and troubleshooting advice, right where you need it–next to the step itself.

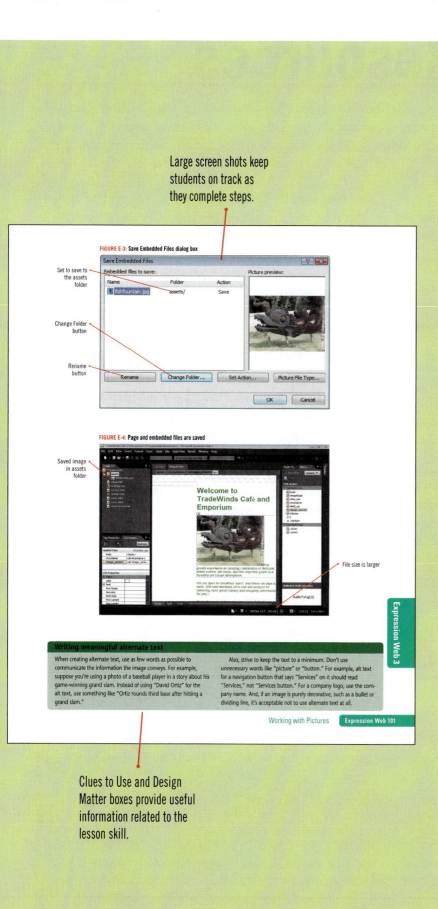

Large screen shots keep students on track as they complete steps.

Clues to Use and Design Matter boxes provide useful information related to the lesson skill.

Assignments

The lessons use TradeWinds Cafe as the case study. The assignments on the yellow pages at the end of each unit increase in difficulty. Data files and case studies provide a variety of interesting and relevant business applications. Assignments include:

- **Concepts Review** consists of multiple choice, matching, and screen identification questions.

- **Skills Review** provides additional hands-on, step-by-step reinforcement.

- **Independent Challenges** are case projects requiring critical thinking and application of the unit skills. In each Independent Challenge, students create a Web site that builds from unit to unit. The Independent Challenges increase in difficulty, with the first one in each unit being the easiest. Independent Challenges 2 and 3 become increasingly open-ended, requiring more independent problem solving.

- **Real Life Independent Challenges** are practical exercises in which students perform activities to help them with their everyday lives.

- **Advanced Challenge Exercises** set within Independent Challenges provide optional steps for more advanced students.

- **Visual Workshops** are practical, self-graded capstone projects that require independent problem solving.

Instructor Resources

The Instructor Resources CD is Course Technology's way of putting the resources and information needed to teach and learn effectively into your hands. With an integrated array of teaching and learning tools that offer you and your students a broad range of technology-based instructional options, we believe this CD represents the highest quality and most cutting edge resources available to instructors today. The resources available with this book are:

- **Instructor's Manual**—Available as an electronic file, the Instructor's Manual includes detailed lecture topics with teaching tips for each unit.

- **Sample Syllabus**—Prepare and customize your course easily using this sample course outline.

- **PowerPoint Presentations**—Each unit has a corresponding PowerPoint presentation that you can use in lecture, distribute to your students, or customize to suit your course.

- **Figure Files**—The figures in the text are provided on the Instructor Resources CD to help you illustrate key topics or concepts. You can create traditional overhead transparencies by printing the figure files. Or you can create electronic slide shows by using the figures in a presentation program such as PowerPoint.

- **Solutions to Exercises**—Solutions to Exercises contains every file students are asked to create or modify in the lessons and end-of-unit material. Also provided in this section, there is a document outlining the solutions for the end-of-unit Concepts Review, Skills Review, and Independent Challenges. An Annotated Solution File and Grading Rubric accompany each file and can be used together for quick and easy grading.

- **Data Files for Students**—To complete most of the units in this book, your students will need Data Files. You can post the Data Files on a file server for students to copy. The Data Files are available on the Instructor Resources CD-ROM, the Review Pack, and can also be downloaded from www.cengage.com/coursetechnology.

Instruct students to use the Data Files List included on the Review Pack and the Instructor Resources CD. This list gives instructions on copying and organizing files.

- **ExamView**—ExamView is a powerful testing software package that allows you to create and administer printed, computer (LAN-based), and Internet exams. ExamView includes hundreds of questions that correspond to the topics covered in this text, enabling students to generate detailed study guides that include page references for further review. The computer-based and Internet testing components allow students to take exams at their computers, and also saves you time by grading each exam automatically.

COURSECASTS   **Learning on the Go. Always Available…Always Relevant.**

Our fast-paced world is driven by technology. You know because you are an active participant—always on the go, always keeping up with technological trends, and always learning new ways to embrace technology to power your life. Let CourseCasts, hosted by Ken Baldauf of Florida State University, be your guide into weekly updates in this ever-changing space. These timely, relevant podcasts are produced weekly and are available for download at http://coursecasts.course.com or directly from iTunes (search by CourseCasts). CourseCasts are a perfect solution to getting students (and even instructors) to learn on the go!

Acknowledgements

Author Acknowledgements

Julie Riley Writing or revising a book is not a solo effort. I've been fortunate to work with a talented and dedicated team to bring this edition to print. Thanks to Marjorie Hunt for giving me the opportunity to work on such a rewarding project. Quality Assurance testers John Freitas and Susan Whalen meticulously tested each unit and greatly improved the quality and accuracy of what you hold in your hands. Christina Kling-Garrett and Cathie DiMassa skillfully guided the book through development and production. MT Cozzola provided her magical editorial touch to make each lesson clearer and more meaningful than they would otherwise have been. MT, I greatly respect your ability to uphold your high standards, maintain your poise, and keep your sense of humor even through difficult times. Thank you to my friends and family for their love and support. And a special thanks to my husband Brian, who is unfailingly supportive and who once again took up the household slack so I could work on "The Book."

Read This Before You Begin

Frequently Asked Questions

What are Data Files?

A Data File is a Web site, text file, image file, or another type of file that you use to complete the steps in the units and exercises to create the final Web site that you submit to your instructor.

Where are the Data Files?

Your instructor will provide the Data Files to you or direct you to a location on a network drive from which you can download them. Alternatively, you can follow the instructions on the next page to download the Data Files from this book's Web page.

What software was used to write and test this book?

This book was written using a typical installation of Microsoft Expression Web 3 installed on a computer with a typical installation of Windows Vista. It was tested using a typical installation of Expression Web 3 and Windows 7.

The browser used for any steps that require a browser is Internet Explorer 8.

Do I need to be connected to the Internet to complete the steps and exercises in this book?

Some of the exercises in this book assume that your computer is connected to the Internet. If you are not connected to the Internet, see your instructor for information on how to complete the exercises. We recommend using Microsoft Internet Explorer 8 or later or Mozilla Firefox 3.5 or later.

Creating Web sites that have not been built through previous consecutive units

If you begin an assignment that requires a Web site that you did not create or maintain before this unit, you must perform the following steps:

1. Copy the Solution Files folder from the preceding unit for the Web site you wish to create on the hard drive, Zip drive, or USB storage device. For example, if you are working on Unit D, you need the Solution files folder from Unit C. Your instructor will furnish this folder to you.

2. Start Expression Web, click File on the menu bar, then click Open Site.

3. Navigate to the location where you placed your Solution Files, then click the root folder for the site you are working on. For example, the root folder for the ConnectUp site is called connectup.

4. Click the local root folder, then click Open.

Downloading Data Files

In order to complete many of the lesson steps and exercises in this book, you are asked to open and save Data Files. A **Data File** is a partially completed file that you use as a starting point to complete the steps in the units and exercises. The benefit of using a Data File is that it saves you the time and effort needed to create a file; you can simply open a Data File, save it with a new name (so the original file remains intact), then make changes to it to complete lesson steps or an exercise. Your instructor will provide the Data Files to you or direct you to a location on a network drive from which you can download them. Alternatively, you can follow the instructions in this lesson to download the Data Files from this book's Web page.

1. Start Internet Explorer, type www.cengage.com/coursetechnology/ in the address bar, then press [Enter]

2. Click in the Enter ISBN Search text box, type 9780538750417, then click Search

3. When the page opens for this textbook, click the About this Product link for the Student, point to Student Downloads to expand the menu, and then click the Data Files for Students link

4. If the File Download – Security Warning dialog box opens, click Save (If no dialog box appears, skip this step and go to Step 6)

5. If the Save As dialog box opens, click the Save in list arrow at the top of the dialog box, select a folder on your USB drive or hard disk to download the file to, then click Save

6. Close Internet Explorer and then open My Computer or Windows Explorer and display the contents of the drive and folder to which you downloaded the file

7. Double-click the file 750417.exe in the drive or folder, then, if the Open File – Security Warning dialog box opens, click Run

8. In the WinZip Self-Extractor window, navigate to the drive and folder where you want to unzip the files to, then click Unzip

9. When the WinZip Self-Extractor displays a dialog box listing the number of files that have unzipped successfully, click OK, click Close in the WinZip Self-Extractor dialog box, then close Windows Explorer or My Computer

You are now ready to open the required files.

Getting Started with Microsoft Expression Web 3.0

Microsoft Expression Web 3 is a Web design program for creating modern, standards-compliant Web sites. Expression Web is part of a suite of programs called Expression Studio. The other programs in Expression Studio include Expression Design (for creating graphics), Expression Blend (for designing Web-based user interfaces), and Expression Encoder (for preparing videos for the Web).  You recently have been hired to redesign the Web site for TradeWinds, a store and café in Florida. Catalina Romero, the owner of TradeWinds, wants a more visually appealing site that reflects the fun spirit of TradeWinds. You begin by getting familiar with Expression Web.

OBJECTIVES

Understand Web design software

Start Microsoft Expression Web

Explore the Expression Web workspace

Open a Web page and preview it in a browser

Work with views and panels

View Web page elements and visual aids

Get help

Print and close a page and exit Expression Web

Understanding Web Design Software

Microsoft Expression Web allows you to design, publish, and manage professional-looking, modern Web sites. You decide to learn more about Expression Web.

Using Expression Web, you can:

- ### Create Web pages and Web sites

  You can use Expression Web to create a single Web page or an entire Web site. A **Web page** is essentially a text file, usually written in a language called **HTML (HyperText Markup Language)**. The code within the file often references images and other multimedia files that appear in the page. In Expression Web, HTML Web pages are saved by default with the file extension ".html." A **Web site** is a collection of related Web pages, linked together. Web pages are viewed through a **Web browser**, software that interprets HTML code and displays it as the text and images. Popular browsers include Microsoft Internet Explorer, Mozilla Firefox, Apple Safari, and Google Chrome.

- ### See what your site will look like as you design it

  Expression Web is a **WYSIWYG** program (pronounced WIZ-EE-WIG), which stands for "What You See Is What You Get." WYSIWYG programs make Web design much faster by showing you what your page will look like in a Web browser as you are designing it. They also allow you to create Web pages without knowing any HTML code.

- ### Add text, images, multimedia files, and scripts to your Web pages

  Web pages today are much more than just text. Expression Web allows you to add images and JavaScript behaviors to add interactivity and interest to your site.

- ### Create Web sites that adhere to Web standards

  The Internet thrives because almost any computer with any browser can view any Web site. This flexibility is a result of organizations developing recommendations for creating Web pages, called **Web standards**. Designing a Web page is similar to writing; if you want readers to understand what you write, you must use proper grammar and spelling. But Web browsers are less forgiving than readers of a written document; if the syntax in an HTML file is wrong, the browser won't display it at all—or at least not in the way you expected. Expression Web works behind the scenes to write code that correctly follows Web standards.

- ### Create Cascading Style Sheets to format and lay out your pages

  Cascading Style Sheets (CSS), often called just **style sheets**, are rules that describe the presentation and visual design of a page, including fonts, colors, and often the layout and positioning of elements on the page. See Figure A-1 for an example of how style sheets change the appearance and layout of a Web site. Expression Web has outstanding tools to help you design and manage styles.

- ### Manage your Web site

  Keeping a Web site in good working order requires you to manage many files. Larger Web sites may have thousands of files to keep track of, including HTML files, CSS files, image and other multimedia files, and scripts. When you create a Web site in Expression Web, the program helps you to organize the files and to make sure that any links between files are not broken if you move them to different folders.

- ### Publish your Web site

  People will not be able to visit your Web site until you publish it to a Web server. A **Web server** is a computer connected to the Internet that stores Web pages and other Web content and displays it to a Web browser. When you **publish** your site, you copy the Web pages and related files from your computer to a Web server. Expression Web makes it easy to publish your site.

QUICK TIP

Before WYSIWYG programs existed, Web designers had to type HTML code, save the file, and then open the file in a browser to see what it looked like.

FIGURE A-1: Web page with and without a style sheet applied

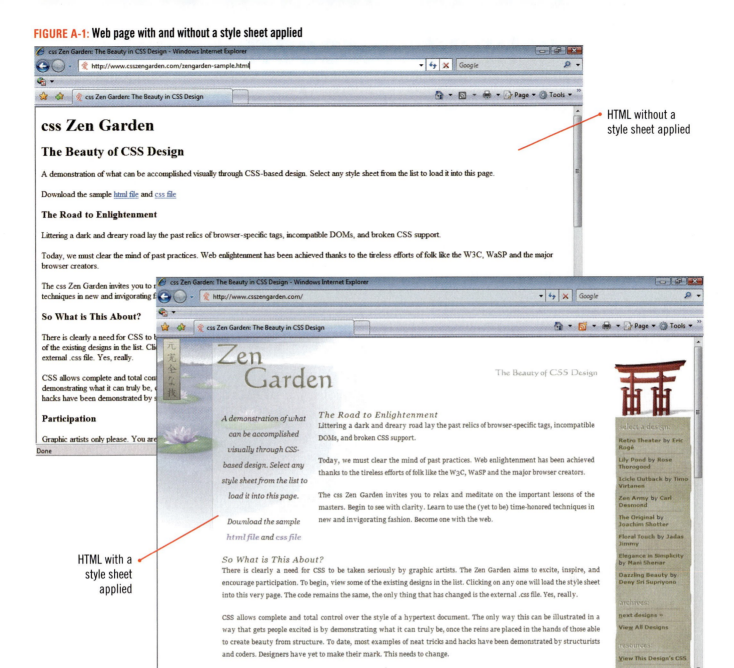

Understanding Web standards

In the early days of the Web, designers used HTML code that was optimized for certain browsers. Many Web sites displayed "Best Viewed in Internet Explorer" or "Best Viewed in Netscape" banners to encourage visitors to use that particular browser to view the site. Thankfully those days, known as the "browser wars," are past. The modern way to design sites is to create code that complies with standards set by the **World Wide Web Consortium (W3C)** and other organizations, rather than code that targets a specific browser. The advantages include knowing that your Web pages will be viewable by future versions of browsers, increasing their accessibility to visitors with disabilities, and making your site more visible and friendly to search engines. That's why it's so important that Expression Web creates standards-compliant code. For more information on Web standards, visit the Web Standards Project (WaSP) Web site at www.webstandards.org.

Starting Microsoft Expression Web

Your first step in using Expression Web is to start the program. You can start Expression Web by using the Start button on the Windows taskbar or by double-clicking a shortcut located on the Windows desktop. If you need additional assistance, contact your instructor or technical support person. You decide to launch Expression Web so you can explore the interface.

STEPS

QUICK TIP

You can also open the program by clicking the Start button, typing the first few letters of the program name into the search box, then choosing Microsoft Expression Web 3 from the list that displays.

TROUBLE

If a Web Site tab appears in the Expression Web window when it opens, click Site on the menu bar, then click Close.

1. **Click the Start button** on the taskbar
   The Start menu opens.

2. **Point to All Programs on the Start menu**
   The All Programs menu opens, listing the programs installed on your computer in alphabetical order.

3. **Click Microsoft Expression on the All Programs menu**
   The Microsoft Expression Studio programs installed on your computer appear, as shown in Figure A-2.

4. **Click Microsoft Expression Web 3**
   The Expression Web program window opens, as shown in Figure A-3.

5. **If necessary, click the Maximize button on the Expression Web program window**
   The program window fills the screen.

Starting Expression Web quickly

Windows provides several options to quickly start Expression Web. One method is via the Recently Opened Programs pane on the Start menu. When you open the Start menu, the programs you recently opened are listed in the left pane. If you use Expression Web frequently, it may show up in this list, allowing you to open it without scrolling to the Microsoft Expression folder on the All Programs menu. You can also set Expression Web to always show up at the top of the Start Menu. To do this, right-click the program name in the Start menu, then click Pin to Start Menu. A third way is to add a shortcut to your Windows desktop. To do this, click the Start button, point to All Programs, click the Microsoft Expression folder, then right-click Microsoft Expression Web 3. Point to Send to, then click Desktop (create shortcut). The shortcut is added to the Windows desktop, and you can double-click it to start the program.

FIGURE A-2: Starting Microsoft Expression Web

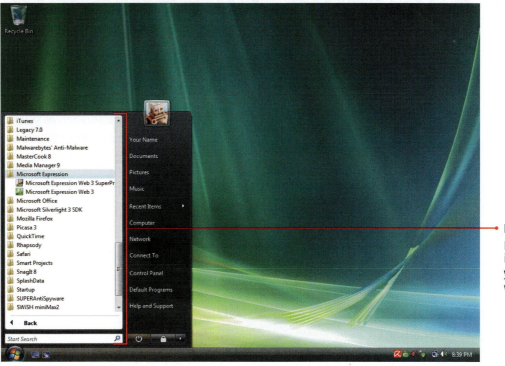

List of all programs installed; your list will differ

FIGURE A-3: Expression Web program window

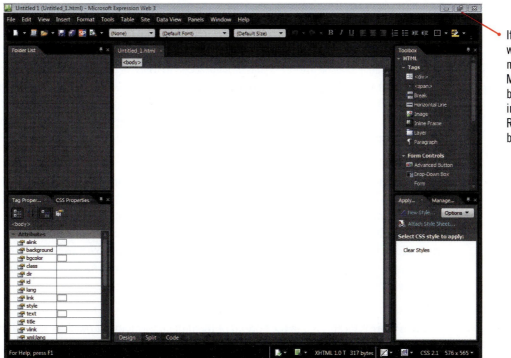

If program window is not maximized, Maximize button appears instead of Restore Down button

Exploring the Expression Web Workspace

The Expression Web workspace is where you create and edit Web pages. The program window consists of a title bar, menu bar, Common toolbar, editing window, panels, and a status bar. As you work in the program, you'll see that all the elements work together to provide an integrated approach to designing and organizing your site.  You spend some time exploring the Expression Web workspace.

DETAILS

Using Figure A-4 as a guide, familiarize yourself with the following elements:

- **Title bar**

  The **title bar** appears at the very top of the program window. It shows the title of the current Web site (if a site is open) or the current Web page (if only a page is open), the file path of the current site or page enclosed in parentheses, and the name of the program. Buttons for minimizing, resizing, and closing the program window are located on the right side of the title bar.

- **Menu bar**

  The **menu bar**, located under the title bar, includes all Expression Web commands organized into menus such as File and Edit. Many of these commands are also available in other locations in the program, such as in a panel or toolbar, or can be activated through keyboard shortcuts.

- **Common toolbar**

  The **Common toolbar**, located under the menu bar, provides access to common tasks in Expression Web. Tasks include creating a new page, saving and opening files, and common text formatting options such as font, font size, bold, and italic. You can also insert a table, picture, or hyperlink using the Common toolbar. This toolbar is one of many available in Expression Web, but it's the only toolbar displayed by default. For a description of the toolbars available in Expression Web, see Table A-1.

- **Panels**

  Panels are small, moveable windows that provide access to tools for specific tasks. They appear on either side of the Expression Web window. Four panels are displayed by default: Folder List in the top left, Tag Properties in the bottom left, Toolbox in the top right, and Apply Styles in the bottom right. Many panels appear as **merged panels**. These panels occupy the same space and appear one in front of the other. For example, the Apply Styles and Manage Styles panels are merged. The panel title bar displays the name of the currently active panel.

- **Editing window**

  The **editing window** is the large area under the Common toolbar where you do most of your design work. A tab appears at the top of the editing window to indicate that one Web page (with the default filename Untitled_1.html) is currently open. If you open additional Web pages, additional tabs appear here. If you open a Web site, an additional tab appears here. The **quick tag selector bar** is located just below the tab area; it allows you to easily select and edit specific HTML tags on your Web page. In the bottom-left corner of the editing window, you can access the **Show Design View**, **Show Split View**, and **Show Code View** buttons, which allow you to view the Web page you are editing in different ways.

- **Status bar**

  The **status bar** is located along the bottom of the program window. It provides helpful information such as any errors or incompatibilities detected in your code, instructions for getting help, and current settings such as Visual Aids mode and Style Application mode—features that help you to place and format elements on a Web page. For the page you are currently editing, the status bar also indicates the file size, the page dimensions, and which versions of HTML and CSS are being used to create your Web page.

FIGURE A-4: Expression Web workspace

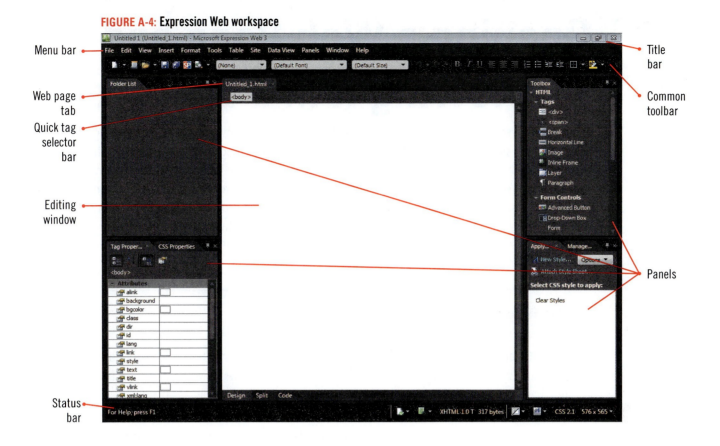

Menu bar
Web page tab
Quick tag selector bar
Editing window
Status bar
Title bar
Common toolbar
Panels

TABLE A-1: Toolbars available in Expression Web

toolbar	use to
Standard	Perform basic functions such as Open, New Document, Undo, and Redo
Formatting	Format text
Code View	Work directly in the HTML code
Common	Easily access commonly used tools from Formatting and Standard toolbars
Dynamic Web Template	Quickly navigate within a Dynamic Web Template
Master Page	Navigate and edit Master Pages
Pictures	Change appearance of pictures in your Web page
Positioning	Set size and positioning of page elements
Style	Apply, rename, and remove styles
Style Application	Control how styles are applied manually to page elements
Tables	Create and modify tables within a Web page

Expression Web 3

Thinking like a designer

Becoming a good Web designer involves more than learning the tools of a program like Expression Web. You also learn to think more closely about design itself. As you visit Web sites, evaluate what you like or don't like about them. Notice the color scheme, font and typography, images, content, layout, and navigation. Does the visual design appeal to you? Is the type easy to read? How easily can you find what you're looking for? What exactly is it about the design, content, or site structure that is successful or not successful? If it's a site you visit often, what aspects of the site draw you back for another visit? By thinking critically about Web sites, you'll start to develop an eye for details that you can use when you create your own sites.

Opening a Web Page and Previewing It in a Browser

In Expression Web, you can open either individual Web pages or an entire site at once. Opening a Web page opens a single page and displays it in the editing window. Opening a Web site displays the list of files included in that site in the Folder List panel and also opens a Web site tab in the editing window. A frustrating aspect of Web design is that no design looks exactly the same in every browser. Expression Web does a good job at approximating what your page will look like in a Web browser, but you will want to check the appearance of your page in different browsers that your visitors might be using. You can use the **Preview** feature to check your pages as you work. You open the TradeWinds home page to view the current design, and preview it in a browser.

STEPS

1. **Click File on the menu bar, then click Open**

   The Open File dialog box opens.

2. **In the Open File dialog box, navigate to the drive and folder where you store your Data Files**

   Many students store files on a flash drive, but you can also store files on your computer, a network drive, or any storage device indicated by your instructor or technical support person.

   TROUBLE

   If your system is set to not display file extensions, you won't see those in your file list; this is not a problem.

3. **Double-click the Unit A folder**

   See Figure A-5. The folder opens, displaying a list of files. Web site files need to be named in a certain way so that they can be used on any type of Web server. When you name any file that is part of a Web site, including HTML files, CSS files, and image files, you should use only lowercase letters, numbers, or underscores. Don't use spaces, capital letters, or special characters such as # or *. By following these rules, you ensure that your site will function on any server.

4. **Click the file a_1.html, then click Open**

   The TradeWinds home page opens in Expression Web, as shown in Figure A-6. This is the home page of the Web site you have been hired to redesign. Catalina is unhappy with this design and wants a look that is more fun and appealing to visitors.

   QUICK TIP

   If you are editing a Web page, you must save it before you preview it. You haven't made any changes to this page, so you don't need to save it first.

5. **Click the Preview button list arrow on the Common toolbar**

   A menu of options for opening installed browsers in different window sizes opens, as shown in Figure A-7. Your list of options varies depending on which browsers are installed on your computer; you may see more or fewer options than those in the figure, and your default browser and window size might vary. The window size options represent common screen resolutions that site visitors may be using. Two of the most common screen resolutions are 1024 × 768 and 800 × 600. Web pages look different in different browsers and at different resolutions, so you should preview a page in several combinations as you work on a design.

   QUICK TIP

   To add a browser to the Preview list, click the Preview button list arrow, choose Edit Browser List, click Add, click Browse, navigate to the .exe file for the browser you wish to add (likely located in the Program Files folder), click Open, type the browser name in the Name box, then click OK twice.

6. **Click the first option in the list**

   The TradeWinds home page opens in a browser window. You can return to Expression Web and choose another option from the list to view your page using a different available browser and window size. If more than one browser is installed on your computer, you can also choose the option to Preview in Multiple Browsers. If you choose this option, Expression Web previews the current page in all available browsers at once by opening multiple browser windows. If you click directly on the Preview button instead of on the list arrow, your page opens in the last option you chose.

7. **Click the Close button on the browser title bar**

   The browser window closes and you return to the Expression Web workspace.

FIGURE A-5: Open File dialog box

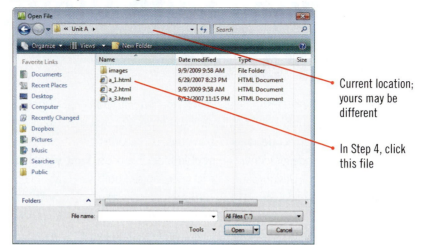

Current location; yours may be different

In Step 4, click this file

FIGURE A-6: Current TradeWinds home page

FIGURE A-7: Preview button list

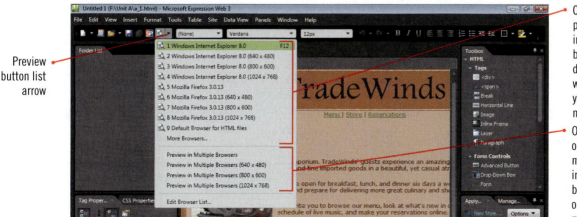

Preview button list arrow

Options to open page in any installed browser at different window sizes; your list may differ

Options to open page in multiple installed browsers at once; your list may differ

Working with Views and Panels

Expression Web includes three views for working with a page: Design, Code, and Split. **Design view** shows what a page will look like when viewed in a browser. This is the default view in Expression Web and the view you work in most often. **Code view** displays the HTML code that the page is written in, so it's useful if you are writing or revising code, or identifying trouble spots in a page. **Split view** is a combination view; it displays both a Code pane and a Design pane so that you can see both views at once when necessary. Panels appear in all views. They consolidate tools related to specific tasks essential to building a Web site, such as modifying styles or selecting HTML tag properties. Panels can be rearranged to suit your working style. You experiment with viewing Web pages in different ways and opening and closing panels.

STEPS

1. **Click the Show Code View button at the bottom of the editing window**

   The HTML code for the open Web page appears, as shown in Figure A-8. When using Expression Web, you do not need to actually write any HTML code, but any time you make an edit in the editing window in Design view, Expression Web generates the HTML code for the page.

   QUICK TIP

   As you edit in the Design pane, watch the code that Expression Web generates in the Code pane. You can pick up a surprising amount of knowledge about the underlying code just by observing.

2. **Click the Show Split View button at the bottom of the editing window**

   Split view shows a combined view of the current page in Code view at the top of the editing window and in Design view at the bottom. It's useful for debugging a page because you can make changes in the Design view window and see the resulting code in the Code view window.

3. **Click the Show Design View button at the bottom of the editing window**

   The page now appears in Design view, the default view.

4. **Click the Tag Properties tab on the Tag Properties panel, drag it to the editing window, then release the mouse button, as shown in Figure A-9**

   The Tag Properties panel is now floating in the middle of the screen. You can drag it with your mouse if you want it in a different location.

   QUICK TIP

   You can place the panel above the editing pane, above or below existing panels, or merge it with another panel.

5. **Click the Tag Properties tab, drag it with your mouse to the upper-right corner of the screen until you see a blue outline appear, then release the mouse button**

   The Tag Properties panel moves to where you dragged it. Re-arranging panels can be helpful in customizing the workspace to reflect your work style.

6. **Click the Turn on AutoHide button** 🔲 **on the CSS Properties panel, then click the Turn on AutoHide button** 🔲 **on the Folder List panel**

   See Figure A-10. Folder List and CSS Properties panels collapse to the left edge of the screen. You can see the title of each of them but the contents have been hidden. This is useful if you are working on a small screen and need to free up space.

7. **Point to Folder List on the left edge of the screen, point to CSS Properties on the left edge of the screen, then point to the editing window**

   As you point to each panel, the panel opens and its contents are revealed. When you move your mouse away from the panel, the panel collapses. This is called AutoHide.

   QUICK TIP

   To AutoHide all panels at once, click Panels on the menu bar, then click AutoHide All Panels.

8. **Click the Turn off AutoHide button** 🔲 **on the CSS properties panel, then click the Turn off AutoHide button on the Folder List panel**

   The panels now remain open.

9. **Click Panels on the menu bar, then click Reset Workspace Layout**

   The panels return to their original positions. The Reset Workspace Layout command restores all panels to their default locations and sizes. It does not affect menus or toolbars.

FIGURE A-8: Code view

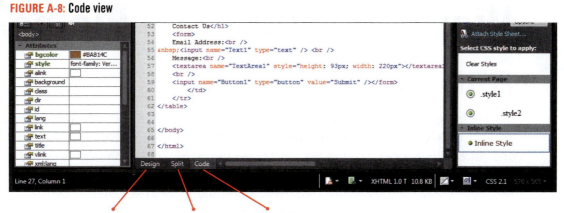

Show Design View button Show Split View button Show Code View button

FIGURE A-9: Relocated Tag Properties panel

Relocated Tag Properties panel

Tag Properties tab

FIGURE A-10: Panels with AutoHide on

Panels are collapsed

Viewing Web Page Elements and Visual Aids

Most Web pages are made up of many different elements, including the HTML page itself, images, tables, and text. Many of these elements are not normally visible in Design view; they only show up in Code view. The **visual aids** in Expression Web allow you to see and modify empty or invisible elements of your page while in Design view so you do not have to work in Code view. Visual aids do not affect the content of your files, only the way that you view them on screen.  You decide to examine how the current TradeWinds home page is constructed and what elements the page uses.

STEPS

TROUBLE

If a visual aid does not appear, click View in the menu bar, point to Visual Aids, then click Show.

1. **Click anywhere within the first paragraph of text, click the <table> tag on the quick tag selector bar, then scroll to the top of the page if necessary**

   Clicking anywhere within an element on a page displays the visual aids for that element. Clicking the <table> tag highlights the table and displays a visual aid indicating that this is a table, as shown in Figure A-11. Expression Web also outlines the table with visible dashed borders so you can see the structure. The Tag Properties panel on the left side of the screen now displays the properties of the selected table, including the width and alignment. From this, you determine that the entire page is laid out using a table. A **table** is a grid-like container with rows and columns. It can be used to display data or to lay out elements on a page. The preferred method of laying out pages uses CSS, not tables. When you redesign this site, you want to change the page to a CSS-based layout.

2. **Click anywhere within the text Welcome! at the top of the page, then click the h1 tab on the visual aid that appears**

   See Figure A-12. The visual aid "h1" indicates that this text is a Heading 1. HTML provides six levels of **headings**. Heading 1 is the highest level and text at this level is usually the largest; Heading 6 is the least important and text at this level is usually the smallest. The light-colored areas above and below the heading show the margins that have been applied and indicate that the top margin is larger than the bottom margin.

QUICK TIP

Without visual aids, you would have to estimate where elements like forms start and stop on a page.

3. **Click inside the text Email Address**

   A visual aid appears indicating that this text is contained inside a form and outlining the boundaries of the form. A **form** is an HTML element that allows visitors to send information from a Web site.

4. **Click the underlined word Menu directly under the TradeWinds image**

   This is a hyperlink. A **hyperlink**, also called a link, is text or an image that visitors click to open another Web page, Web site, or file.

5. **Click the image of the fish fountain**

   A visual aid appears around the image. The "img" indicates that it is an image, and the ".style1" indicates that a style, named style1, has been applied to it. See Figure A-13. The Tag Properties change to display the properties of this image and style.

Combining software programs for Web design

Web sites rarely consist of only pages of text. Almost all sites include images, and some also feature video, animation, and sound. This is why Web designers and developers use several software programs to create a site. For example, you might use Expression Design to create an illustration, Adobe Flash to create an animation, and Corel Paint Shop Pro to enhance your digital photos. You can then use Expression Web to insert these elements into your Web page. It's not uncommon for Web designers to use four or five different software programs while developing a site.

FIGURE A-11: Table selected showing visual aid

Table tag selected in quick tag selector bar

Tab indicates table element is selected

First paragraph of text

Table tag indicates that Tag Properties displayed apply to the selected table

Scrollbar

Shaded area is the selected table; because the entire Web page is contained in the table, the full page is shaded

FIGURE A-12: h1 element selected showing visual aid

h1 tag selected in quick tag selector

h1 tab on visual aid

h1 tag indicates that Tag Properties displayed apply to the h1 element selected

Shading shows area of the page occupied by the h1 element

Lighter color indicates margins on h1 element; the top margin is wider than the bottom margin

FIGURE A-13: img element selected on page

img tag is selected in quick tag selector

Tab indicates an img (image) element is selected and that a style named style1 has been applied to it

Properties of selected image, including the file path and styles applied

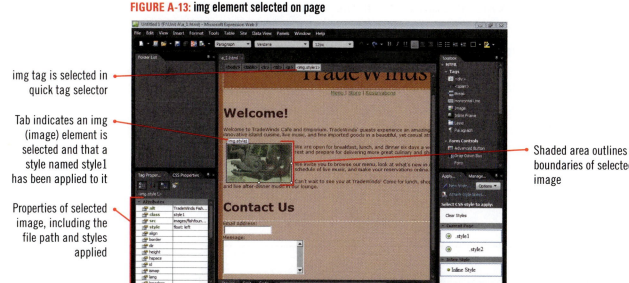

Shaded area outlines boundaries of selected image

Expression Web 3

Getting Help

Expression Web has a User Guide that you can refer to if you have questions or problems. You can press [F1] or click Help on the menu bar and then click User Guide on the Help menu. The User Guide opens where you can search or browse for information and guidance. The Help menu includes additional help resources, such as a Microsoft Expression Web Online command, which you can use to access articles, video tutorials, and discussions with other Expression Web users. You want to learn more about the features available on the status bar in Expression Web, and decide to consult the User Guide.

STEPS

1. **Click Help on the menu bar, then click User Guide**

   The Expression Web User Guide window opens, as shown in Figure A-14. This window includes a toolbar and three tabs, Contents, Index, and Search. You can use the toolbar buttons to navigate through the Help materials, and to change the way the Help window is displayed. To get help, you can click the Contents tab to browse the table of contents, the Index tab to browse an alphabetical list of all topics, or the Search tab to search for a topic.

   QUICK TIP

   When you are working in the Index tab, you can type the first part of a word or phrase and the selection will move to terms starting with those letters in the index.

2. **Click the plus sign next to Getting started, click the plus sign next to Quick start, then click Adjusting your workspace**

   The Adjusting your workspace topic appears. This has some information on the status bar but you want more details.

3. **Click the Index tab, click in the Type in the keyword to find text box if necessary, type stat, then double-click status bar**

   Information about the status bar appears. After you scroll down the page and read the information, you decide to search the user guide to see if you can find any additional information about the status bar.

4. **Click the Search tab, type status bar in the Type in the keyword to find text box, then click List Topics**

   A list of topics related to the status bar appears.

5. **Double-click Check spelling in one or more pages, then scroll down the page**

   See Figure A-15. Information about checking spelling appears. The search term you entered, "status bar," is highlighted in blue in the text to help you find it easily. You decide this information is not helpful to you and you want to return to the previous status topic.

6. **Click the Back button ⬅ on the menu bar**

   TROUBLE

   If your computer is not connected to a printer, you will not be able to complete this step. Contact your technical support person for assistance.

7. **Click the Print button 🖨 on the menu bar, then click Print in the Print dialog box**

   The page you were viewing prints.

8. **Click the Hide button on the menu bar, then click the Show button**

   The tabs are hidden and then shown. This is helpful if you want to make more space to see the topic you are reading.

9. **Click the Close button ❌ on the User Guide window title bar**

   The User Guide window closes and you return to the Expression Web workspace.

FIGURE A-14: Expression Web User Guide window

Toolbar

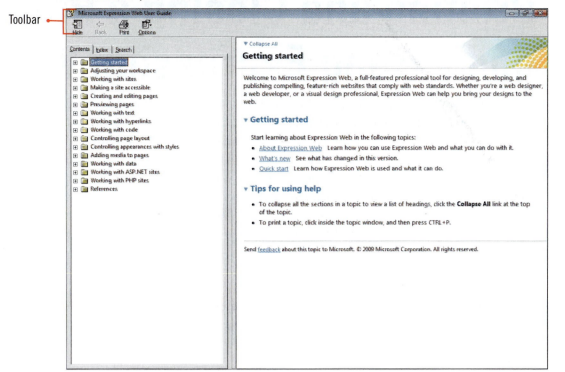

FIGURE A-15: Status bar help topic

Words searched on

Selected topic

Search term is highlighted

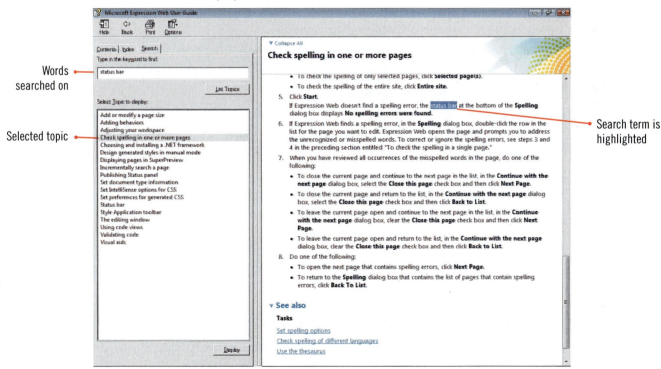

Printing and Closing a Page and Exiting Expression Web

When printing a Web page in Expression Web, background colors and images do not print. (Printing the page exactly as it looks in Design view or in a browser would strain your printer's ink resources.) However, printing can be useful for reference or for marking up a page with design comments. When you launch Expression Web, it opens the last Web page or site you were working on, so it's a good idea to close your Web page or site before you exit Expression Web. That way if you are sharing a computer with others, Expression Web won't try to open files that might no longer be available (if, for instance, the files are stored on a flash drive that's been removed from the computer).  You are finished reviewing the TradeWinds site, so you decide to print and close the TradeWinds home page and exit Expression Web.

STEPS

QUICK TIP

The Print Page Setup dialog box uses variables in the header and footer boxes to indicate what to print; for example, "&T" means titles and "&P" means page number.

1. **Click File on the menu bar, then point to Print**

   The Print submenu opens displaying the commands Print, Print Preview, and Page Setup, as shown in Figure A-16. Clicking Print opens the Print dialog box and prints the Web page as it would print from the Internet Explorer browser. Clicking Print Preview shows you what the page will look like when printed. Clicking Page Setup gives you options to change the page margins and the header and footer. By default, the page title prints in the header and the page number prints in the footer. You can replace these with your own text if you'd like.

2. **Click Print Preview on the Print submenu**

   The Print Preview window opens, displaying a preview of the Web page, as shown in Figure A-17. This view shows you what your page will like when printed. In this mode, background colors and background images do not appear, although regular images such as the fish fountain do appear. Using the buttons on the Print Preview toolbar, you can print the page, close Print Preview, navigate between pages if the Web page will span more than one printed page, and zoom in on the page.

3. **Click Print at the top of the Print preview window**

   The Print dialog box opens.

TROUBLE

If your computer is not connected to a printer, you will not be able to print the Web page. Contact your technical support person for assistance.

4. **Click OK in the Print dialog box**

   The page prints. Print Preview closes and you return to the editing window in Design view.

5. **Click File on the menu bar, then click Close as shown in Figure A-18; if you are prompted to save changes, click No**

   You did not make any intentional changes to this page, so you do not need to save changes. The Web page closes. The title bar now displays "Microsoft Expression Web 3," indicating that no Web page or Web site is currently open.

6. **Click File on the menu bar, then click Exit**

   Expression Web closes.

Saving and closing files

If you try to close a Web page that you have made changes to, a message box opens asking if you want to save your changes. If you click Yes and the page has been saved previously, Expression Web saves your changes to the file. If you click Yes and the file has not been saved previously, Expression Web opens the Save As dialog box so that you can save a copy of the file with a different filename, in a different location, or both. This is useful when you want to create a new Web page that contains text or design elements from a previous page but you need to keep the original file intact. If you click No in the message box, Expression Web closes the file, and any changes are lost. Clicking Cancel cancels the closing of the Web page and returns you to the Expression Web workspace.

FIGURE A-16: Print submenu

Print submenu

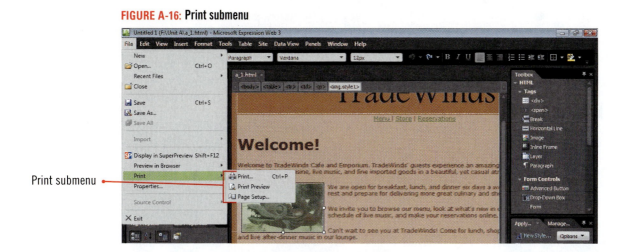

FIGURE A-17: Print preview of TradeWinds home page

Print button

Zoom In button

Close button

Page title prints in header by default

Page is white because background colors and images do not print

Page number prints in footer by default

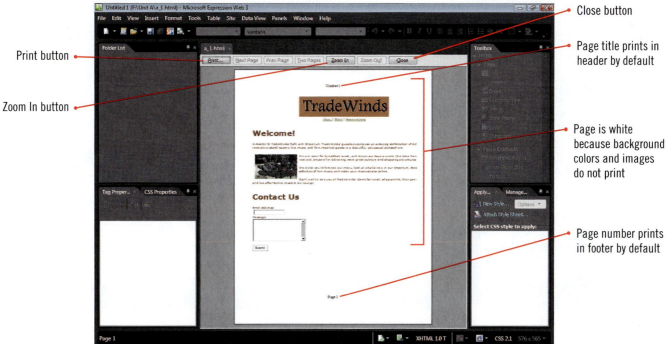

FIGURE A-18: File menu

Close command

Practice

SAM

For current SAM information including versions and content details, visit SAM Central (http://samcentral.course.com). If you have a SAM user profile, you may have access to hands-on instruction, practice, and assessment of the skills covered in this unit. Since we support various versions of SAM throughout the life of this text, you will want to check with your instructor for instructions and the correct URL/Web site to access those assignments.

Concepts Review

Label each element in the Expression Web workspace shown in Figure A-19.

FIGURE A-19

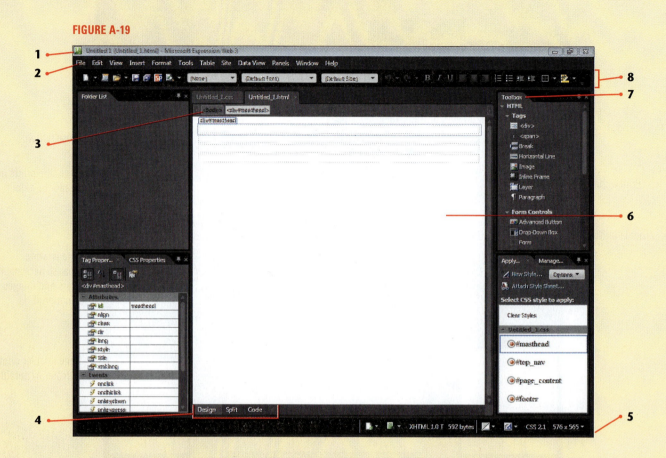

Match each term with the statement that best describes it.

9. **Panel**	**a.** Displays the HTML code for the active Web page
10. **Menu bar**	**b.** Displays the active Web page as it will look in a Web browser
11. **Editing window**	**c.** Allows you to select individual HTML tags
12. **Common toolbar**	**d.** Small window that provides access to tools for specific tasks
13. **Code view**	**e.** Includes all the Expression Web commands
14. **Quick tag selector bar**	**f.** Provides access to common tasks and formatting options
15. **Design view**	**g.** Main area where you edit Web pages

Select the best answer from the list of choices.

16. **The ability to see what your Web page would look like in a browser as you edit it is called:**
    a. Cascading Style Sheets.
    c. WYSIWYG.
    b. Visual aids.
    d. Editing window.

17. **Recommendations for creating Web sites that are written by organizations such as the W3C are called:**
    a. Programming rules.
    c. Web standards.
    b. Cascading Style Sheets.
    d. Code views.

18. **Copying Web site files from your computer to a Web server is called:**
    a. Publishing.
    c. Code View.
    b. Developing.
    d. Hyperlinking.

19. **A computer that stores and displays Web pages and other content is a:**
    a. Web browser.
    c. Web site.
    b. Web standard.
    d. Web server.

20. **Rules that describe the presentation and formatting of a Web page are:**
    a. Cascading Style Sheets.
    c. HTML files.
    b. JavaScript files.
    d. Image files.

Skills Review

1. **Start Microsoft Expression Web and explore the Expression Web workspace.**
   a. Launch Expression Web.
   b. If a Web site opens automatically, close it.
   c. Locate the title bar.
   d. Locate the menu bar.
   e. Locate the Common toolbar.
   f. Locate the editing window.
   g. Locate the status bar.

2. **Open a Web page and preview it in a browser.**
   a. Open the Open File dialog box.
   b. Navigate to the drive and folder where you store your Data Files, then double-click a_2.html in the Unit A folder. Your screen should resemble Figure A-20.
   c. Preview the page in the Internet Explorer browser in an 800 × 600 window. If this option is not available on your computer, choose a different resolution.

FIGURE A-20

3. **Work with views and panels.**
   a. Switch to Code view.
   b. Switch to Split view.
   c. Switch to Design view.
   d. Move the Tag Properties panel to the top of the editing window.
   e. Turn on AutoHide for the CSS Properties panel.
   f. Turn off AutoHide for the CSS Properties panel.
   g. Reset your workspace to the default layout.

4. **View Web page elements and visual aids.**
   a. Click anywhere in the first paragraph, then click the div#column_l tab on the quick tag selector bar.
   b. Click inside the text **Why we're different**.
   c. Click the word **Home** near the top of the page.
   d. Click the photo of the man.

Skills Review (continued)

5. **Get help.**
   a. Open the Expression Web User Guide.
   b. In the Index tab, browse for information on images.
   c. Find a topic related to images that interests you and double-click on it.
   d. Read the information on the page.
   e. Close the Expression Web User Guide window.

6. **Print and close a page and exit Expression Web.**
   a. Use Print Preview to preview the page.
   b. Print the page.
   c. Close the Web page; if prompted, do not save changes to the page.
   d. Exit Expression Web.

Independent Challenge 1

As part of your redesign of the TradeWinds Web site, you decide to review the music page. You need to view the current music page and start considering what changes you want to make.

a. Start Expression Web.
b. Open file a_3.html from the drive and folder where you store your Data Files. Your screen should resemble Figure A-21.
c. Select elements on the page and notice the visual aids that appear. Select a table, a hyperlink, and an HTML heading.
d. Move the Tag Properties panel to the bottom right of the screen.
e. AutoHide the Manage Styles panel.
f. Restore the workspace to its original layout.
g. Change the view to Split view.
h. Change the view to Design view.
i. Write down three changes you would make to improve the appearance and functionality of this page. These can include changes to the design or content.
j. Close the Web page, then exit Expression Web.

FIGURE A-21

Independent Challenge 2

Note: This Independent Challenge requires an Internet connection.

You have been hired as a Web designer for *Get Real*, an online news magazine. Your manager, Rex Treger, has asked you to find ways to reduce the costs of running the Web site by making it easier to maintain. You have read a little about Web standards and think that redesigning the site to be more standards-compliant could help the company meet this goal. You also think that the company could benefit in other ways from applying Web standards.

a. Go to your favorite search engine and search on the term **Web standards business case**.
b. Find at least two good articles that describe the "business case" for Web standards—in other words, articles that describe how businesses can save money or benefit in other ways by building standards-compliant sites.
c. Write at least two paragraphs for your manager, explaining all the business benefits of using Web standards.

Independent Challenge 2 (continued)

Advanced Challenge Exercise

- Find additional articles explaining the reasons organizations don't build sites that comply with Web standards.
- Based on your additional research, write a paragraph explaining why companies sometimes resist using Web standards. Add a sentence or two expressing why you do or do not feel these are good arguments against using Web standards.

Independent Challenge 3

Note: This Independent Challenge requires an Internet connection.

Designers today are creating beautiful sites using Cascading Style Sheets to control the design and layout. Many Web sites feature sample CSS-based designs, and Web designers often visit these gallery sites for inspiration. Most galleries feature snapshots of the sites and allow visitors to comment on the design. Hone your design skills by visiting some CSS-based Web sites and evaluating them.

a. Go to your favorite search engine and type **CSS design gallery**.

b. Follow some of the links until you find one or two sites that are galleries of CSS-based Web site designs. You may have to click a page called "gallery," "showcase," or something similar to find the Web site examples.

c. Browse the thumbnail images and find two that catch your interest.

d. Read any comments that visitors have written about both of the sites that you chose.

e. Click the thumbnail images to visit both sites.

f. Take notes about what you like or don't like about the design and content of both sites.

g. Write a paragraph about each site that includes the topic of the site, who you feel the intended audience is, and what you liked and didn't like about the design.

Advanced Challenge Exercise

- For each Web site, write a paragraph describing why you think the sites either deserve or don't deserve to be showcased in a CSS gallery.
- For each Web site, write a description of the changes you would make if you were redesigning the site.

Real Life Independent Challenge

Note: This Independent Challenge requires an Internet connection.

Developing a Web site is a great way to publicize your business or hobby. For this challenge, you will build a Web site of your choosing. You will pick not only the topic but also the audience. You will start by evaluating the design of sites that cover the same subject or audience. Throughout this book, you will design and build the site.

This Real Life Independent Challenge will build from unit to unit, so you must complete the Real Life Independent Challenge in each unit to complete your Web site.

a. Write down the topic and the audience for your Web site. Describe the audience's demographics—age, gender, interests, and any other important characteristics.

b. Go online and find at least two sites that cover the same topic as the one you plan to design.

c. Evaluate the page layout, navigation, content, color scheme, typography, and use of images, video, or animations.

d. Write a paragraph describing which elements of the sites (from the preceding list) you felt were well-designed and which were poorly designed, and why.

e. Find at least two sites that target the same audience as yours but cover a different topic. For example, if you are planning to develop a music site for women over age 40, find sites targeting this group but covering topics other than music.

f. For the two sites with similar audiences, write two paragraphs discussing whether the color, layout, content, navigation, and use of imagery and multimedia were appropriate for the sites' intended audiences. Explain why they were appropriate or inappropriate for the audience.

Expression Web 3

Visual Workshop

Launch Expression Web. Rearrange your workspace to match Figure A-22. When you have finished, press [Print Screen], paste the image into a word-processing program, add your name at the top of the document, print the document, close the word processor without saving changes, then exit Expression Web. If you are prompted to save your changes, click No.

FIGURE A-22

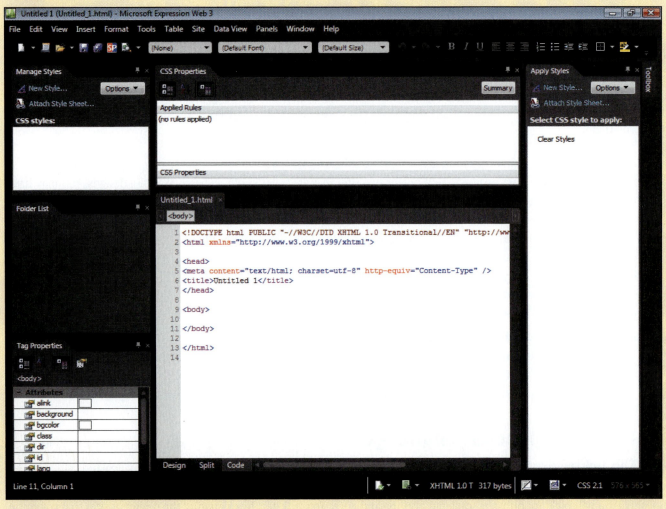

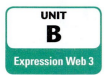

Creating a Web Site

If you want your site to accomplish certain goals, such as selling products or sharing family photos, you need to do some planning and research up front. In this unit, you learn about the Web site planning process and its role in developing a successful Web site. You also learn how to use the tools in Expression Web to create and manage a Web site and an individual Web page.  You meet with Catalina Romero to discuss her expectations and goals for the TradeWinds site redesign, and then you begin developing the new site.

OBJECTIVES

Research and plan a Web site

Plan the page layout

Create a Web site

Create a Web page and set CSS options

Add a title, page description, and keywords

Import Web pages

Manage Web pages and folders

Change the Web site view

Researching and Planning a Web Site

The Web site development process can be organized into six phases, as shown in Figure B-1: research and plan, design, build, test, publish, and market. By researching and planning a site before you begin building it, you can use the information to guide your design decisions along the way. ▰▰▰ You meet with Catalina to better understand her business goals. After some additional research, you create a plan for the site.

DETAILS

Developing a Web site involves these steps:

QUICK TIP

Also consider the maintenance factor; for example, don't plan a daily news feature if the site doesn't have the staff or resources to maintain it.

• ### Research and plan the site

The goals for your Web site drive the entire research and planning process. Consider the goals of both the site owner and the site visitor. For example, your new design should satisfy Catalina's goals to promote live entertainment and new products, and her visitors' goals of getting directions and contact information.

Next, learn as much as possible about your intended audience. Table B-1 describes some methods you can use to gather this information. Catalina's market research reveals that most site visitors are age 30 to 55, and many access the site using a dial-up connection.

Based on your analysis of the site's goals and audience, decide what features are important. You decide that features important to the TradeWinds site include: a section on the store page highlighting new products, a schedule of live music, and a section on the home page to promote products and/or events.

QUICK TIP

Visiting other Web sites targeted to your audience can help you quickly get an idea for an appropriate look and feel.

• ### Design the site

Consider the characteristics of both the business and the audience when designing a site's look and feel. For example, an insurance company site might need a conservative design to communicate stability, while a music site geared toward teens might want a wild color scheme to convey a more irreverent attitude. You want the TradeWinds design to look polished and worldly, yet fun and casual.

The next stage involves creating a **site map**, a diagram depicting the structure of the Web site—that is, how the pages are organized within the site, and where the links are between pages. The TradeWinds site map is shown in Figure B-2. Finally, design the **page layout**, the placement of content, graphics, and navigation on each page in the site.

QUICK TIP

More people are using cell phones and other small devices to visit sites rather than a desktop or laptop computer.

• ### Build and test the site

Building the site means creating the site and each page within Expression Web. This also includes writing the content and creating or gathering graphics.

It is critical to test your site before you publish it. Although Design view in Expression Web approximates the way a site will look in a browser, the only way to really know how it looks is to view the site in each individual browser. Test it on different browsers, different screen sizes, and different operating systems (Mac and PC), at different connection speeds, and, if possible, on cell phones and other handheld devices.

• ### Publish and market the site

When you are satisfied that your site is ready, you publish it to a Web server so visitors can access the site. Once your site is published, you can promote it to attract visitors. Registering the site with search engines, placing ads online or in print, and asking for links from other sites are all effective ways to market a Web site.

Organizing your site

Most sites are organized around topics, audiences, tasks, or dates. If you also organize the content on your site around one of these commonly used structures, visitors will be familiar with the structure and able to find what they need more easily. It can be helpful to visit sites with content that is similar to yours and see how they are structured before you develop your site map. Be sure to include navigation that allows visitors to easily move back and forth between sections and pages of the site as well as a link back to the home page.

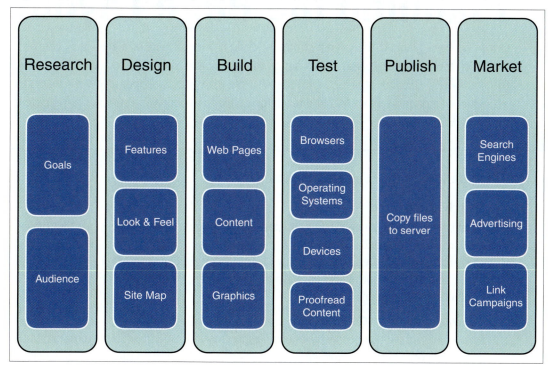

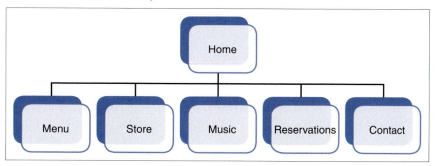

TABLE B-1: Methods of profiling a Web site audience

method	description	good for finding out...
Focus group	In-person discussion with a small group of current or potential Web site visitors	Subjective information about visitors' attitudes and initial reactions to site designs and features
Visitor survey	Questionnaire posted on the site that visitors can fill out online	Demographics and technology use, likes/dislikes of site features and design
Market research	Reports and articles published by companies describing a particular target market or trends in a specific industry	Big-picture data about the market or audience
Traffic analysis	Use of traffic analysis software, which tracks frequency of site visits, pages visited, etc.	How visitors use your site, what areas of your site are the most popular, what browsers and screen sizes visitors use

Planning the Page Layout

Once you have planned the overall structure, design, and content of a Web site, you need to plan the layout of the individual pages. Your design of each page should reflect and support your goals for the site. Catalina is pleased with the Web site plan you developed. Now she wants to see what the individual Web pages will look like. You reach for a paper and pencil and start sketching potential layouts for the TradeWinds site.

DETAILS

When designing the Web page layout:

- **Sketch it first**

    It can be tempting to immediately start Expression Web and begin creating a page, but the best tools to start with are paper and pencil. By sketching on paper first, you can quickly and easily refine your ideas. Once you're happy with the design, you're ready to start working in Expression Web. Figure B-3 shows your planned layout for the TradeWinds home page. If you are a graphic artist, you can also perform this first step using a graphics editing program.

- **Draw on existing conventions**

    Research has shown that people have certain expectations of Web sites. They expect to find the logo and the link to the home page in the top left, internal links and navigation on the left, a search field in the top right, and copyright and contact information at the bottom, as shown in Figure B-4. You can instantly make people feel comfortable in your site by using these design conventions.

- **Be consistent**

    Place elements in the same spot on every page, and maintain a consistent color scheme. This helps visitors quickly learn to use your site, and also makes the site "hang together" visually. Very large sites sometimes vary their color schemes from section to section, essentially creating several smaller sites within the larger one. But for small to medium-sized sites, it's best to be consistent.

- **Keep it simple**

    Work toward a simple, clean design that shows off your content and lets visitors accomplish their tasks.

- **Focus on navigation**

    Design effective navigation that helps visitors find what they need; otherwise, they may not stay long enough to figure out where things are. Label your navigation clearly with terms that visitors will understand.

- **Decide on a size**

    There are essentially two approaches to Web page size—fixed and liquid. A **fixed page design** means that the page is the same width on every visitor's computer no matter how large their screen is. A **liquid page design** shrinks or expands to fit the size of the visitor's screen. Each option has its pros and cons, but liquid designs can be more difficult to implement. If you want to use a fixed design, you need to decide what screen resolution to target.

Using basic page layouts

The Web is a very boxy place. Because of the rectangular nature of HTML elements and digital images, Web page layouts are almost always based on a grid pattern. Some basic layouts are used repeatedly because they work well and are easy to navigate. For example, most Web pages include a masthead running along the top of the page, internal navigation in a column on the left, content in the middle, and perhaps a third column on the right. A footer at the bottom often contains copyright information and text links to contact information, privacy policies, and other information. Even sites that look very different at first glance usually use an embellished version of this same basic layout.

FIGURE B-3: Sketch of TradeWinds Web page layout

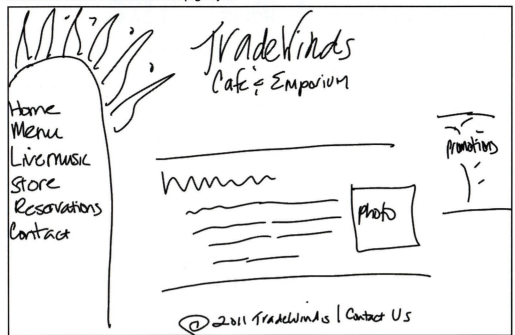

FIGURE B-4: Basic page layout structure familiar to Web visitors

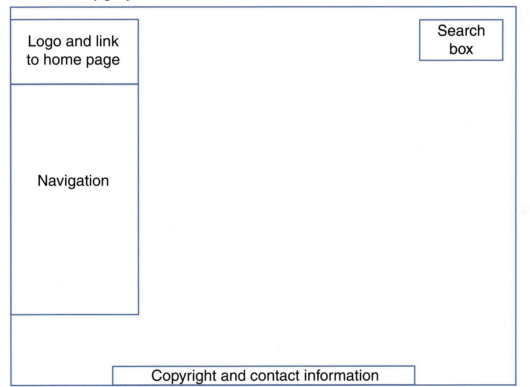

Avoiding a dated design

It can be fun to jump on the latest design fad to give your site an up-to-the-minute look. But what is cool today could be considered "so 2012" in just a few years. Some Web design crazes that have come and gone include blinking text, hit counters, rainbow-colored horizontal bars, heavily beveled buttons, heavy drop shadows, "splash" pages that open before the actual home page, distracting background patterns, "under construction" signs, and pages with tiny fonts and dashed content borders. Ouch. Don't let this happen to you. For a professional-looking site that's easy to use, stick to clean, simple, attractive designs that stand the test of time. If you want to step back in Internet time, visit the Wayback Machine at http://www.archive.org where you can see literally billions of archived Web pages dating from 1996 to the present.

Creating a Web Site

The first step in building a Web site in Expression Web is to organize your files, including HTML files, CSS files, and images, into a root folder. The **root folder** is a folder on your hard drive, USB drive, or network drive that stores all the files that make up your site. Expression Web includes three options for creating sites. You can create an empty Web site to which you can add your own pages, a simple Web site with one blank page, or an entire Web site at once based on templates that generate all the pages for you.  For the TradeWinds site, you decide to create a new empty Web site and root folder, to which you can add your own pages later.

STEPS

TROUBLE

If a Web site is already open when you start Expression Web, click Site on the menu bar, then click Close.

1. **Start Expression Web, click Site on the menu bar, then click New Site**

   The New dialog box opens. See Figure B-5.

2. **Click General in the list on the left, if it is not already selected**

   The left area lists two categories, General and Templates. The middle area lists the types of new sites available for the currently selected category. The General category includes three types of sites: a One Page Site, an Empty Site, and the Import Site Wizard, which lets you import an existing set of Web site files. If you click the Templates category, you can create a Web site using one of the available templates.

3. **Click Empty Site in the middle area of the dialog box**

   The Description in the right area explains that this option creates an empty Web site, with nothing in it.

4. **Click Browse next to the Specify the name and location of the new site box**

   The New Site Location dialog box opens.

QUICK TIP

If you store your Web site files on a USB drive, remember to back them up somewhere else, too, such as onto your home computer, a second USB drive, or a school server, so that if you lose your drive or it fails, you have a copy of the files.

5. **In the New Site Location dialog box, navigate to the location where you store your Data Files, then click Open**

   You return to the New dialog box.

6. **Click twice after the last backslash in the Specify the name and location of the new site box, type tradewinds, then compare your screen to Figure B-6**

   When naming any files or folders that are part of your Web site, use all lowercase, no spaces, and no characters except numbers, letters, or underscores. If you don't follow these rules, your Web pages may not work when you publish them to the server. The folder name, in this case tradewinds, also appears in the Name text box by default. But you can change the name to something more descriptive such as TradeWinds New Design. The name is only used by Expression Web to help you identify the site and will not be seen by visitors.

7. **Click OK**

   Expression Web creates a folder named tradewinds in the location you specified and a new Web site within the new tradewinds folder. The Create New Site window opens, then closes quickly. The new Web site files appear in the Folder List panel, and a Site View tab is added to the editing window, as shown in Figure B-7.

Using Expression Web templates to build a site

The Templates category in the New Site dialog box includes 19 Web site templates that allow you to build a complete site in a matter of minutes. Expression Web includes six templates for sites for organizations such as clubs, seven for personal sites, and six for small business sites. Each template adds different types of pages that are appropriate to the site's purpose, such as news and calendar pages for the organization site, or resume and photo gallery pages for a personal site. Creating a template-based site can be a good way to learn more about Expression Web. Be aware that the templates included with Expression Web are all based on **Dynamic Web Templates**, which help maintain a consistent design across the pages in a site and allow you to make changes across several pages in a site at once. However, working with them requires some familiarity with additional concepts and tools. To learn more about working with Dynamic Web Templates, refer to Expression Web Help.

FIGURE B-5: New Site dialog box

General category

Options within the selected category

Location of root folder for Web site

Name text box

Description of the type of Web site that will be created

Browse button

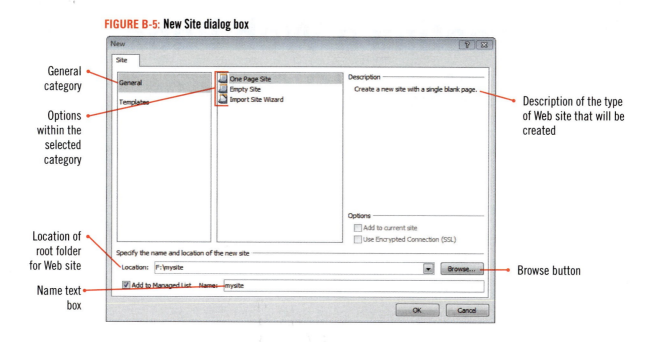

FIGURE B-6: New Site dialog box after choosing Web site type and location

General category selected

Empty Site type selected

Your path will vary, but \tradewinds should appear at the end of the path

The folder name will appear here but you can change it

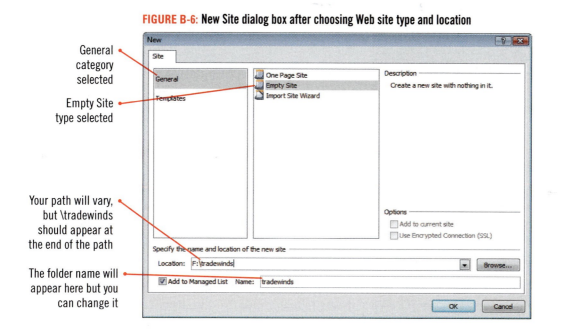

FIGURE B-7: Creating a new Web site

Path to root folder

Folder List panel showing path to tradewinds root folder

Site View tab

Creating a Web Site

Creating a Web Page and Setting CSS Options

While creating the basic layout structure of Web pages is probably the least glamorous part of designing a Web site, it provides the foundation for the rest of your design. To create the basic layout structure of a Web page, it's best to use CSS positioning. You could also use layout tables or frames, but these are not recommended because they can cause problems for visitors with disabilities and those using handheld devices. When you use **CSS positioning**, you create an HTML document that contains content placeholders, and you use style sheets to position the placeholders on the page. It can be difficult to come up with a design that works well in all browsers, but Expression Web takes out much of the work by including prestructured, browser-tested CSS page layouts.  You are ready to create the first page in your site.

STEPS

1. **Click File on the menu bar, point to New, then click Page**

   The New dialog box opens, with options for choosing a type of page and other options.

2. **Click CSS Layouts in the list on the left, then click the first Header, nav, 2 columns, footer option in the list of layouts, as shown in Figure B-8**

   > **QUICK TIP**
   > You can also set the CSS Page Editor Options by clicking the CSS Mode button on the status bar, then clicking CSS Options.

3. **Click the Page Editor Options link, click the CSS tab, then click Reset Defaults, as shown in Figure B-9**

   By resetting the defaults on the CSS tab of the Page Editor Options dialog box, you ensure that the only changes you make to these settings are the intended ones. When you change the Page Editor Options, all future sites you create in Expression Web will use those settings unless you change them.

4. **Click the Page properties on the <body> tag list arrow, then click CSS (rules)**

5. **Click the Sizing, positioning, and floating list arrow, click CSS (classes), click OK, then click OK in the New dialog box**

   > **TROUBLE**
   > If the page opens in Code view, click the Show Design View button.

   Expression Web creates two new files: an HTML file named Untitled_1.html and a CSS (style sheet) file named Untitled_1.css. The HTML file contains **divs**, which are rectangular areas you can position on a page to hold content, including text and images. The CSS file contains style rules that describe how those divs should be positioned on the page. Expression Web also creates a link from the HTML file to the style sheet.

6. **Click in the page_content div on the Untitled_1.html page, as shown in Figure B-10**

   A visual aid appears when you click in the div, indicating that this div is named page_content.

7. **Type Welcome to TradeWinds, click File on the menu bar, then click Save**

   > **TROUBLE**
   > If your system is set to hide file extensions, you will not see the .html extension in the File name box; this is not a problem.

   This is the first page you are saving in the Web site, so default.html is entered automatically in the File name box, indicating that this will be saved as the **home page**, the first page a visitor sees when entering your Web site address in a browser. You could change this, but since you want this file to be your home page, you don't need to.

8. **Click Save**

   Expression Web also recognizes that the Untitled_1.css file is linked to your page, so it prompts you to save that as well. You don't want to use the default file name for this file.

9. **Type twstyles.css in the File name box, then click Save**

   Expression Web saves the default page and the twstyles style sheet in your root folder, and the Save As dialog box closes.

FIGURE B-8: New dialog box

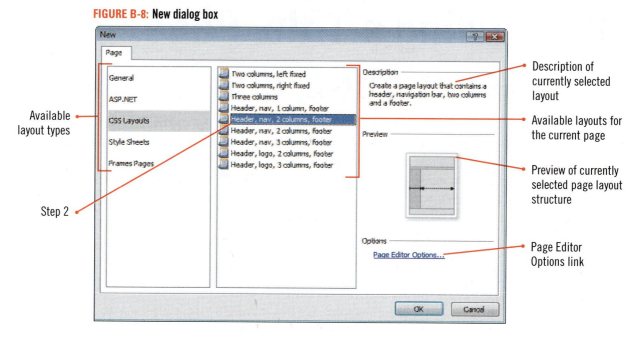

Available layout types

Step 2

Description of currently selected layout

Available layouts for the current page

Preview of currently selected page layout structure

Page Editor Options link

FIGURE B-9: Page Editor Options dialog box with CSS tab open

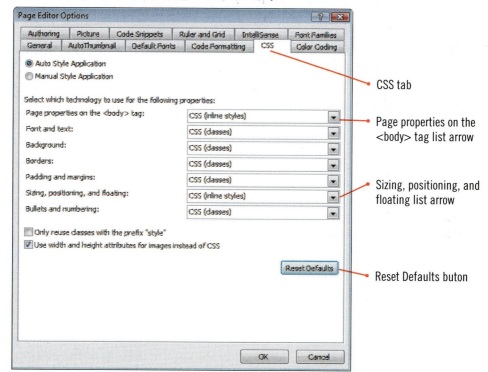

CSS tab

Page properties on the <body> tag list arrow

Sizing, positioning, and floating list arrow

Reset Defaults button

FIGURE B-10: Finished page with page_content div selected

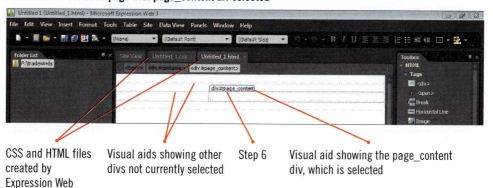

CSS and HTML files created by Expression Web

Visual aids showing other divs not currently selected

Step 6

Visual aid showing the page_content div, which is selected

Adding a Title, Page Description, and Keywords

The title, description, and keyword elements help visitors find your Web site. The **title** is not displayed on the page itself; it appears in the title bar of the visitor's browser and as the title in a browser's list of favorites or bookmarks if a visitor has added it to that list. The description and keywords are used by some search engines to help determine what your site is about.  After consulting with Catalina and researching potential search terms, you come up with a description and keywords for the TradeWinds site. You use the Page Properties feature in Expression Web to add them to your basic Web page.

STEPS

1. **Click the default.html tab in the editing window to make it the active tab**

QUICK TIP
You can also open the Page Properties dialog box by right-clicking in the editing window of an open page in Design view, then clicking Page Properties.

2. **Click File on the menu bar, then click Properties**

   The Page Properties dialog box opens, as shown in Figure B-11. In the General tab of this dialog box, you can set properties such as a title, a description, and keywords for a page. You can use other tabs, such as Formatting and Advanced, to change additional aspects of the page, including the background and link colors, margins, and page language. In general, it is best to let style sheets manage most of these settings, rather than setting the options here.

3. **Select the text Welcome to TradeWinds in the Title text box if necessary, press [Delete], then type TradeWinds Cafe and Emporium**

   The new text replaces the default title. When you save a file, Expression Web gives it a title based on the first text that appears on the page. However, you usually want to change this to a more descriptive page title. Unlike a file name, you can use spaces and capital letters in the title. Search engine results often display the contents of the title element as the link to your site, so it should be reader-friendly and descriptive.

4. **Click in the Page description text box, then type Featuring delicious island cuisine, beautiful imported goods, and live music.**

   Search engine results often display the contents of the description element as the description below the link, so this should be a brief, interesting explanation of what visitors can find at your site. It should motivate them to visit.

5. **Type folk art, jewelry, steel drum music, seafood in the Keywords text box, compare your screen to Figure B-12, then click OK**

   Keywords are a list of terms, separated by commas, that describe the content of your site. You and Catalina have decided that these are terms your site visitors are likely to enter in a search engine when looking for the goods and services TradeWinds has to offer.

6. **Click the Show Code View button at the bottom of the editing window**

   The title, description, and keywords do not show up on the page itself in Design view or when viewed in a browser. But when you look at Code view, as shown in Figure B-13, you see that they have been added to the HTML code, which means that search engines will be able to see them.

7. **Click the Show Design View button at the bottom of the editing window**

   The page is displayed in Design view. An asterisk appears on the tab next to the file name, indicating that changes have been made to the page since the last time you saved it.

QUICK TIP
It's important to save your work frequently as you design a Web site. To save time, use the keyboard shortcut [Ctrl][S] to save the page you are currently editing.

8. **Click the Save button 🖫 on the Common toolbar**

   Expression Web saves your changes to the file, and the asterisk next to the file name on the tab is removed.

FIGURE B-11: Page Properties dialog box

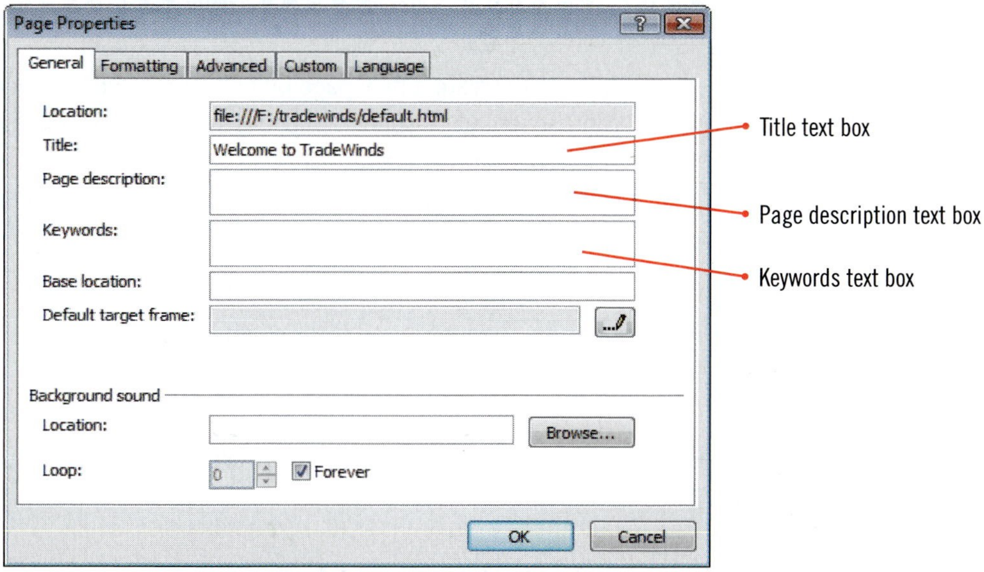
Page Properties
General
Formatting
Advanced
Custom
Language
Location:
file:///F:/tradewinds/default.html
Title:
Welcome to TradeWinds
Page description:
Keywords:
Base location:
Default target frame:
Background sound
Location:
Browse...
Loop:
0
Forever
OK
Cancel
Title text box
Page description text box
Keywords text box

FIGURE B-12: Page Properties dialog box with page properties added

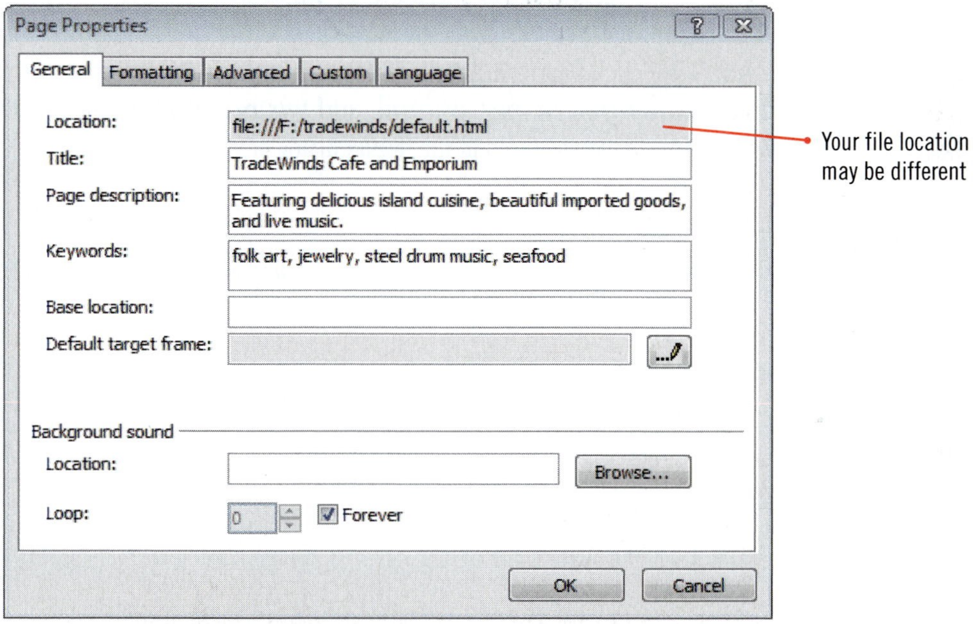
Page Properties
General
Formatting
Advanced
Custom
Language
Location:
file:///F:/tradewinds/default.html
Title:
TradeWinds Cafe and Emporium
Page description:
Featuring delicious island cuisine, beautiful imported goods, and live music.
Keywords:
folk art, jewelry, steel drum music, seafood
Base location:
Default target frame:
Background sound
Location:
Browse...
Loop:
0
Forever
OK
Cancel
Your file location may be different

FIGURE B-13: Code view of TradeWinds home page

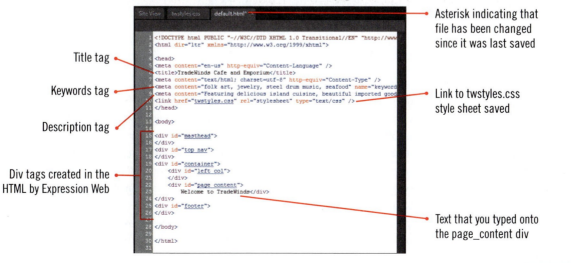

default.html*
<!DOCTYPE html PUBLIC "-//W3C//DTD XHTML 1.0 Transitional//EN" "http://www
<html dir="ltr" xmlns="http://www.w3.org/1999/xhtml">
<head>
<meta content="en-us" http-equiv="Content-Language" />
<title>TradeWinds Cafe and Emporium</title>
<meta content="text/html; charset=utf-8" http-equiv="Content-Type" />
<meta content="folk art, jewelry, steel drum music, seafood" name="keyword
<meta content="Featuring delicious island cuisine, beautiful imported good
<link href="twstyles.css" rel="stylesheet" type="text/css" />
</head>
<body>
<div id="masthead">
</div>
<div id="top_nav">
</div>
<div id="container">
<div id="left_col">
</div>
<div id="page_content">
Welcome to TradeWinds</div>
</div>
<div id="footer">
</div>
</body>
</html>
Title tag
Keywords tag
Description tag
Div tags created in the HTML by Expression Web
Asterisk indicating that file has been changed since it was last saved
Link to twstyles.css style sheet saved
Text that you typed onto the page_content div

Expression Web 3

Importing Web Pages

As you have learned, you can create a new page by using the Page command on the New submenu of the File menu. You can also import existing Web pages into your site. You have only created one page of the TradeWinds site, and the site map calls for several more pages to be developed. Your co-worker Andrew created the rest of the pages and saved them as separate files. You can import those files into the site.

STEPS

1. **Click File on the menu bar, point to Import, then click File**

   The Import dialog box opens. From this box you can choose files or folders to be imported into the Web site.

   > **QUICK TIP**
   > You can use the Remove button to remove any files you add by mistake or decide you do not want to import.

2. **Click Add File, then navigate to the drive where you store your Data Files, as shown in Figure B-14**

3. **Double-click Unit B, click twcontact.html, then click Open**

   The twcontact.html file appears in the Import dialog box.

   > **QUICK TIP**
   > You can press and hold [Ctrl] to select multiple files at once in a dialog box.

4. **Click Add File, click twmenu.html, press and hold [Ctrl], click twmusic.html, twreservations.html, twspecials.html, and twstore.html, release [Ctrl], then click Open**

   See Figure B-15. Six files are listed in the Import dialog box.

   > **QUICK TIP**
   > You can also add pages by creating copies of existing pages. For example, you can right-click on default.html in the Folder List panel, click New From Existing Page, then save the file with a new name.

5. **Click OK**

   The files now appear in the Site View tab and the Folder List panel, as shown in Figure B-16.

Understanding Web site addresses

Web site addresses are also known as URLs. The term **URL** stands for Uniform Resource Locator. A URL is made up of a domain name, a file name, and sometimes folder names. A **domain name** is a name that identifies a particular Web site. For example, the Web site for a school named Central University might be centraluniversity.edu. The three letters after the period indicate what type of site it is or from what country the site originates. For example, .edu indicates an educational institution, .org indicates a nonprofit organization, and .ca indicates that the site originates in Canada. If the Web page with information about library hours at Central University was named hours.htm and was in a subfolder named library, the entire URL for that page would be www.centraluniversity.edu/library/hours.htm. Because file and folder names make up part of the URL, it's important to choose short file names that are descriptive. Try to avoid unnecessarily long URLs such as www.centraluniversity.edu/maincampuslibraryfiles/hours_we_are_open.htm.

FIGURE B-14: Add File to Import List dialog box

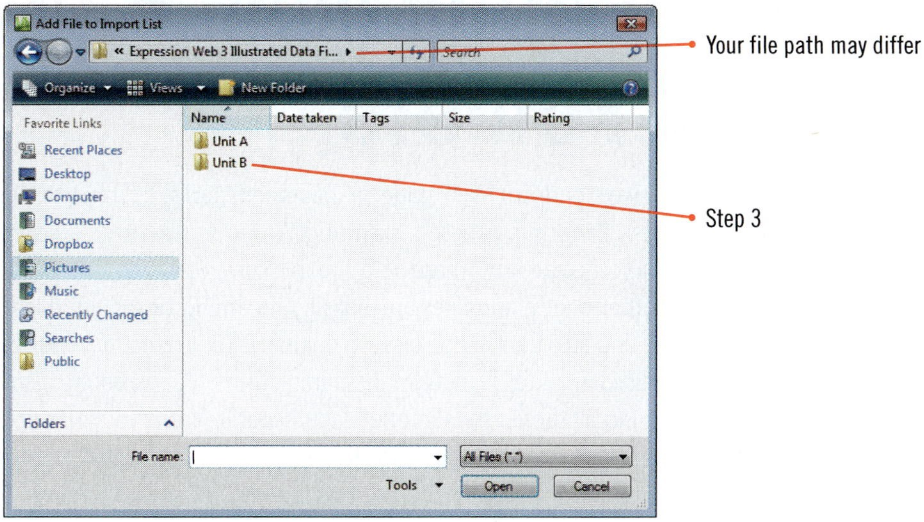

Your file path may differ

Step 3

FIGURE B-15: Files added to Import dialog box

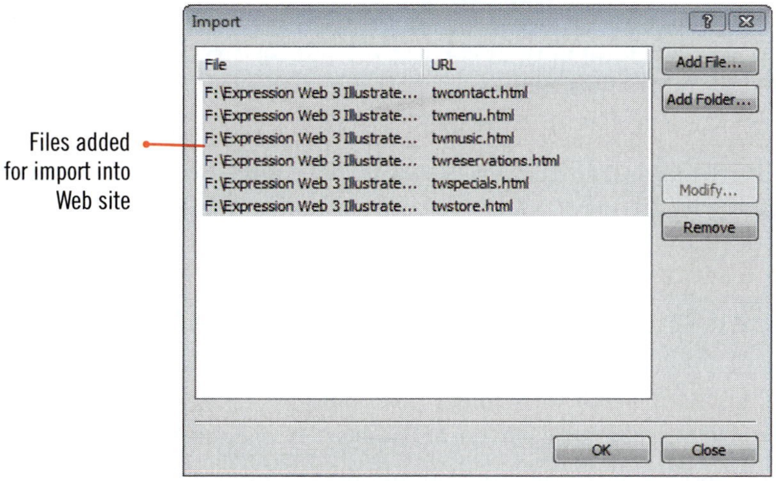

Files added for import into Web site

FIGURE B-16: Folder List panel showing imported files

Imported files

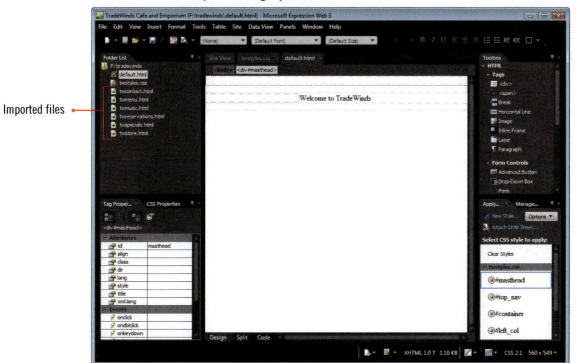

Managing Web Pages and Folders

You should always perform Web page management tasks, such as deleting and renaming pages, within Expression Web. Performing these tasks using Windows Explorer could result in broken links in your Web site. But when you create and manage a site in Expression Web, the program warns you if you delete files with links to other pages, and fixes any links by renaming or moving files. Another smart file management strategy is creating an assets folder, a subfolder in the root directory. **Assets** is a catch-all term for the variety of media files used in a site, such as images, animations, videos, sounds, and more. As your site grows, you'll appreciate having all these assets in one place, separate from your HTML files.  The sitemap doesn't call for a specials page, so you need to delete the specials file. You also want to simplify the names of the other HTML files. In addition, you decide to create an assets folder for the images and other assets you plan to add to the site.

STEPS

1. **Right-click twspecials.html in the Folder List panel, click Delete, then click Yes in the Confirm Delete box**

   The twspecials.html page is no longer listed in the Site View tab or the Folder List panel, and the file is deleted from your disk or hard drive. You can also delete a file by right-clicking it in the Site View tab of the editing window. Files can be open or closed when you rename or delete them. If a file is open in Expression Web when you delete it, the tab for the deleted page in the editing window closes. If you rename an open file, the file name on the tab changes to reflect the new name.

   > **TROUBLE**
   >
   > Be sure to type the file extension after the period; the extension is not added automatically.

2. **Right-click twcontact.html in the Folder List panel, click Rename, type contact.html, then press [Enter]**

   The file is renamed to contact.html. When you click the Rename command, the current file name is highlighted so that you can replace it by typing a new name.

   > **QUICK TIP**
   >
   > When you delete or rename a page using Expression Web, you are making changes to the actual files on your disk, not just within Expression Web, so be careful when using these file management features.

3. **Repeat Step 2 four times to rename the following files:**

original name	rename as
twmenu.html	menu.html
twmusic.html	music.html
twreservations.html	reservations.html
twstore.html	store.html

   The Folder List panel and Site View window show the renamed files, as shown in Figure B-17.

4. **Right-click the path of the root folder in the Folder List panel**

5. **Point to New, then click Folder**

   > **TROUBLE**
   >
   > If the temporary folder name is not highlighted, right-click the new folder, click Rename, then type the new name.

   A new folder is created and the temporary name New_Folder is highlighted so that you can immediately replace it by typing a new name. Whenever you add a new folder, Expression Web creates it within the folder you have selected on the Folder List panel.

6. **Type assets, then press [Enter]**

   The assets folder now appears in the Folder List panel, as shown in Figure B-18, and in the list in the Site View tab of the editing window. As you build your site, you will save any files that are not HTML or CSS files in this folder. See Table B-2 for a description of the typical files in a Web site and their file types.

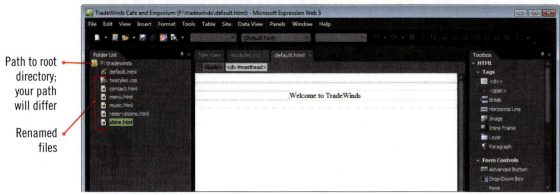

Path to root directory; your path will differ

Renamed files

List of all files currently saved in TradeWinds Web Site

Newly created assets folder

TABLE B-2: Web site file types

file type	description	common file extensions
HTML	HTML pages	.htm, .html
CSS	Cascading Style Sheets	.css
Dynamic	Pages that use a combination of HTML and other languages to display information from a database within a Web page	.aspx, .asp, .jsp, .php, .cfm
Graphics	Photos, illustrations, or other images for a Web site	.jpg, .jpeg, .gif, .png
Audio	Files that play sound when a page loads or that visitors can click to play or download to their computers	.mp3, .mp4, .wav, .ram, .rm, .mid, .midi
Video	Files that play video when a page loads or that visitors can click to play or download to their computers; video files may also include audio	.avi, .mov, .qt, .mpg, .mpeg, .ram, .rm, .flv, .wmv, .mp4
Animation	Animated images such as blinking ad banners or moving illustrations; animated images don't include audio	.swf, .gif

Changing the Web Site View

When the Site View tab is open in the editing window, you can view the current Web site four different ways: Folders, Publishing, Reports, and Hyperlinks. The default view is **Folders**, which displays a list of files and folders in the site. You can use this to navigate your site to locate files. It looks similar to the Folder List panel but includes some additional information such as the file size and type as well as the last modified date. You explore the different Web site views to learn more about working with the TradeWinds site in Expression Web.

STEPS

1. **Click the Site View tab, then click the Publishing View button at the bottom of the editing window, as shown in Figure B-19**

   You switch to Publishing View. **Publishing view** displays a dual list of files, those on the local Web site and those on the remote Web site. The **source** site or **publishing source** is the folder on your hard drive, USB drive, or network drive that contains your Web site files. The destination site is the folder on the Web server that contains your Web site files once you publish them. This view is useful only after you have set up a publishing destination. Because you have not set up a publishing destination for this site, the message "Add a publishing destination…" appears.

2. **Click the Reports View button**

   You switch to Reports view, as shown in Figure B-20. **Reports** view provides an overview of available Web site reports, providing information on broken hyperlinks, slow pages, and much more. The Site Summary report lists basic information such as the number of files in the report, along with links to all the available reports. Notice that the report name, Site Summary, appears just below the Site View tab, and displays a small list arrow. You can click any of the links to view that particular report, or you can click the list arrow next to the report name to open a menu of all available reports, organized into categories. These reports will be more useful later, when the TradeWinds site is more fully developed.

   TROUBLE
   If you do not see the Site Summary report, another report may have opened instead. If this happens, click the list arrow next to the current report name, then click Site Summary.

3. **Click the Recently added files link in the Site Summary report**

   The Recently Added Files report opens, showing all files in the TradeWinds site created within the last 30 days. You can double-click any of the files to open them for viewing or editing.

   QUICK TIP
   The first time you use Reports view during a session, it opens to the Site Summary; the next time during the session you switch to Reports view, it opens to the last report you viewed.

4. **Click the list arrow next to the Recently Added Files report name, point to Problems, then click Unlinked Files**

   A report opens showing all files in the TradeWinds site that are not linked to any other pages in the site. As a general rule, you do not want any pages in your site that are not linked to the others, because visitors will not be able to access them. You take note that you will need to create links between all the Web site pages and run this report again later to make sure none were forgotten.

5. **Click the Hyperlinks View button at the bottom of the editing window**

   You switch to **Hyperlinks view**, which illustrates how one file is linked to other files in your site.

6. **Click the file twstyles.css in the Folder List panel**

   The twstyles.css file opens in Hyperlinks view, as shown in Figure B-21. The TradeWinds style sheet is in the center, with the other Web site files on the left, pointing to the style sheet. This illustrates that all the pages in the site link to the style sheet.

7. **Click the Folders View button**

   You return to Folders view, which is the default view for the Site View tab.

8. **Click Site on the menu bar, click Close, click File on the menu bar, then click Exit**

   The Web site closes, and Expression Web closes.

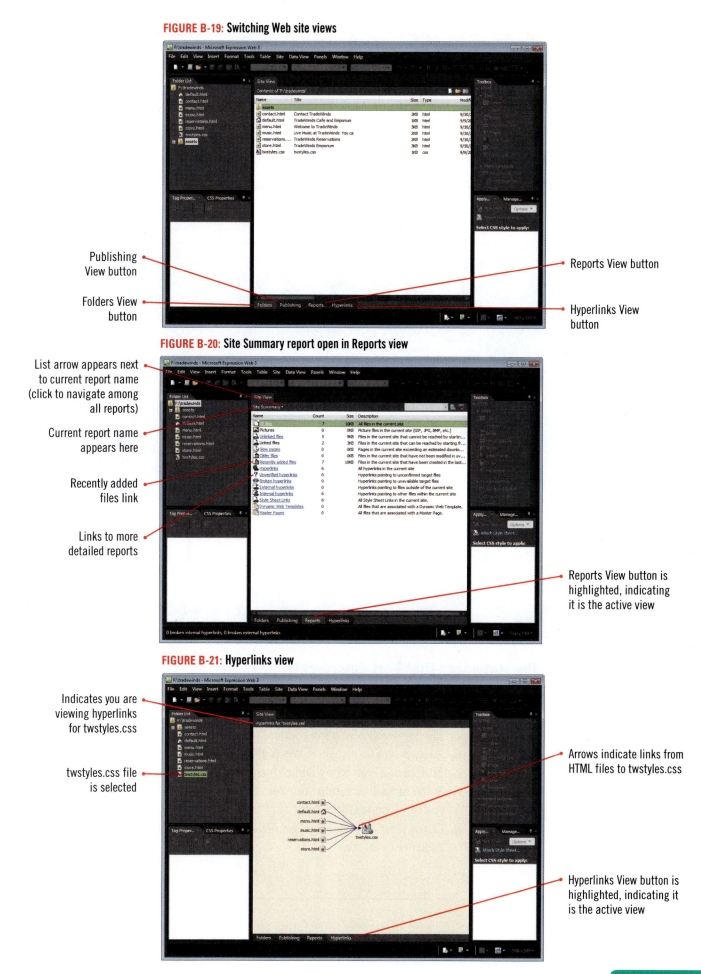

FIGURE B-19: Switching Web site views

Publishing View button

Folders View button

Reports View button

Hyperlinks View button

FIGURE B-20: Site Summary report open in Reports view

List arrow appears next to current report name (click to navigate among all reports)

Current report name appears here

Recently added files link

Links to more detailed reports

Reports View button is highlighted, indicating it is the active view

FIGURE B-21: Hyperlinks view

Indicates you are viewing hyperlinks for twstyles.css

twstyles.css file is selected

Arrows indicate links from HTML files to twstyles.css

Hyperlinks View button is highlighted, indicating it is the active view

Expression Web 3

Creating a Web Site

Expression Web 39

Practice

SAM

For current SAM information including versions and content details, visit SAM Central (http://samcentral.course.com). If you have a SAM user profile, you may have access to hands-on instruction, practice, and assessment of the skills covered in this unit. Since we support various versions of SAM throughout the life of this text, you will want to check with your instructor for instructions and the correct URL/Web site to access those assignments.

Concepts Review

Label each element in the Expression Web window shown in Figure B-22.

FIGURE B-22

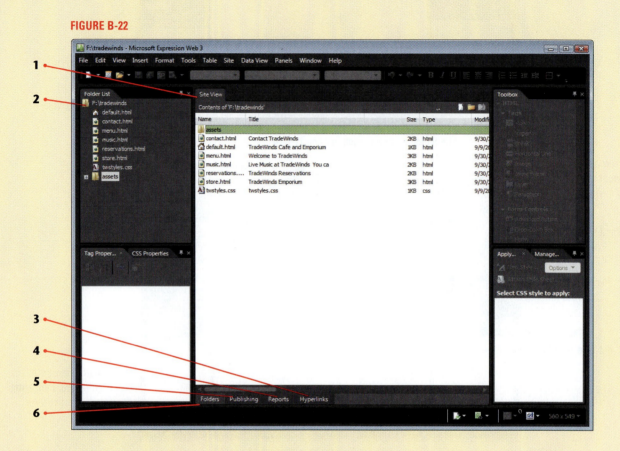

Match each term with the statement that best describes it.

7. **URL**

8. **Div**

9. **Site map**

10. **assets**

11. **Demographics**

12. **default.html**

13. **Destination site**

a. A diagram of a Web site structure

b. The name Expression Web assigns to the home page file of a Web site

c. Also known as a Web site address

d. A folder on a server where you publish your Web site

e. An area of a Web page that holds content, such as text or images

f. Name of a folder within your Web site folder that holds image, sound, video, and other non-HTML files

g. Characteristics such as age, gender, and income level that identify a likely audience or market

Select the best answer from the list of choices.

14. **What do visitors expect to find at the bottom of a Web site?**
    - **a.** Search box
    - **b.** Home page link
    - **c.** Contact us link
    - **d.** Advertisements

15. **In which Web site view can you see a report showing all the slow pages in your site?**
    - **a.** Hyperlinks view
    - **b.** Reports view
    - **c.** Folders view
    - **d.** Publishing view

16. **What is the preferred method for creating a Web page layout?**
    - **a.** Tables
    - **b.** CSS positioning
    - **c.** JavaScript
    - **d.** HTML

17. **What is the first phase of the Web site development process?**
    - **a.** Build
    - **b.** Design
    - **c.** Test
    - **d.** Research and plan

18. **A design that is the same width no matter what size screen the visitor's computer monitor has is called a:**
    - **a.** Fixed design.
    - **b.** Narrow design.
    - **c.** Liquid design.
    - **d.** Table layout.

19. **Which of the following are *not* allowed in a Web site file name?**
    - **a.** Lowercase letters
    - **b.** Spaces
    - **c.** Numbers
    - **d.** Underscores

20. **Which of the following is *not* a good Web design practice?**
    - **a.** Consistency
    - **b.** Effective navigation
    - **c.** Complexity
    - **d.** Using existing conventions

Skills Review

1. **Create a new Web site.**
   - **a.** Launch Expression Web.
   - **b.** Open the New dialog box.
   - **c.** Click the General category if necessary.
   - **d.** Create an Empty site in the drive and folder where your Data Files are stored. Name the root folder **careers**, then click OK to close the New dialog box.

2. **Create a Web page and set CSS options.**
   - **a.** Open the New dialog box.
   - **b.** Create a new page based on the **second** Header, nav, 2 columns, footer layout in the CSS Layouts category. This is the layout with the narrower right column.
   - **c.** Open the Page Editor Options dialog box, switch to the CSS tab, then click Reset Defaults.
   - **d.** Change the Page properties on the <body> tag setting to CSS (rules). Change the Sizing, positioning, and floating setting to CSS (classes).
   - **e.** Click OK to close the Page Editor Options dialog box, then click OK to close the New dialog box.
   - **f.** Click in the page_content div, then type **Welcome to Careers Guaranteed**. (*Hint*: The visual aid reads "div#page_content.") Compare your screen to Figure B-23.
   - **g.** Save the Web page as **default.html** and the style sheet as **cgstyles.css**.

FIGURE B-23

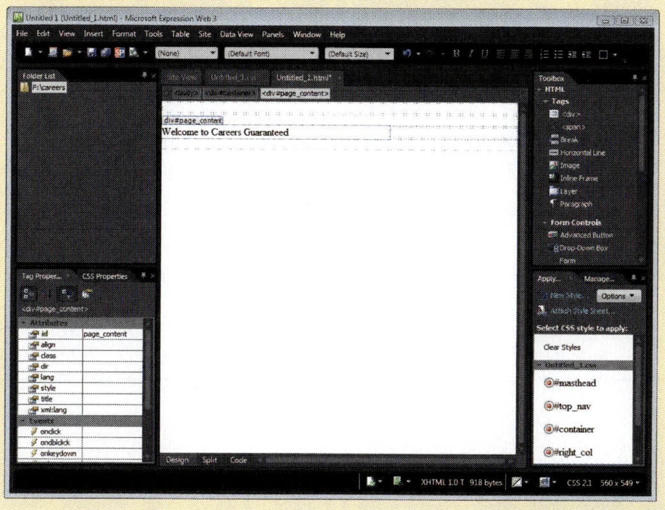

Skills Review (continued)

3. **Add a title, page description, and keywords.**
   a. Open the Page Properties dialog box for the default.html file.
   b. Click the General tab if necessary, then change the title to **Careers Guaranteed**.
   c. Add the following page description: **At Careers Guaranteed, we guarantee we will match you to a job position or we will refund your money**.
   d. Add the following keywords: **careers, guaranteed jobs, job placement, resume, job interview**. Click OK to close the Page Properties dialog box.
   e. View the page in Code view and find the title, keywords, and description tags.
   f. Switch back to Design view.
   g. Save your changes to the file.

4. **Import Web pages.**
   a. Open the Import dialog box.
   b. Import the following files from the location where you store your Data Files: **cgabout.html**, **cgcontact.html**, **cghistory.html**, and **cgservices.html**.

5. **Manage Web pages and folders.**
   a. Delete the **cghistory.html** file.
   b. Rename the remaining files:

File	Rename as
cgabout.html	about.html
cgcontact.html	contact.html
cgservices.html	s.html

   c. Create a new folder within the root folder.
   d. Name the new folder **assets**.

6. **Change the Web site view.**
   a. View the site in Publishing view. (*Hint*: You have to switch to Site View first.)
   b. View the site in Reports view.
   c. View the Recently Added Files report.
   d. View the Unlinked Files report.
   e. Switch to Hyperlinks view, then view the cgstyles.css file in hyperlinks view.
   f. Switch to Folders view, then compare your screen to Figure B-24.
   g. Close the Web site, then exit Expression Web.

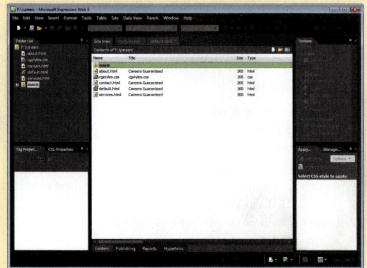

Independent Challenge 1

You have been hired by Tiffany Harris, the marketing manager of a social networking business called ConnectUp, to design the ConnectUp Web site. The site's audience is made up of hip young professionals who want to network with people who can help them advance their careers and also become part of their social network. Tiffany wants a fresh look that will be attractive to their young and trendy audience.

a. Launch Expression Web, then create a new empty site in the folder and drive where your Data Files are stored. Name the root folder **connectup**.

b. Create a new Web page based on the Header, nav, 1 column, footer CSS layout.

c. Save this page as **default.html** in the connectup folder, and save the stylesheet as **custyles.css**.

d. Open the Page Editor Options dialog box for this page. In the CSS tab, reset the defaults and change the Page properties on the <body> tag setting to CSS (rules). Change the Sizing, positioning, and floating setting to CSS (classes).

e. Add the text **Welcome to ConnectUp** to the page_content div. (*Hint*: Use the visual aids to find the right div.)

f. Open the Page Properties dialog box using a command on the File menu. Change the page title to **ConnectUp**, add **Join other young professionals in Connecting Up to a better career and social life.** as the page description, and add **careers, social networking, career networking** as keywords. Save your changes to the page.

g. From the location where you store your Data Files, import the following files into your site: **cujoinup.html**, **cufaq.html**, and **cucontact.html**.

h. Rename the files to **joinup.html**, **faq.html**, and **contact.html**.

i. Create an assets folder for the Web site.

j. Compare your screen to Figure B-25, then save changes to your files, close the Web site, and exit Expression Web.

FIGURE B-25

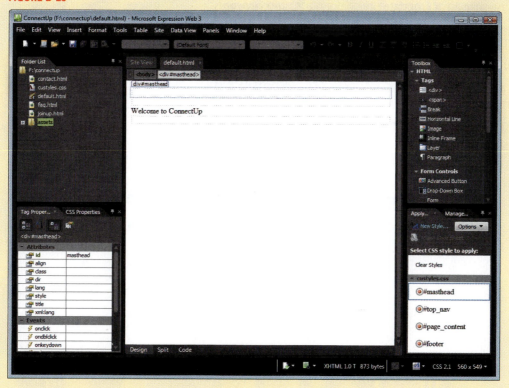

Independent Challenge 2

You have been hired to create a Web site for Memories Restored, a company in Alberta, Canada that specializes in digital restoration of family photographs. Brian Edwards, the owner of the company, would like a site that showcases their photo restoration work and customer testimonials, educates visitors about the process of submitting a scanned or physical photo, and broadens their market reach beyond Alberta to other parts of Canada, the United States, and Europe. Many people are nervous about turning over their family photos to a stranger, so the Web site needs to present the business as credible and trustworthy. After doing some research and planning, you create a site map, shown in Figure B-26.

a. Launch Expression Web, then create an empty Web site and root folder named **memories** in Expression Web for Memories Restored.

b. Create a new page based on the Header, logo, 2 columns, footer CSS layout. On the CSS tab of the Page Editor options dialog box, reset the defaults, then change the Page properties on the <body> tag setting to CSS (rules) and the Sizing, positioning, and floating setting to CSS (classes).

c. Click in the page_content div and type **Welcome to Memories Restored**.

d. Save this page as **default.html**, and save the style sheet with an appropriate name.

e. Give the page a descriptive title. Add a description that briefly explains the services Memories Restored offers, and keywords targeted to likely visitors who are looking for photo restoration services.

f. Create four additional pages based on the default page, using the New From Existing Page command. (*Hint*: Right-click default.html in the Folder List panel.) Save each page, using the site map in Figure B-26 as a guide in naming the pages but following correct file naming rules.

Advanced Challenge Exercise

- Import the Data File mrac.html into the site. This page will feature tips for people who want to try to restore digital photos at home.
- Rename the page with a more descriptive but short name.
- Give the page an appropriate title, description, and keywords.

g. Create an assets folder in the root directory of the site.

h. Save your work, close the Web site, then exit Expression Web.

FIGURE B-26

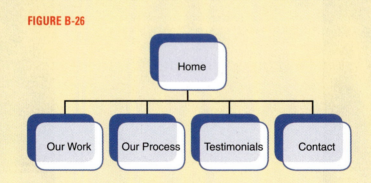

Independent Challenge 3

Note: This Independent Challenge requires an Internet connection.

A local nonprofit organization, Technology For All, needs to redesign their Web site. The organization collects cast-off computers, repairs and upgrades them, and then donates the refurbished machines to low-income students. You have volunteered to help the organization by conducting a design audit. As part of the audit, you decide to research some new ways to organize the site. You posted a survey for Web site visitors, and many people wrote that the site was poorly organized and difficult to navigate. You know that the four most common ways to organize a Web site are based on topic or category, audience, task, and date. You want to examine some real-world examples of how designers implement these structures. You decide to start by more closely examining sites that you visit frequently.

a. Make a list of at least 10 Web sites you like to visit. Try to think of a mix of sites, including educational sites, news sites, shopping sites, entertainment sites, and corporate sites.

b. Visit the sites and spend a few minutes analyzing how each site is structured and how the navigation is organized. Write down which category of site organization the site fits into. Some sites may use a combination of methods.

c. Write a site survey based on your research. Choose one site from each site organization category you researched. For each site chosen, write the site name, URL, and one paragraph explaining why you think the site designer chose that method for organizing the site. Your document should include descriptions of four sites.

Advanced Challenge Exercise

■ Choose one of the sites that you think was poorly structured or could use improvement.

■ Write a paragraph explaining what is lacking in the structure and navigation.

■ Draw a site map or create an outline illustrating how you would restructure the site.

d. Add your name to the document and print it.

Real Life Independent Challenge

This assignment builds on the personal Web site you started planning in Unit A. In this project, you will create a Web site in Expression Web, create your site pages, and add titles, keywords, and descriptions to your pages.

a. Write down at least three goals for your site.

b. Sketch a site map and page layout for your site.

c. In Expression Web, create a Web site and root folder.

d. Create a new Web page for your site, using one of the CSS layout options, and save it as **default.html**.

e. Add a title, description, and keywords to your home page.

f. Use the New From Existing Page command to create new pages based on the default.html page. Create as many pages as you need for your site and save them with appropriate file names.

g. Create an assets folder to hold additional Web site files.

h. Begin collecting or creating content and images for your site. Save these files in a separate folder outside your web site so you can access them later.

i. When you are finished, close the Web site, then exit Expression Web.

Visual Workshop

Launch Expression Web, then create an empty Web site in the drive and folder where your Data Files are stored. Name the root folder **ecotours**. Create a Web page based on the Header, nav, 1 column, footer CSS layout. Add the title, keywords, and description shown in Figure B-27. Save your home page and style sheet with the names shown in the figure. Import etcontact. html, etdestinations.html, and etpackages.html from the location where you store your Data files. Rename the files with the file names shown, create an assets folder, then close all Web pages so your editing window matches the figure. When you have finished, press [Print Screen], paste the image into a word-processing program, add your name at the top of the document, print the document, close the word processor without saving changes, then exit Expression Web.

FIGURE B-27

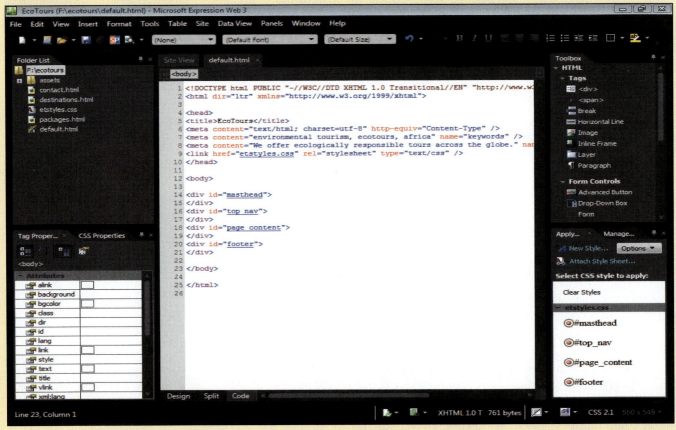

Adding Text and Links

Beneath the sophisticated layouts, colorful graphics, and engaging video, Web pages have a supporting foundation of text and links. Text might not seem as exciting as pictures or videos, but it's the simplest and most common way to communicate with Web site visitors. In fact, the Web originated as a way for scientists and researchers to exchange text-based documents. The inventors of the Web also came up with a way to navigate from one document to another: hyperlinks, also known simply as links. Links allow you to surf from one Web site to another or among pages in a single site; they're the glue that holds the Web together.  Catalina has e-mailed you some content for the new TradeWinds site. You decide to add it to the Web pages you laid out earlier.

OBJECTIVES

Paste text into a Web page

Type text and insert symbols

Check spelling and use the thesaurus

Create an internal link

Create an external link

Create and link to a bookmark

Create an e-mail link

Copy and paste content between pages

Pasting Text into a Web Page

You can add text to a Web page by typing directly in Expression Web, or by pasting text from an existing document, such as one created in Microsoft Word. You simply open the Word document, copy the text you want, and then switch to Expression Web and paste the selection into the Web page.  Catalina has sent you a file with the content for the home page in Microsoft Word format. You copy and paste the content from Word into Expression Web.

STEPS

1. **Launch Expression Web, then open the tradewinds Web site from the location where you store your Data Files**

   The tradewinds Web site you created in Unit B opens in Design view.

2. **Double-click default.html in the Folder List panel or the Site View tab, switch to Design view if necessary, then click in the page_content div**

   The page_content div is the main content container for your page. Any content or graphics that are not part of the navigation, footer, or masthead should be inserted in this div. So far, this div contains only the text you typed, "Welcome to TradeWinds," as shown in Figure C-1.

3. **Point to <div#page_content> on the quick tag selector bar, click the <div#page_content> list arrow, then click Select Tag Contents**

   This selects the contents of the div but not the div itself, so only the words are highlighted.

4. **Press [Delete]**

   The text is deleted.

> **TROUBLE**
> If Microsoft Word 2007 is not installed on your computer, consult your technical support person.

5. **Launch Microsoft Word, open the Open dialog box, navigate to where you store your Data Files, double-click the Unit C folder, then double-click tw_home.docx**

   The tw_home.docx file opens in Microsoft Word. The text is formatted with font colors and sizes.

6. **Press [Ctrl][A] to select all the text, press [Ctrl][C] to copy the text, then click the Close button ▬✖▬ on the Word program window to exit Word**

   The text is copied to the **Windows Clipboard**, a temporary storage area in your computer's memory. The formatting is copied along with the text. Both Word and the tw_home.docx file close and you return to Expression Web.

> **QUICK TIP**
> Be careful when you add content to ensure that you add it to the correct div; use the visual aids and the quick tag selector to help verify that your cursor is correctly placed.

7. **Right-click in the blank page_content div, then click Paste**

   See Figure C-2. The formatted text is pasted into the page_content div on the home page, and the **Paste Options button** appears, allowing you to choose how to format the pasted text. Word uses style sheets and HTML code to create formatting such as fonts and colors. These Word styles can conflict with the styles you create and apply to your Web pages, causing unpredictable or undesirable results.

> **TROUBLE**
> If you don't see the Paste Options button, click the Tools menu, click Page Editor Options, click the General tab, then click the check box next to Show Paste Options buttons.

8. **Click the Paste Options button 📋**

   The Paste Options menu offers several options for controlling how much, if any, formatting you wish to include with the text. The available options depend on the program you copied the text from and the format of the text where you are pasting.

9. **Click Keep Text Only, click Normal paragraphs without line breaks, click OK, then save the page**

   See Figure C-3. The formatting is removed from the pasted text. Choosing Normal paragraphs without line breaks in the Paste Text dialog box preserves the structure of your text by creating paragraph containers, but strips away the formatting; this is usually the safest option when pasting text only into a Web page. Later, you will create and apply styles in Expression Web to format the text.

FIGURE C-1: TradeWinds home page

<div#page_content> is light gray, indicating cursor is in page_content div

page_content div and visual aid

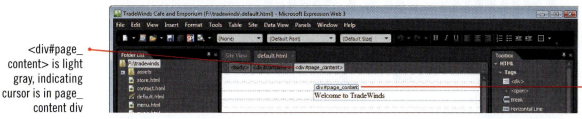

FIGURE C-2: Content from tw_home.docx pasted into default.html

Formatting from Microsoft Word is pasted along with content

Paste Options button

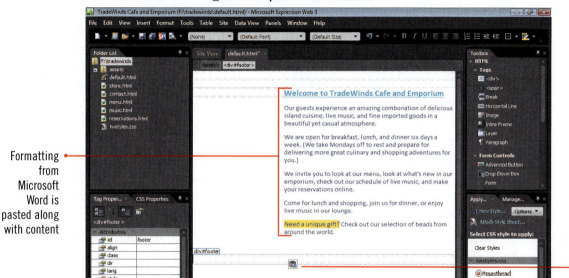

FIGURE C-3: Content pasted from tw_home document

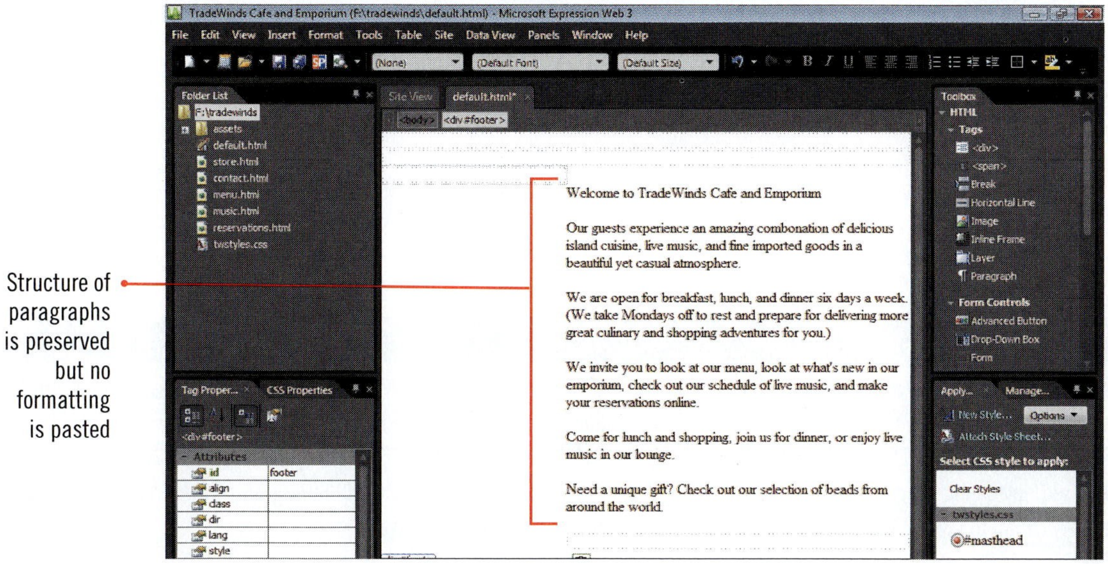

Structure of paragraphs is preserved but no formatting is pasted

Typing Text and Inserting Symbols

In addition to copying and pasting from other files, you can type and edit text directly in the page in Expression Web. You sometimes need to insert symbols in addition to regular text. For example, many Web sites include an area at the bottom of each page called the **footer**, which usually contains contact information and a copyright statement.  Although you plan to add navigation buttons along the left side of the page, you want to add some text in the footer of the home page that will serve as text-based navigation. You also need to add a copyright statement to the page and fix the spelling of "café".

STEPS

QUICK TIP
Be sure to type a space between each word and pipe symbol.

1. **In the default.html page, click anywhere in the footer div, type Home | Menu | Live Music | Store | Reservations | Contact Us, press [Enter], then type 2013 TradeWinds**

   Pressing [Enter] creates a new line. Compare your screen to Figure C-4. The vertical lines between the words are called **pipes**; usually, this symbol shares a key with the backslash symbol. Certain symbols and special characters, such as the copyright symbol, foreign letters, and scientific notation, cannot be typed using a standard keyboard; to add these, you use the Symbol command on the Insert menu.

2. **Position the insertion point in front of the text 2013 you just typed, click Insert on the menu bar, then click Symbol**

   The Symbol dialog box opens, as shown in Figure C-5. The Font is automatically set to the font surrounding the insertion point, in this case Times New Roman. More symbols are available than are visible in the dialog box; you can use the scroll bar to find more. To jump more quickly among sets of symbols, you can click the Subset list arrow and click a different subset.

QUICK TIP
If the Symbol dialog box is in the way, click and hold the title bar of the Symbol dialog box, then drag it out of the way until you can see the text.

3. **Scroll down until you see the copyright sign (©), click ©, then click Insert**

   The symbol is inserted into your page. The Symbol dialog box remains open and the Cancel button changes to a Close button.

4. **Click Close on the Symbol dialog box, then press [Spacebar]**

   The Symbol dialog box closes and a space is added between the copyright symbol and 2013.

5. **In the page content div, in the first line of text, select the e in Cafe, press [Delete], click Insert on the menu bar, then click Symbol**

   The "e" is deleted and the Symbol dialog box opens.

6. **Scroll down and find the é (LATIN SMALL LETTER E WITH ACUTE), click é, click Insert, click Close, then compare your screen to Figure C-6**

7. **Save the page**

Text-based navigation

Many Web sites use images linked to internal pages for navigation, often along the side or top of the page. It's also a good idea to include text-only navigation links at the bottom of each page that duplicate the image-based navigation found elsewhere. This text-based navigation can be helpful to visitors with disabilities and those accessing the site with handheld devices or cell phones. It also provides a convenient way to move to another page without having to scroll back up to the top of the current page. Text-only links also help search engines to find all the pages on your Web site so they show up in search results.

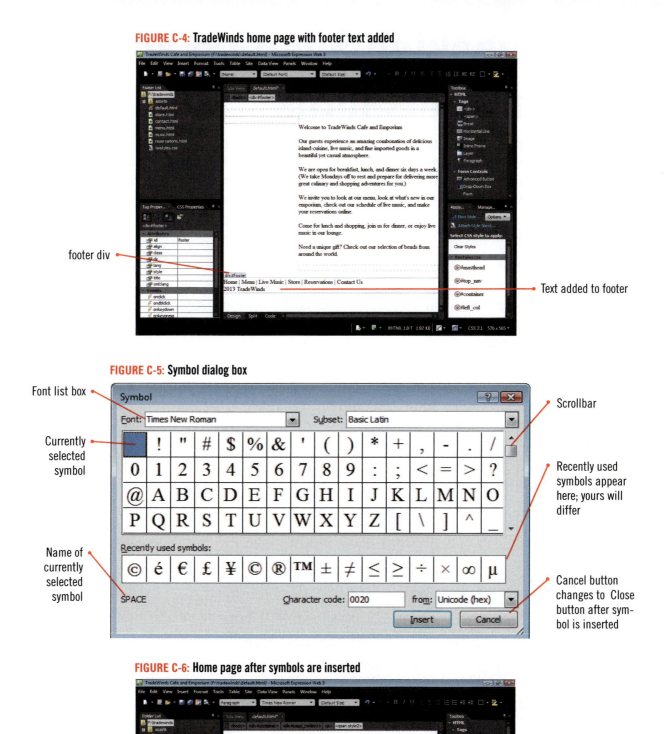

FIGURE C-4: TradeWinds home page with footer text added

footer div

Text added to footer

FIGURE C-5: Symbol dialog box

Font list box

Currently selected symbol

Name of currently selected symbol

Scrollbar

Recently used symbols appear here; yours will differ

Cancel button changes to Close button after symbol is inserted

FIGURE C-6: Home page after symbols are inserted

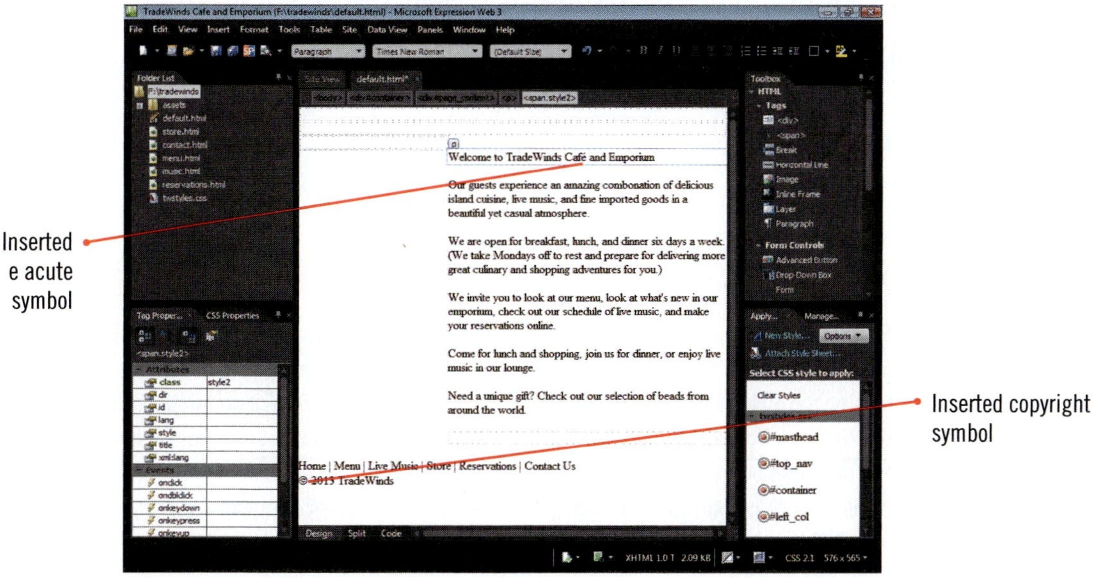

Inserted e acute symbol

Inserted copyright symbol

Expression Web 3

Checking Spelling and Using the Thesaurus

Visitors judge the credibility of a Web site not only on the design, but also on the quality and accuracy of the content. Expression Web includes a robust spelling feature that can help you identify and correct spelling errors either on individual pages or in an entire Web site. The Thesaurus feature allows you to look up synonyms of a word or phrase and substitute them for your text.  You noticed a few errors in the home page text, so you use the Spelling feature in Expression Web to correct them. You also decide to use the Thesaurus feature to help add variety to the wording of the text.

STEPS

1. **Click Tools on the menu bar, point to Spelling, click Spelling Options, click the Check spelling as you type checkbox if necessary, then click OK**

   The words "TradeWinds" and "combonation" are now underlined with a red wavy line, indicating potential spelling errors.

2. **Right-click the word combonation in the page_content div, as shown in Figure C-7**

   The shortcut menu offers alternatives to the misspelled word. It also displays options to Ignore All (if you want Expression Web to stop flagging this word as misspelled) and Add (if you would like to add this word as it is spelled to the custom dictionary).

3. **Click combination on the shortcut menu**

   The shortcut menu closes and the word "combination" replaces the misspelled word.

4. **Select the words look at in the phrase look at our menu, click Tools on the menu bar, then click Thesaurus**

   The Thesaurus dialog box opens, as shown in Figure C-8. The Meanings list displays words or phrases that are close in meaning to the word or phrase you selected, in this case, "look at." When you choose an option in the Meanings list, more words and phrases with meanings similar to the selected word appear in the Replace with Synonym list. You can choose one to replace the phrase.

5. **Click explore (verb) in the Meanings list, then click Replace**

   The Thesaurus dialog box closes, and "look at" is replaced by "explore."

6. **Right-click the word TradeWinds, then click Add**

   Your page should look like Figure C-9. The word "TradeWinds" is added to the custom dictionary and will no longer be flagged as misspelled in Expression Web.

7. **Save your changes to the page**

> **QUICK TIP**
> To remove an added word from the custom dictionary, click Tools, point to Spelling, click Spelling Options, click Custom Dictionaries, click Edit Word List, select the word, click Delete, then click OK three times in the dialog boxes.

Checking the spelling in an entire Web site

In addition to checking individual words on a page, you can check the spelling in a Web page or in an entire Web site at once. To check spelling in the current page, click Tools on the menu bar, point to Spelling, then click Spelling. To check spelling throughout all pages in a site, click the Site View tab to select it, click Tools on the menu bar, point to Spelling, then click Spelling. The Spelling dialog box opens, giving you the option of checking the spelling for selected pages or the entire site. If you choose the entire site, Expression Web displays a list of pages containing errors. Double-click the page name and Expression Web will open it and step through each possible error, allowing you to choose a replacement, ignore it, or add it to the custom dictionary. In addition to using the Spelling feature, you should always proofread each page in a site to check for any errors that were not recognized by the Spelling feature.

FIGURE C-7: Spelling shortcut menu

Red, wavy underlines indicate words that are possibly misspelled

Shortcut menu with spelling options

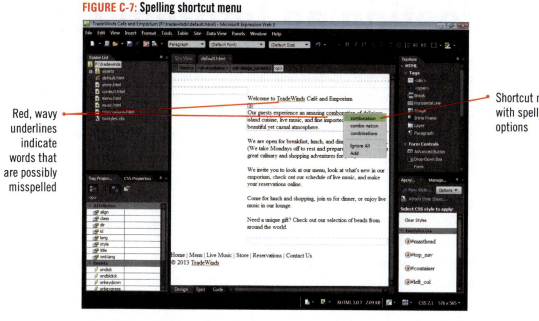

FIGURE C-8: Thesaurus dialog box

Text that was selected when Thesaurus dialog box opened

Meanings list displays synonyms for selected text

Selected meaning is highlighted

Word or phrase that will replace selected text if Replace button is clicked

Synonyms or equivalent meanings for currently selected meaning

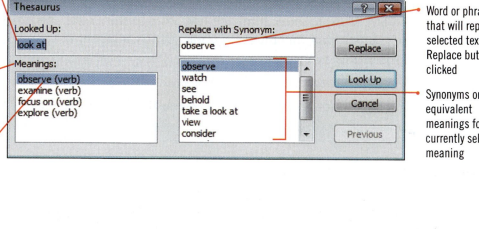

FIGURE C-9: TradeWinds home page after checking spelling and using the Thesauras

The word "TradeWinds" is no longer flagged as possible misspelling

The word "explore" replaces "look at"

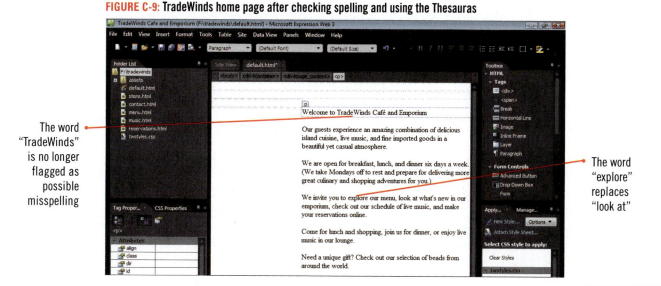

Adding Text and Links

Creating an Internal Link

You can create both internal and external links in Expression Web. **Internal links** are links between pages or files within the same Web site. **External links** are links to Web pages or files on a different Web site. A working link has two parts, called **anchors**. The first part is the **source anchor**, which is the word, phrase, or image on a Web page that leads to another page or file when a visitor clicks the link. The second part is the **destination anchor**, which is the file or page that opens when a visitor clicks the link.  You need to create the internal links for your text-based navigation at the bottom of the home page.

STEPS

1. **Select the word Home in the footer**

   Make sure to select only the word and not the space on either side, or the link underline will extend past the word. (It will still work, but will look a bit sloppy.)

2. **Right-click the selected word, then click Hyperlink on the shortcut menu**

   The Insert Hyperlink dialog box opens, as shown in Figure C-10. The text you selected, "Home," appears in the Text to display box.

   > **QUICK TIP**
   > You can create a link to any type of file, including movies, PDF files, and PowerPoint files; however, if you link to any type of file besides an image or Web page, visitors must have the necessary software installed on their computer in order to view the file.

3. **Click Existing File or Web Page under Link to if necessary, click Current Folder under Look in if necessary, click default.html (open), then click OK**

   The Insert Hyperlink dialog box closes. Home is now formatted in blue and underlined, indicating that it is a link. The default style is blue and underlined for links that have not yet been clicked and purple and underlined for links that have already been clicked.

4. **Using Steps 1–3 as a guide, link the text Menu in the footer to menu.html, the text Live Music to music.html, the text Store to store.html, the text Reservations to reservations.html, and the text Contact Us to contact.html**

   Your links are created, but you cannot test them in Design view. Testing links requires a Web browser.

5. **Click File on the menu bar, then click Save**

6. **Click the Preview in Browser button 🖼 on the Common toolbar**

   The home page opens in a browser window, as shown in Figure C-11. Your browser type and window size may differ from the one shown.

7. **Click the Store link at the bottom of the page**

   The Store page opens in the same browser window, indicating that the link is working.

8. **Close the browser, then return to Expression Web**

Maintaining your links

Creating an entire Web site in Expression Web, rather than just individual pages, makes it much easier to manage your Web site files. When you create links between pages, the file location and name are both part of the link URL. Normally, this means that if you move the file or rename it, the link will break and will no longer work.

However, if you rename and move your files within Expression Web, its site management features will update the links for you automatically. So be sure to always do your file management in Expression Web and not in Windows Explorer.

FIGURE C-10: Insert Hyperlink dialog box

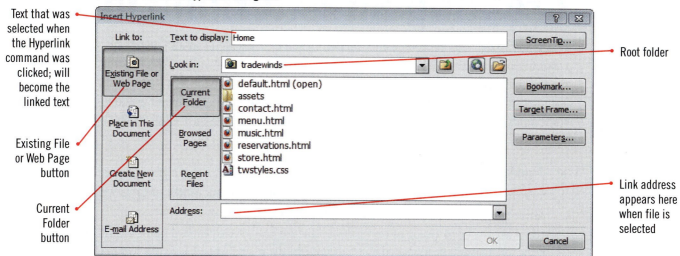

Text that was selected when the Hyperlink command was clicked; will become the linked text

Root folder

Existing File or Web Page button

Current Folder button

Link address appears here when file is selected

FIGURE C-11: Home page in browser with internal links in page footer

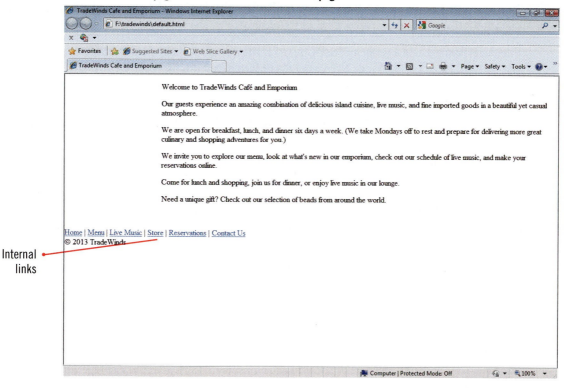

Internal links

Understanding absolute and relative URLs

A URL defines the location of a file. External files use **absolute URLs** containing a path that describes the protocol (such as http://), the domain name (such as centraluniversity.com), and the file path (such as /library/hours.html) to make up a complete URL such as http://centraluniversity.com/library/hours.html. Internal links use **relative URLs**, which contain a path that describes only the location of the file being linked relative to the source file. An example of a relative URL would be ../contact.html. This URL indicates that the file being linked to is one folder up (../) and is named contact.html. Notice that no protocol or domain name are included.

To grasp the concept of absolute versus relative URLs, consider the different ways you might give people directions to your house. You might give a friend relative directions, telling her to turn right out of her driveway, take a right at the next street, then turn in to the second house on the left. Those directions are relative to her starting point, in this case her house. On the other hand, you might give her absolute directions, telling her to go to 134 Chestnut Street. She would be able to find your house no matter where she started because this is an absolute address and it is not relative to her starting point.

Creating an External Link

In addition to defining the source and the destination of a link, you can also determine a link's target. The **target** is the browser window or frame in which the destination file opens. You can target internal or external links but not e-mail links.  Catalina requests that you create a link to a quilt museum Web site from the store page. You decide to create the link so it opens in a new browser window. This will leave the TradeWinds page open so a visitor can easily return after visiting the quilt museum site.

STEPS

1. **Double-click store.html in the Folder List panel to open the page**

2. **Select the text National Quilt Museum Web site near the middle of the page under Americana, right-click the selection, then click Hyperlink**

   The Insert Hyperlink dialog box opens, with the text you selected entered in the Text to display field. This is the text that will be formatted as a hyperlink on the page; if you change this text in the dialog box, you edit the text on the page. You can type a URL in the Address box to create a link to an external Web site. All external links must start with http://, but Expression Web will fill it in for you if you forget.

3. **In the Address box, type http://www.quiltmuseum.org, as shown in Figure C-12**

4. **Click Target Frame**

   The Target Frame dialog box opens. See Figure C-13. The left area lists any frames-based pages currently in the site. Since you aren't using frames to construct your Web pages, this list is empty. The right area lists options for targeting the link. Same Frame, Whole Page, and Parent Frame only apply to frames-based pages. New Window can be used on any type of page and opens the destination link in a new browser window. Page Default (none) resets the target to the default, meaning that it opens as a regular link would—in the same browser window as the source page.

TROUBLE

If you accidentally close the window before clicking the Target Frame button, right-click the link in Design view, then click Hyperlink Properties on the shortcut menu.

5. **Click New Window in the Common targets list**

   The text "_blank" appears in the Target setting box, indicating that the link will open in a blank, or new, browser window. Note that many people use software known as a pop-up blocker that prevents new browser windows from opening. Some pop-up blockers only block windows that open automatically without user intervention, such as annoying ads, but others prevent any new windows from opening, even when a visitor clicks the link. You are targeting this link to open in a new window, but you should be aware of this issue when you are browsing the Web. When in doubt, play it safe and don't open a link in a new window.

6. **Click OK, then click OK again**

   The dialog boxes close and you return to the store.html tab in the editing window. The text "National Quilt Museum" is blue and underlined, indicating a link.

QUICK TIP

If you need to make changes to an existing hyperlink, right-click the link in Design view, then select Hyperlink Properties from the shortcut menu.

7. **Save the page, then click the Preview in Browser button 📷 on the Common toolbar**

   The Store page opens in a browser window, as shown in Figure C-14. Your browser type and size may be different from the one shown; this is not a problem. Any browser type and size works fine for testing the links.

8. **Click the link National Quilt Museum Web site near the middle of the page**

   The National Quilt Museum Web site opens in a new browser window. The TradeWinds Store page is still open in the first browser window. (You may have to minimize the Museum browser window to see it.)

9. **Close both browser windows, then return to Expression Web**

FIGURE C-12: Insert Hyperlink dialog box

Text to display as the hyperlink

Address text box with URL filled in

Browse the Web button

Bookmark button

Target Frame button

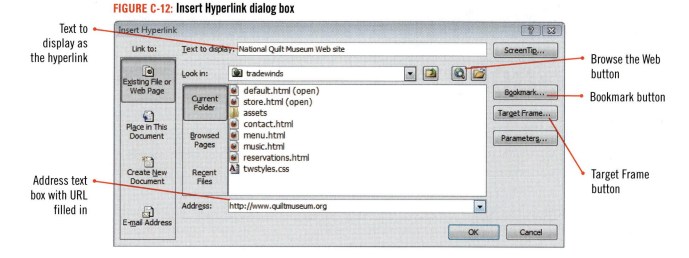

FIGURE C-13: Target Frame dialog box

New Window option

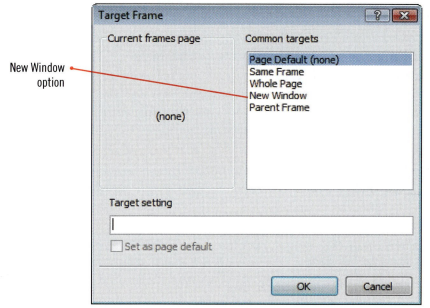

FIGURE C-14: Store page open in browser

Link to http:// www.quiltmuseum.org

Ensuring accuracy of URLs

Accurately typing a URL can be tricky—and if one character is wrong, the link won't work. To ensure that your link URLs are accurate, you can use one of two methods. You can visit the site in a browser and copy the URL from the browser's address window, then paste it into the Address text box when you insert the hyperlink in Expression Web. Or, you can save time by using the Browse the Web button 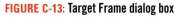 in the Insert Hyperlink dialog box. Click the button to open your default browser. Surf to the page you want to link to, then leave the browser open and return to Expression Web. The Insert Hyperlink dialog box is displayed again and the address of the site automatically appears in the Address text box—like magic!

Creating and Linking to a Bookmark

A **bookmark**, also known as a **named anchor**, is a marker at a specific spot on a Web page that can be used as a destination anchor. Designers often use bookmarks to create a table of contents at the top of a long, scrolling page so that when visitors click a link, they jump down the page to that particular section. Bookmarks can also be used to link from one page to a specific section of a different page. Creating a bookmark is a two-part process: first you create a bookmark for the text that will serve as the destination anchor; then you create the link to the bookmark.  You want to link information on the home page about beads to the bead section of the store page. First you need to create the bookmark on the store page, and then you can create the link on the home page to the bookmark.

STEPS

1. **If necessary, click the store.html tab to make it the active page**

2. **Select the text World Bead Collection approximately one-third of the way down the page, click Insert on the menu bar, then click Bookmark**
    The Bookmark dialog box opens, as shown in Figure C-15. The Bookmark name text box displays a suggested name for the bookmark based on the text you selected. You decide the name World_Bead_Collection is fine. A bookmark name cannot contain any spaces or special characters, and no two bookmarks on the same page can have the same name.

3. **Click OK**
    The Bookmark dialog box closes. A visual aid consisting of a dashed line appears under the text "World Bead Collection," indicating that this is a bookmark. See Figure C-16. The visual aid is only to help you see the bookmark, which would otherwise be invisible. The dashed line will not appear when the page is viewed in a browser.

4. **Save your changes to store.html, click the default.html tab, then select the text selection of beads in the last sentence**
    This is the text you wish to link to the World_Bead_Collection bookmark on the Store page.

5. **Right-click the selection, click Hyperlink on the shortcut menu, in the Insert Hyperlink dialog box click Existing File or Web Page under Link to if necessary, click Current Folder under Look in if necessary, then click store.html (open)**

6. **Click Bookmark, click World_Bead_Collection, then click OK**
    The Select Place in Document dialog box closes. See Figure C-17. The relative URL shows up in the Address box. Links to bookmarks are constructed by adding # and the name of the bookmark to the end of the file name in which the bookmark is inserted.

7. **Click OK**
    The Insert Hyperlink dialog box closes. The text "selection of beads" is now linked.

8. **Save your changes, click the Preview in Browser button ■ on the Common toolbar, then click the selection of beads link**
    The Store page opens in your Web browser. Because the link is to the bookmark, the page opens so that World Bead Collection is at the top of the page.

9. **Close the browser and return to Expression Web**
    Your bookmark name may have an extra underscore at the end (e.g., "World_Bead_Collection_") if you also selected the space after "Collection"; this is fine.

FIGURE C-15: Bookmark dialog box

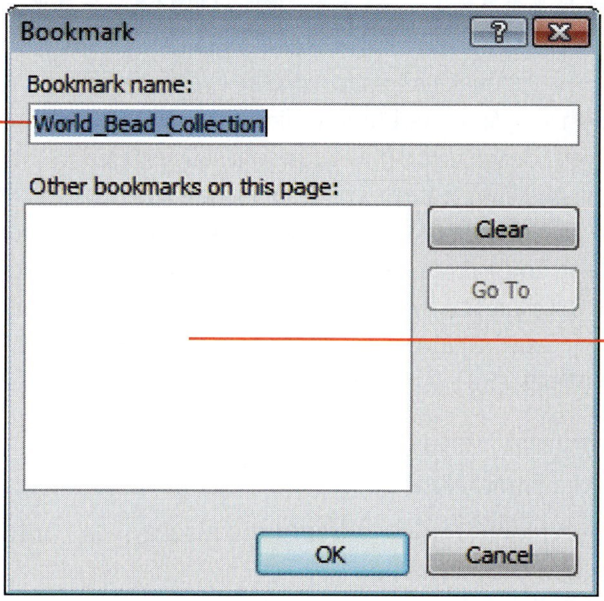

Bookmark name text box →

Bookmark

Bookmark name:
World_Bead_Collection

Other bookmarks on this page:

Clear

Go To

← If there were other bookmarks on this page, they would be listed here

OK   Cancel

FIGURE C-16: Store page after bookmark is inserted

Dashed line indicates bookmark; this line will not appear in a browser →

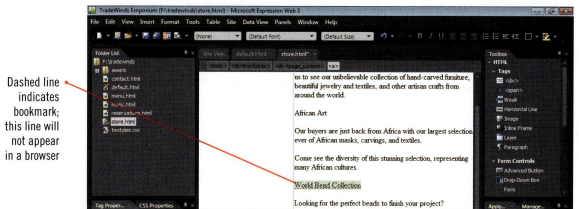

FIGURE C-17: Creating a link to the bookmark

Text that will display in link →

Address or URL of bookmark on Store page →

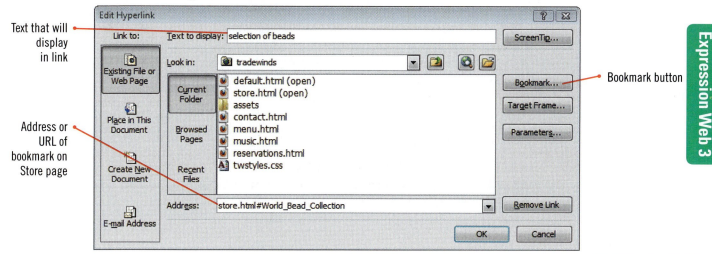

← Bookmark button

Creating an E-Mail Link

Including an e-mail link on your contact page or elsewhere on your Web site makes it easy for visitors to communicate with you. An **e-mail link** is a link that opens an e-mail message in the visitor's default e-mail program, with your designated e-mail address already entered in the To line. Visitors to a site often use e-mail links to ask questions, note problems, or request additional information. While putting an e-mail link on a Web page can increase the amount of **spam**, or bulk unsolicited e-mail, received, many Web sites include e-mail links. To create an e-mail link, you select the text or image that you want visitors to click, and then format the selection as a hyperlink and specify the information that should appear in the e-mail message that is generated when a visitor clicks the link. Catalina is eager to receive feedback from visitors to the TradeWinds Web site, so you decide to create an e-mail link on the contact page.

STEPS

1. **Double-click contact.html in the Folder List panel to open the page**

2. **Select the text info@tradewindsemporium.com at the bottom of the page, right-click the selection, then click Hyperlink**

   The Insert Hyperlink dialog box opens. For link text, you can use a phrase such as "Email us" instead of the address; however, using the e-mail address as the link text ensures that people can read the address even if there's a problem opening the link with their e-mail program or if they print the page.

3. **Click the E-mail Address button under Link to**

4. **Type info@tradewindsemporium.com in the E-mail address text box, type Web Site Contact in the Subject text box, then compare your screen to Figure C-18**

   As you type the email address, the "mailto:" protocol is automatically inserted in front of the address. This completes the html code required to make the link work properly in the Web site.

5. **Click OK, then click away from the link to deselect it**

   The Insert Hyperlink dialog box closes. The e-mail address is linked and appears as blue, underlined text, as shown in Figure C-19. When visitors click the e-mail link, a new e-mail outgoing message window will open on their computer, with the e-mail address and subject line already filled in. They can then complete the message and send it.

6. **Save changes to the page**

   Creating a subject line for the e-mail message makes it easy for the person who receives the messages to see e-mails that have originated from the Web site; however, visitors can change the subject line in their e-mail program.

Writing good link text

Writing good link text is an art. Clear, accurate link text minimizes any distraction from the content and lets the visitor know what to expect when they click a link. Some general guidelines include:
• Write naturally, but plan for placement of the link.
• When possible, place link text toward the end of a sentence.
• Make the link text meaningful and obvious.
• Don't use "click here" in link text.
This last point deserves special attention. Avoid using "click here" because:
• When out of context, it is meaningless. If visitors are scanning the page and "click here" repeatedly catches their eye, the phrase provides no additional information about the page.

• It is device-dependent. Not all users "click" to follow a link; navigation varies with different devices.
• It lowers search engine rankings for your site. Search engines give weight to link text, and "click here" offers no clue to help the search engine software decide what your site is all about.
• It makes your site less accessible to those who have visual impairments and who use screen readers to hear content, including links. A series of links labeled "click here" doesn't clarify the surrounding context for a screen reader system, making navigation difficult.

FIGURE C-18: Creating the e-mail link

E-mail address text box

Subject text box

E-mail Address button

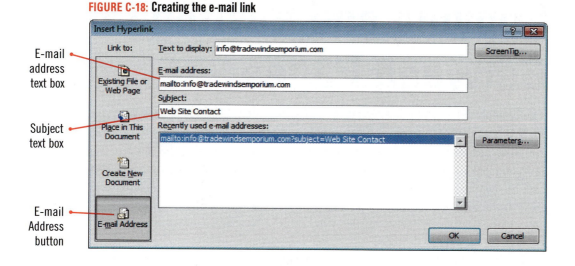

FIGURE C-19: E-mail link on contact page

E-mail link

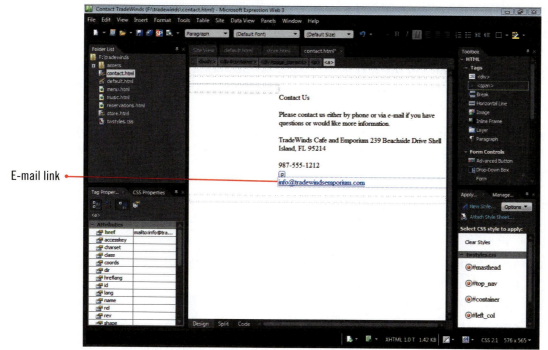

Avoiding spam generated by e-mail links

While it is convenient for both you and your visitors to have an e-mail link on your Web site, it can be an open invitation for a flood of spam. Spammers use software called "harvesters" to crawl through Web pages and find linked e-mail addresses. They then add those addresses to their mailing lists, and the unfortunate recipient can begin to receive hundreds or thousands of unwanted e-mails a day. To protect yourself from spam, consider using an HTML form instead of providing a direct link to your e-mail address.

Copying and Pasting Content Between Pages

It is common to have text that repeats on every page of a Web site. To save you having to manually type the text again on each page, you can simply copy text from one page and paste it into another. When you paste between pages, the formatting and links are maintained.  You want to create a set of navigation links in the footer of each page in the site. To save time, you decide to copy the e-mail address from the contact page into the home page footer, and then copy the complete navigation and copyright notice from the home page footer to all the other pages in the site.

STEPS

TROUBLE
Be sure to right-click the highlighted text. If you click outside the text, it will be deselected. If this happens, select it again, then right-click the selected text.

1. **On the contact.html page, select the info@tradewindsemporium.com link, right-click, then click Copy on the shortcut menu**
   The text is copied to the Windows Clipboard.

2. **Click the default.html tab, click at the end of the copyright line in the footer div, press [Spacebar], type [|], press [Spacebar] again, right-click after the space, then click Paste**
   The text is pasted with the hyperlink intact, as shown in Figure C-20. The home page now has a complete footer with a top row of text-based navigation and a bottom row containing the copyright notice and e-mail address separated by a vertical pipe. You want this same footer on every page, but you don't want to have to type it into every page and re-create all the links.

QUICK TIP
Remember to use the visual aids and quick tag selector bar to make sure the cursor is in the correct div.

3. **Select both lines of the text in the footer div beginning with Home | and ending with info@tradewindsemporium.com, right-click, then click Copy on the shortcut menu**
   The selected text is copied to the Windows Clipboard.

4. **Make store.html the active page, click in the footer div, right-click, then click Paste**
   The entire footer from the home page, with links intact, is on the store page. See Figure C-21.

TROUBLE
If one or more of these pages are not open, double-click the file name in the Folder List panel or Web site tab.

5. **Using Step 4 four as a guide, open each page and paste the footer text and links into the footer of the contact, menu, music, and reservations pages**
   You don't need to copy the selection again, because it remains in the Windows Clipboard until you cut or copy a new selection, or until you exit Expression Web.

6. **Save changes to all pages, click the music.html tab, then click the Preview in Browser button** on the Common toolbar
   The music page opens in the Web browser window. See Figure C-22.

7. **Click the Store link at the bottom of the page**
   The store page opens in the browser window, indicating that the link is working.

8. **Close the browser, then return to Expression Web**

9. **Close the Web site, save any changes to your pages if prompted, then exit Expression Web**

FIGURE C-20: Home page with pasted e-mail address link

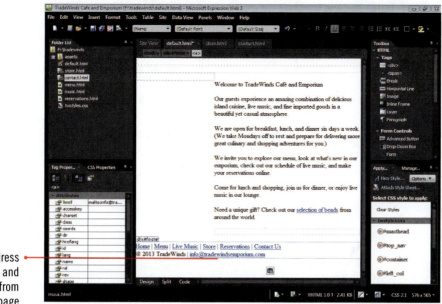

E-mail address copied and pasted from Contact Us page

FIGURE C-21: Store page

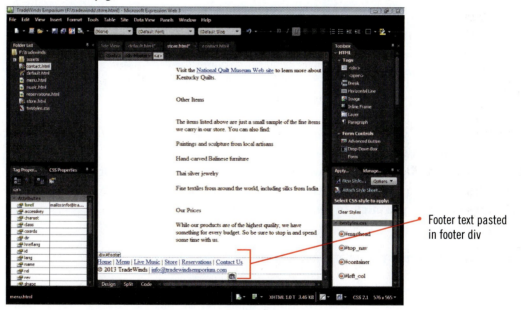

Footer text pasted in footer div

FIGURE C-22: Music page with footer open in browser

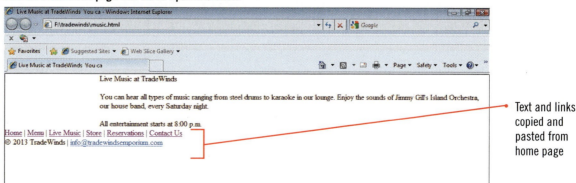

Text and links copied and pasted from home page

Practice

For current SAM information including versions and content details, visit SAM Central (http://samcentral.course.com). If you have a SAM user profile, you may have access to hands-on instruction, practice, and assessment of the skills covered in this unit. Since we support various versions of SAM throughout the life of this text, you will want to check with your instructor for instructions and the correct URL/Web site to access those assignments.

Concepts Review

Use Figure C-23 to answer the following questions.

FIGURE C-23

1. Which element do you click to create a link that will allow visitors to contact you from your Web site?
2. Which element do you type in to create an external link?
3. Which element do you click to change in which browser window a link opens?
4. Which element displays the text that will display as the source link?
5. Which element do you click to link to a particular area on a page?

Match each term with the statement that best describes it.

6. **Bookmark**   **a.** Allows visitors to send e-mail from a Web site

7. **Internal link**   **b.** Uses absolute URL

8. **External link**   **c.** Uses relative URL

9. **Spam**   **d.** Also known as a named anchor

10. **E-mail link**   **e.** Unsolicited bulk e-mail

Select the best answer from the list of choices.

11. The safest option to choose when pasting text if you want to avoid conflicts later with CSS styles is:
    a. Match Destination Formatting.
    c. Keep HTML Only.
    b. Keep Source Formatting.
    d. Keep Text Only.

12. The spelling tools in Expression Web allow you to:
    a. Check the spelling in an entire Web site.
    c. Add your own words to the custom dictionary.
    b. Check the spelling on a single Web page.
    d. All of the above

13. If you create a link from your personal Web site to the Microsoft Web site, this would be considered:
    a. An internal link.
    c. An external link.
    b. A source anchor.
    d. A destination anchor.

14. Which of the following are not allowed as part of a bookmark name?
    a. Spaces
    c. Special characters
    b. Uppercase letters
    d. Both a and c are correct

15. A bookmark is also known as:
    a. an external link.
    c. a source link.
    b. an absolute URL.
    d. a named anchor.

Skills Review

1. **Paste text into a Web page.**
    a. Launch Expression Web, then open the careers Web site.
    b. Open the default.html page, use the quick tag selector to select the contents of the page_content div, then delete the contents.
    c. Launch Microsoft Word, open the Open dialog box, navigate to the folder where you store your Data Files, open the Unit C folder, then open the cg_home.docx file.
    d. Select all the text, then copy it to the Windows Clipboard.
    e. Close Microsoft Word and return to Expression Web.
    f. Paste the text into the page_content div in the default.html page as Keep text only and as Normal paragraphs without line breaks.
    g. Save the page.

2. **Type text into a Web page and insert symbols.**
    a. In the footer div of the home page, type **Home | Services | About | Contact**.
    b. Press [Enter], then type **2013 Careers Guaranteed**.
    c. Use the Symbol dialog box to insert a copyright symbol and a space in front of the text **2013**.
    d. Save your changes to the file.

3. **Check spelling and use the thesaurus.**
    a. Correct the spelling error on the home page.
    b. Use the Thesaurus feature to find another word or phrase to replace the word **work** in the sentence "You know how those other career sites work." (*Hint:* You will have many options; be sure to choose one that makes sense in the context of the sentence.)
    c. Save your changes to the file.

4. **Create an internal link.**
    a. Create a link from the word **Home** in the footer div of the home page to the same page, default.html. (*Hint*: You want the option to link to an existing page.)
    b. Create a link from the word **Services** in the footer div of the home page to the services.html page.
    c. Create a link from the word **About** in the footer div of the home page to the about.html page.
    d. Create a link from the word **Contact** in the footer div of the home page to the contact.html page.
    e. Save your changes to the page, then preview the home page in a browser and check each link.

Skills Review (continued)

5. Create an external link.

   a. Open the about page.

   b. In the paragraph under Tina Russo, Chief Technology Officer, link the text **vintage synthesizers** to **http://www.synthmuseum.com** and set the link to open in a new window.

   c. Save your changes.

   d. Preview the about page and click the link to test it. When you are finished, close both browser windows.

6. Create a bookmark and link to it.

   a. Open the services page.

   b. Select the text **Help with career planning:** and insert a bookmark.

   c. Save the page.

   d. Switch to the home page.

   e. Select the text **career exploration tools**, then create a link to the bookmark in the services.html page.

   f. Save the page.

   g. Preview the home page in a browser and test the link.

7. Create an e-mail link.

   a. Open the contact page.

   b. Select the text **info@careersguaranteed.com**.

   c. Link the selected text as an e-mail link to info@careersguaranteed.com with a subject line of **Web site e-mail**.

   d. Save the page.

8. Copy and paste content between pages.

   a. In the contact page, copy the **info@careersguaranteed.com e-mail** link to the Clipboard.

   b. Switch to the home page.

   c. In the last line of the footer div, click after the word **Guaranteed**, press [Spacebar], type **[|]**, then press [Spacebar] again.

   d. Paste the e-mail link at the location of the insertion point.

   e. Select the entire contents of the footer. This includes both lines of text, the navigation, and the copyright notice with e-mail link.

   f. Paste this into the footer div on all pages of the site.

   g. Save all pages.

   h. Preview the Home page in a browser, then test the links. Your page should look similar to Figure C-24.

   i. Close the browser window, close the Web site, then exit Expression Web.

FIGURE C-24

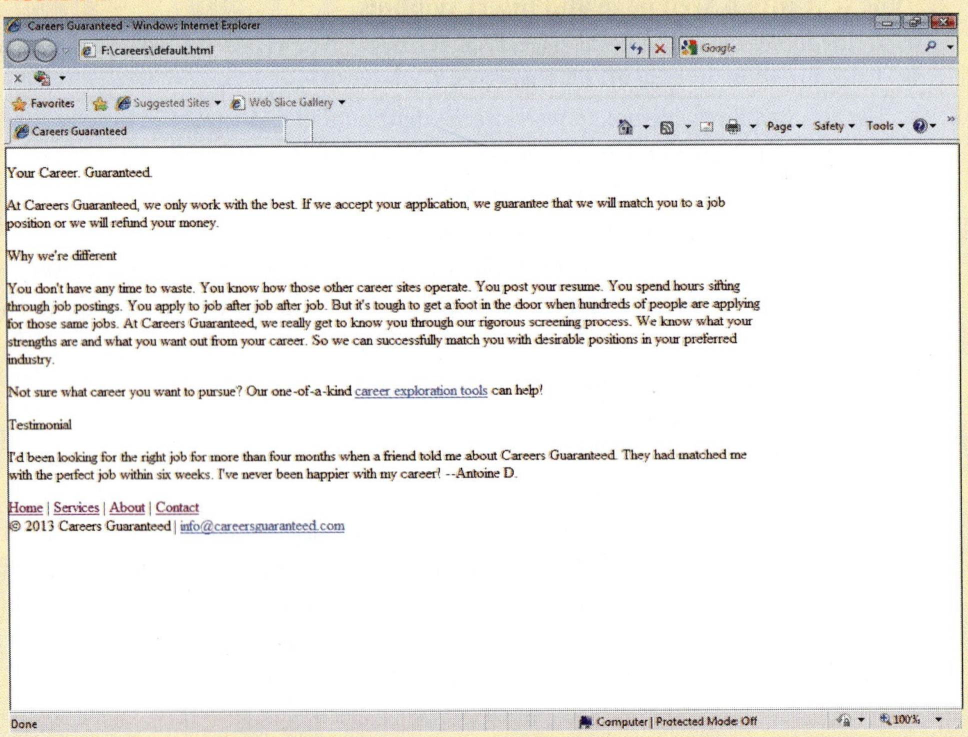

Independent Challenge 1

In this project, you continue your work on the ConnectUp Web site. Tiffany has provided you with content that you need to add to the site. You also want to add some navigation links at the bottom of the pages.

a. Launch Expression Web, then open the connectup Web site.

b. Open the home page, delete the contents of the page_content div, then copy the contents of cu_home.docx from within Microsoft Word and paste it as text only, Normal paragraphs without line breaks, into the page_content div.

c. On the home page, add the following text in the footer div: **Home | Join Up | FAQ | Contact Us**.

d. On a new line under the new text, add a copyright statement that includes a copyright symbol.

e. Check the spelling on the home page and correct any misspellings. Add ConnectUp to the custom dictionary so it is no longer flagged as a misspelled word.

f. Use the Insert Hyperlink function to link the name of each page in the footer div of the home page to the appropriate Web page in the site.

g. On the faq page, link the words **Charity Navigator** to http://www.charitynavigator.org; target the link to open in a new window.

h. On the faq page, select the word **Membership**, insert a bookmark, then save the page.

i. On the joinup page, link the text **Frequently Asked Questions** to the bookmark you created on the faq page.

j. On the contact page, select the text **info@connectupyourlife.com**, then create an e-mail link with a subject line of your choosing.

k. Copy the e-mail link from the contact page into the footer of the home page after the copyright statement. (*Hint*: Add some space and a pipe to separate the two and make them easier to read.)

l. Copy and paste the content of the footer div on the home page into the other pages. (*Hint*: You should have two lines of text to paste.)

m. Save changes to all pages, then preview the joinup page in a browser and check all the links. Your screen should look similar to Figure C-25.

n. Close the browser windows, close the Web site, then exit Expression Web.

FIGURE C-25

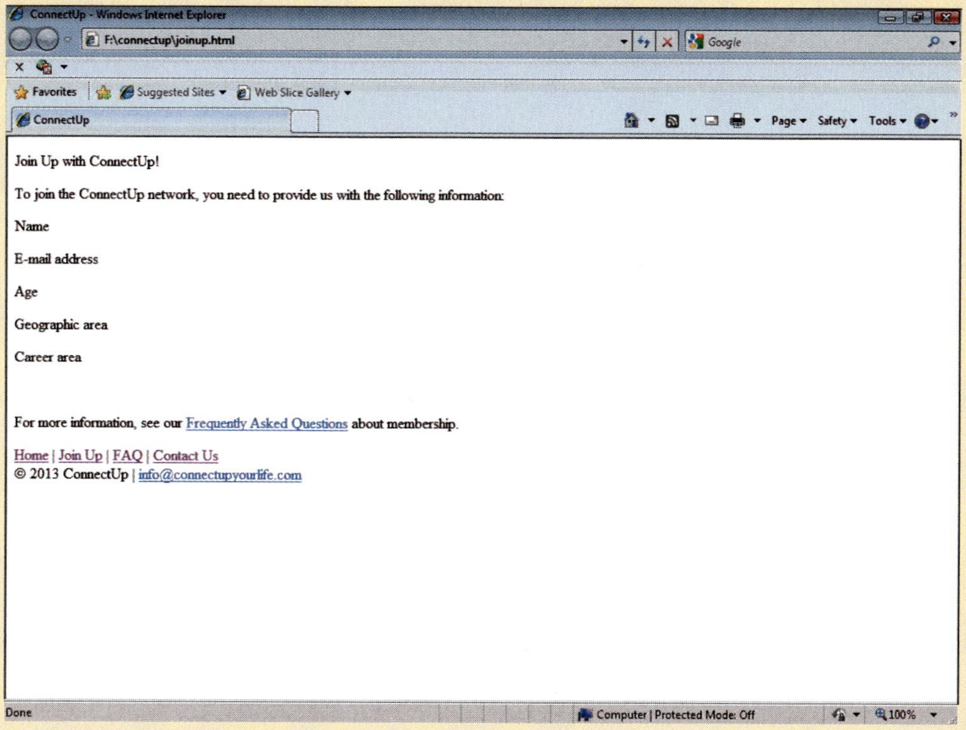

Independent Challenge 2

In this project, you continue your work on the Memories Restored Web site. Brian has sent you the content so that you can start adding it to the pages.

   a. Launch Expression Web, then open the Memories Restored Web site.

   b. Add the contents of the mr_home.docx file to the home page, replacing the contents of the page_content div. (*Hint*: Be sure to choose your paste options wisely to avoid bringing in formatting along with the text.)

   c. Add the contents of mr_contact.docx, mr_process.docx, mr_testimonials.docx, and mr_work.docx to the appropriate files.

   d. On the home page, check the spelling and correct any errors. If you like, use the Thesaurus feature to make changes to the text.

   e. Link the e-mail address on the contact page.

   f. On the home page, create a footer that contains links to all pages in the site, a copyright statement, and an e-mail link.

   g. Copy the footer and paste it into the footer of all other pages in the site.

   h. Add an external link that opens in a new window to a page of your choosing. (*Hint*: Check the process page for an idea for an external link relating to payment for services.)

   i. Add a bookmark to a page, then create a link to the bookmark either from the same page or a different one. (*Hint*: One method is to link from the home page to the testimonials from organizations text at the bottom of the testimonials page.)

Advanced Challenge Exercise

- Copy the contents of the mr_ace_tips.docx file into the tips page you created.
- Enter **photo restoration tips** into your favorite search engine, and look through the results to find a site you like that provides advice on restoring photos.
- Under the inserted text in the page_content div, type **Resources**, then add text describing the site you found and an external link to the site.

   j. Save your work, then preview your pages in a browser and check the links. When you are finished, close the Web site, then exit Expression Web.

Independent Challenge 3

Note: This Independent Challenge requires an Internet connection.

Technology for All has asked you to research some guidelines their editors and writers can use when developing content for the company's Web site.

a. Enter the phrase **writing for the web** into your favorite search engine. From the search results, choose and read at least three articles from three different authors related to how to write for the Web. (*Hint*: You may need to go past the first page of search results to find three quality articles.) If you find an article that doesn't seem credible, find another. Take notes while you're reading.

b. Based on the information you read, create a summary that lists at least five principles the editors and writers at Technology for All can use when writing content for the Web. Briefly explain each principle. Add one paragraph explaining why writing for the Web is different from writing for a print publication.

Advanced Challenge Exercise

- Visit two of the four sites you wrote about in Unit B, and spend some time looking at how the content is written and structured.
- Evaluate the content based on the guidelines you created.
- Write a paragraph on each site evaluating how well it met or didn't meet your guidelines.

c. Add your name to the document, save it, and print it.

d. Close your Web browser and your word processing program.

Real Life Independent Challenge

This assignment builds on the personal Web site you started planning in Unit A and created in Unit B. In this project, you add text and links to your Web pages.

a. Add a heading describing the page (for example, About this Site) and at least one paragraph of text to each of your Web pages.

b. If you copy and paste the text from other sources, use the appropriate options to paste only the text and not the formatting.

c. Check the spelling of all your content to be sure you don't have any misspellings.

d. Create an e-mail link so visitors can contact you.

e. Add text-based navigation at the bottom of each page to link the pages together.

f. Add at least one external link and one bookmark link to your site.

g. Preview your pages in a browser, and test the links to be sure they work.

h. Begin collecting or creating images for your site.

i. Begin thinking of a color scheme for your site.

j. When you are finished, close the Web site, then exit Expression Web.

Visual Workshop

Launch Expression Web, then open the **ecotours** Web site. Add the content from the et_home.docx file, located in the drive and folder where you store your Data Files, to the page_content div on the home page. Make any necessary additions so that when you your page in a Web browser, it looks like Figure C-26. Print a copy of the page using your browser's Print feature. Save the page, close the Web site, then exit Expression Web.

FIGURE C-26

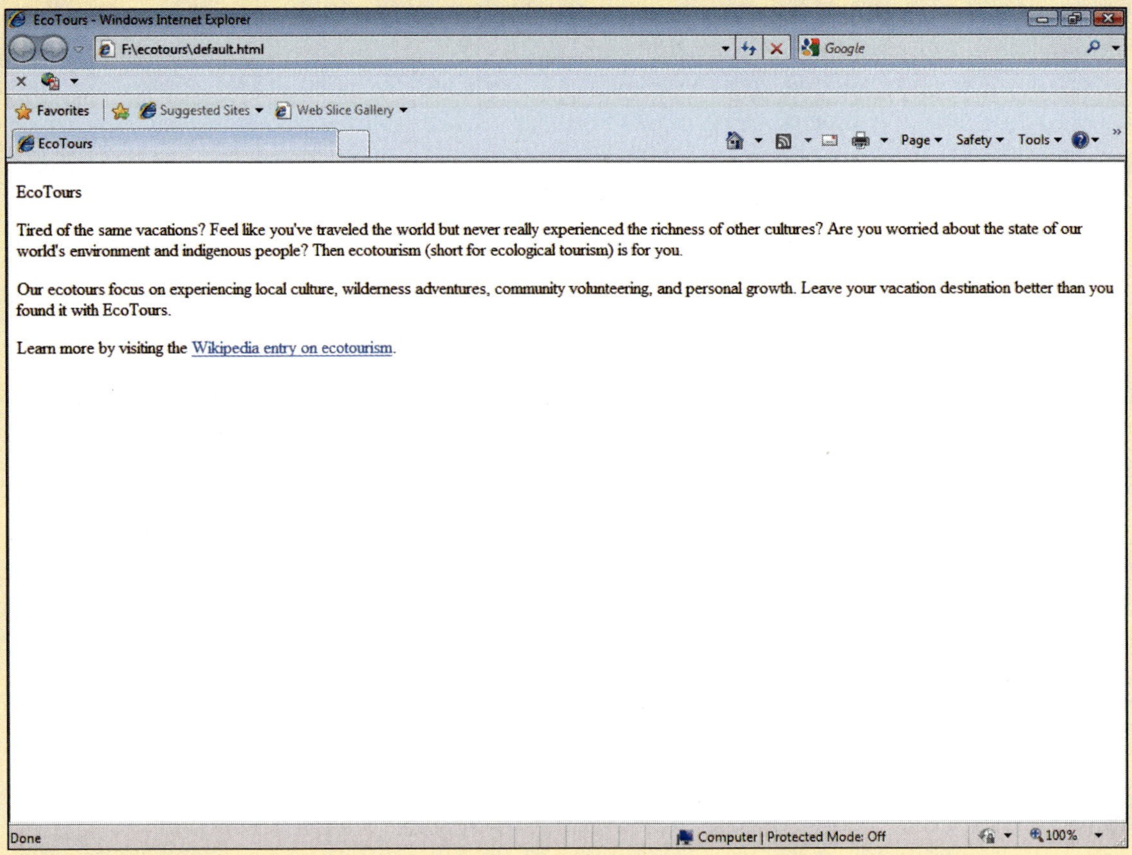
EcoTours - Windows Internet Explorer
F:\ecotours\default.html
Google
Favorites
Suggested Sites
Web Slice Gallery
EcoTours
Page
Safety
Tools
EcoTours
Tired of the same vacations? Feel like you've traveled the world but never really experienced the richness of other cultures? Are you worried about the state of our world's environment and indigenous people? Then ecotourism (short for ecological tourism) is for you.
Our ecotours focus on experiencing local culture, wilderness adventures, community volunteering, and personal growth. Leave your vacation destination better than you found it with EcoTours.
Learn more by visiting the Wikipedia entry on ecotourism.
Done
Computer | Protected Mode: Off
100%

Structuring and Styling Text

In order to practice good, standard-based Web design, you need to separate structure from visual design. This means using HTML to meaningfully define a document's structure by identifying pieces of text as paragraphs, quotes, lists, headings, or other elements. Once you've structured the content, you use CSS to control its presentation by defining visual properties such as fonts, colors, margins, and the position of elements on the page. By keeping the structure and presentation separate, you have more flexibility in how you use the content. For example, you can create a special style sheet to present a less heavily formatted version of your site to visitors accessing it through their cell phones. Using CSS, you can also easily update your site by making a change to one style and applying it to all the pages in a site at once.  You have added all the text to the TradeWinds site. Now it's time to create structure for the text and to create styles to control its presentation.

OBJECTIVES

Structure content with HTML

Create paragraphs and line breaks

Create headings

Create lists

Understand Cascading Style Sheets

Create an element-based style rule

Modify a style rule

Create a class-based style rule

Apply and remove a class-based style rule

Structuring Content with HTML

Structuring your HTML documents properly is the key to a reliable, well-built Web site. If you take the time to use appropriate HTML markup, you will have more flexibility in the way you work with content later, fewer hassles when it comes to updating your site, and an easier time creating and applying CSS styles.  You spend some time studying the way HTML documents are structured so you can logically structure the content for the TradeWinds site.

DETAILS

To understand HTML document structure, review the following concepts:

- **HTML tags and elements**

  Using HTML allows you to add tags to a document to denote meaning and structure. **HTML tags** are simply text enclosed in angle brackets; they identify each piece of Web page content. For example, in the code `<li>study for test</li>`, the `<li>` tags indicate that "study for test" is a list item. Most HTML tags surround the content they define with an opening tag and a closing tag. The closing tag is the same as the opening tag with the addition of a "/" before the tag name.

  The combination of an opening tag, content, and a closing tag is known as an **element**. Elements can also have **attributes**, which describe other properties of the element. For example, in Figure D-1, the attribute "class" specifies that the element belongs to the style class "important." While it's helpful to understand the concept behind how HTML works, the tools in Expression Web allow you to create well-structured content without knowing how to write HTML tags. Lucky you! The use of tags to describe the structure of a document is known as **markup**. This accounts for the "M" in HTML (HyperText Markup Language).

QUICK TIP
Semantic means "related to meaning."

- **Semantic markup**

  Following principles of **semantic markup**—that is, using HTML tags to mark up elements in a meaningful and descriptive way—is important. See Figure D-2 for an example of a well-structured document. Because semantic markup was used to create the Web page, the structure is clear even without applying a style sheet. Although people who visit your site don't see your code, the devices they use do. Browsers, search engines, and assistive devices for people with disabilities all use HTML code to help interpret your Web page.

  The concept of meaningful markup is probably easiest to understand by considering an example of non-semantic markup, or markup that is used solely for presentation rather than for structure or meaning. An example would be the first line of text on a Web page, which usually serves as a heading. A nonsemantic approach to marking up the text would be to create a style to display it as bold and red, without also applying an `<h1>` tag to mark the text as a first-level heading. Using this method, the text may look like a heading, but it has no structural meaning without the HTML tag and devices will not recognize it as a heading.

QUICK TIP
HTML includes many other tags that can be used to structure content, but most of them are fairly obscure and rarely used.

- **Common text elements**

  All content on a Web page should be contained in an element, so that it can be controlled using CSS. The elements used most often are shown in Table D-1.

FIGURE D-1: HTML element

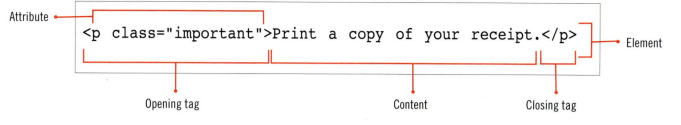

Attribute

`<p class="important">Print a copy of your receipt.</p>`

Element

Opening tag   Content   Closing tag

FIGURE D-2: A well-structured HTML document with styles disabled

Body text and three levels of headings are apparent even without style sheet applied

> css Zen Garden: The Beauty in CSS Design - Windows Internet Explorer
>
> http://www.csszengarden.com/zengarden-sample.html   Google
>
> Favorites   Suggested Sites ▾   Web Slice Gallery ▾
>
> css Zen Garden: The Beauty in CSS Design   Page ▾ Safety ▾ Tools ▾
>
> ## css Zen Garden
>
> ### The Beauty of CSS Design
>
> A demonstration of what can be accomplished visually through CSS-based design. Select any style sheet from the list to load it into this page.
>
> Download the sample html file and css file
>
> ### The Road to Enlightenment
>
> Littering a dark and dreary road lay the past relics of browser-specific tags, incompatible DOMs, and broken CSS support.
>
> Today, we must clear the mind of past practices. Web enlightenment has been achieved thanks to the tireless efforts of folk like the W3C, WaSP and the major browser creators.
>
> The css Zen Garden invites you to relax and meditate on the important lessons of the masters. Begin to see with clarity. Learn to use the (yet to be) time-honored techniques in new and invigorating fashion. Become one with the web.
>
> ### So What is This About?
>
> There is clearly a need for CSS to be taken seriously by graphic artists. The Zen Garden aims to excite, inspire, and encourage participation. To begin, view some of the existing designs in the list. Clicking on any one will load the style sheet into this very page. The code remains the same, the only thing that has changed is the external .css file. Yes, really.

TABLE D-1: Common HTML text elements

element	tag	purpose
paragraph	`<p>`	Creates a paragraph of text
line break	` `	Creates a line break to force text to the next line, while still keeping it in the same paragraph
unordered list	`<ul>`	Creates a bulleted list
ordered list	`<ol>`	Creates a numbered list
headings `<h1>` through `<h6>`	`<h1>`, `<h2>`, `<h3>`, `<h4>`, `<h5>`, `<h6>`	Creates headings with `<h1>` being the highest level and `<h6>` being the lowest

Understanding screen readers

People who are blind or have severely impaired eyesight use software called a **screen reader** to help them use a computer. Screen readers use a synthesized voice to read aloud the text that is on the screen. Built-in controls on most screen readers allow the user to navigate through the content. However, these controls rely on the document being well structured. When a screen reader encounters a tag indicating the presence of a list, for example, it activates controls that allow the user to skip to the next list item. If the structural HTML tags are absent or incorrectly applied, it makes it difficult or impossible for visitors who use screen readers to navigate through the content.

Expression Web 3

Creating Paragraphs and Line Breaks

The most basic structural elements for text are paragraphs and line breaks. In HTML, the <p> tag is used to denote a paragraph element. The <br /> element is used to create a new line of text within an existing paragraph without creating a new paragraph. You don't need to use line breaks often, but they can come in handy when you want to force text to the next line without creating a new paragraph.  You notice that the TradeWinds address on the contact page is not listed on separate lines. You decide to add line breaks to make it more readable.

1. **Launch Expression Web, open the tradewinds site, then open contact.html**

TROUBLE
If all the formatting marks do not appear, click View in the menu bar, point to Formatting Marks, then click Show.

2. **Click the Show Split View button at the bottom of the editing window, click View on the menu bar, point to Formatting Marks, then click Show**

   Using Split view, you can continue to work in the Design pane and see the code generated by Expression Web. Showing formatting marks allows you to see paragraph and line break marks in Design view.

3. **In the Design pane, click in front of the text 239 in the TradeWinds address**

   See Figure D-3. The Code pane shows that all the address text is contained in a single paragraph tag with no line breaks. The Design pane shows that the address text runs together, breaking to the next line only when it reaches the right edge of the editing window.

QUICK TIP
All text within a paragraph element wraps automatically according to the size of the page, so there's no need to hyphenate text.

4. **Press [Enter]**

   A new paragraph element is inserted, as shown in Figure D-4. A visual aid appears with a p in the tab, indicating the new paragraph. Expression Web creates a new paragraph any time you press [Enter] while in Design view, when the insertion point is in a paragraph. Browsers usually display text contained in a <p> tag with no indentation and with top and bottom margins that create white space above and below the paragraph. Although you want the text to break to a new line, you do not want to create a new paragraph.

5. **Click Edit on the menu bar, then click Undo Insert**

   The paragraph element is removed.

QUICK TIP
If you press [Shift] [Enter] when your cursor is in Code view, you create a line break in the code itself, not a <br/> tag in the page.

6. **Press [Shift][Enter]**

   The street address appears on a new line with no extra white space, and a <br /> tag appears in the Code pane. Expression Web inserts a line break whenever you press [Shift][Enter] rather than [Enter]. A line break has no visual aid or closing tag, since it doesn't hold any content and is considered an empty element.

7. **Click in front of the word Shell in the Design pane, then press [Shift] [Enter]**

   In the Design pane, the city, state, and zip code appear on a new line. In the Code pane, a <br /> tag is inserted. See Figure D-5.

8. **Click the Show Design View button, click View on the menu bar, point to Formatting Marks, then click Show**

   You return to Design view and formatting marks no longer appear. You can insert HTML tags without working in Split view. Sometimes it helps to be able to see the code, but it's your choice as to how you want to work.

9. **Save your changes**

FIGURE D-3: Viewing the text in Split view

Entire address enclosed in one paragraph with no break tags

Address does not display with line breaks

Show Split View button

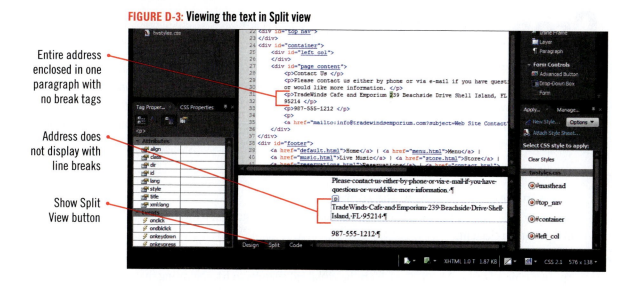

FIGURE D-4: Results of inserting a paragraph break

Pressing [Enter] creates a new paragraph

Visual aid tab

Visual aid showing new paragraph

Paragraph mark

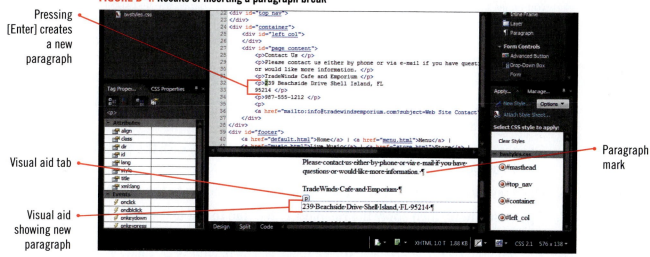

FIGURE D-5: Results of inserting a line break

Break tags

Line break

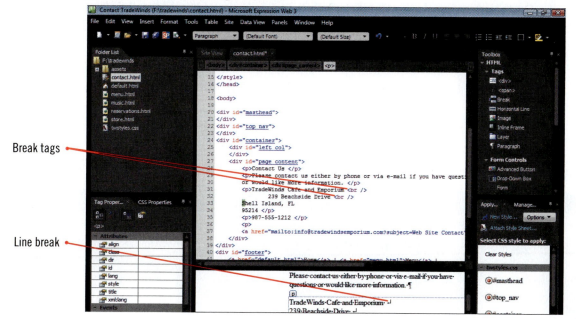

Expression Web 3

Creating Headings

Using the tools in Expression Web, you can easily add HTML tags to create structure in your document without having to write code. The Style list box on the Common toolbar allows you to choose from a list of common structural elements and apply them to your content.  You review the pages in the TradeWinds site and notice that some text on the pages is meant to serve as page headings and subheadings. You add markup to create the headings.

STEPS

QUICK TIP
Although HTML has six levels of headings, you generally won't use more than three or four levels unless you have very long, highly structured documents on your site.

1. **Select the text Contact Us on the contact page**
   See Figure D-6. The text is selected and the p in the tab on the visual aid indicates that this text is contained in a paragraph element.

2. **Click the Style list arrow on the Common toolbar, then click Heading 1 <h1>**
   The text is now large and bold. The tab on the visual aid changes to h1, indicating that the text is now contained in an <h1> element. Design view displays text the way it will look in most browsers. Browsers generally display <h1> elements as very large and bold, with subsequent lower level headings decreasing in text size. If you prefer smaller text for a heading, it's better to write a style to change the text size than to mark up the main heading with an <h2> tag, which is intended to mark up subheadings. Remember that the purpose of the markup is to describe this text as a first-level heading, not to dictate the display properties.

TROUBLE
Don't be confused by the name of the Style list box; it actually applies HTML tags, not CSS, to your content.

3. **Open default.html, select the text Welcome to TradeWinds Café and Emporium, click the Style list arrow on the Common toolbar, then click Heading 1 <h1>**

4. **Open menu.html, select the text TradeWinds Menu, click the Style list arrow, then click Heading 1 <h1>**

5. **Open music.html, select the text Live Music at TradeWinds, click the Style list arrow, then click Heading 1 <h1>**

6. **Open reservations.html, then apply the Heading 1 <h1> tag to the text Reservations**

7. **Open store.html, then apply the Heading 1 <h1> tag to the text What's New in the TradeWinds Emporium**

8. **Select the text African Art, click the Style list arrow, then click Heading 2 <h2>**
   The text is now larger and bolder than the body text but not as large as the text in the <h1> element. The tab on the visual aid changes to h2, indicating that the text is now contained in an <h2> element.

9. **On this page, apply the Heading 2 <h2> tag to the text World Bead Collection, Americana, Other Items, and Our Prices, compare your screen to Figure D-7, then save your changes to all open pages**

Creating a visual hierarchy

You can use CSS to override any default HTML tag style, including, for example, making your sixth-level headings larger than your third-level headings. This is a bad idea, though. Part of an aesthetically pleasing and user-friendly design is creating a **visual hierarchy** on the page. This means varying the size of text elements in relationship to their importance. So first-level headings should be the largest and most eye-catching, with second-level headings being less visually prominent. This helps readers quickly scan the page and grasp the structure of the content.

FIGURE D-6: Contact page with text highlighted

Style list box

Style list arrow

Selected text

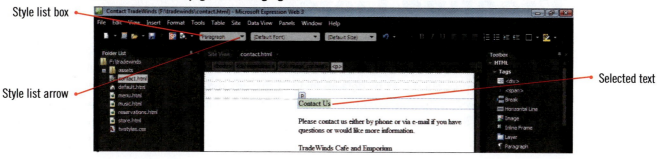

FIGURE D-7: Text with <h2> tag applied

Heading 2 style results in <h2> tag

Quick tag selector indicating <h2> tag

Heading 2 text

Visual aid indicating <h2> tag has been applied

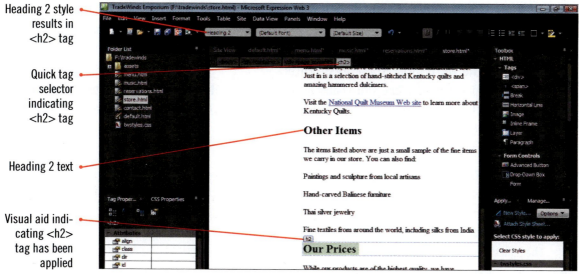

Introducing XHTML

In this book, we refer to HTML as the primary Web development language. By default, Expression Web actually uses **XHTML** (Extensible HyperText Markup Language) when generating code for your Web pages. XHTML is a newer version of HTML that has slightly different rules and tags; however, XHTML files still use the ".htm" or ".html" extension. It's fine to refer to both languages as HTML, but if you want to impress your geeky friends, you can start referring to your code as XHTML.

Creating Lists

If you have text on a page that lists two or more items, you should always mark it up as a list with HTML tags. HTML provides three types of list elements: ordered list, unordered list, and definition list. Items in **ordered lists** appear numbered by default. Items in **unordered lists** appear with bullets beside them by default. **Definition lists** are used to list terms and their definitions; they are not used as often as the other types. ▰▰▰▰ The store page contains text that is marked up as paragraphs but intended to be a list of items. You decide to fix this. Catalina has also requested that you add an item to the list.

STEPS

1. **On the store page, select the four lines of text starting with Paintings and sculpture and ending with silks from India**

   See Figure D-8. No visual aid appears because you have selected more than one element. Visual aids only appear when you select a single element. Each line of text is currently contained within its own <p> element.

2. **Click the Style list arrow on the Common toolbar, then click Ordered List <ol>**

   See Figure D-9. The visual aid tab changes to ol, indicating an ordered list. The items are now listed numerically on the page. When marking up text, choose the list type based on the purpose of the list rather than how it might initially look; you can always adjust the formatting later. You decide to change this to an unordered list, since these items aren't in any particular sequence.

3. **Click the Style list arrow, then click Unordered List <ul>**

   The tab on the visual aid changes to ul, indicating an unordered list. The list items now have bullets instead of numbers beside them. You now need to add the new item to the list.

4. **Click after the word India, then press [Enter]**

   The cursor appears on a new line with a bullet beside it. The li on the visual aid tab indicates that this is a list item. Lists are defined by marking up the entire list with the list tag (<ul>, for example), then marking up each item with an <li> tag.

5. **Type Mexican glassware, then compare your screen to Figure D-10**

   QUICK TIP
   To finish a list without creating a new list item, you can click anywhere outside the list.

6. **Press [Enter]**

   Expression Web created a new list item, but you are finished with this list and realize you don't need a new list item.

7. **Press [Backspace]**

   The bullet is removed.

8. **Save your changes**

Using lists for site navigation

Many Web designers mark up the navigation links on a Web site as a list. This makes sense, since the navigation is essentially a list of locations you can choose to visit. No one wants their navigation to actually look like a bulleted list, so this option wouldn't be very popular if designers could not override the default list style. Through the magic of CSS, designers can remove the bullets or numbers, make list items appear side-by-side rather than on separate lines, and add background colors and borders. By the time the lists have had the styles applied, they are unrecognizable as lists when viewed in a browser. However, the list markup is still in the HTML so screen readers and other devices can make use of it.

Selected text

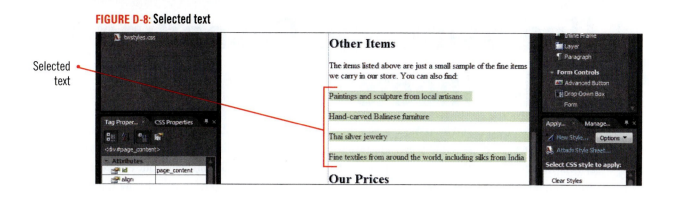

FIGURE D-9: Numbered list

Ordered list

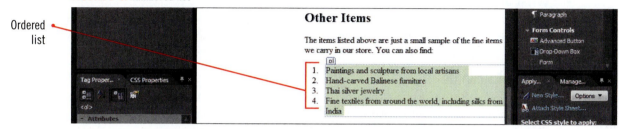

FIGURE D-10: Bulleted list with new list item

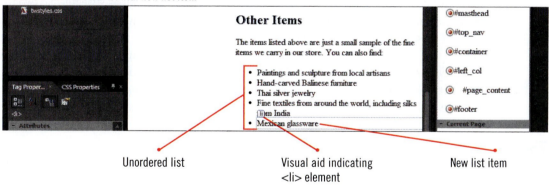

Unordered list   Visual aid indicating \<li\> element   New list item

Understanding browser defaults

Each Web browser uses its own built-in styles to decide how to display HTML elements. These styles are commonly referred to as the **browser defaults**. The default displays are fairly consistent across all browsers. The \<p\> or paragraph tag is a good example. In printed materials, paragraphs are generally indented and don't have an extra line of white space between them. Almost all browsers, though, display any content that's wrapped in a \<p\> tag with top and bottom margins and no indentation. If you don't specifically apply a style to an element, it will display using the browser defaults of the visitor's Web browser. You can override any default by creating and applying your own style. You could, for example, write a style to display paragraphs with no margins, which would remove the extra space between them. While defaults have some consistency from browser to browser, there is enough variation that you want to be sure to check the way your pages display in several different browsers.

Understanding Cascading Style Sheets

The CSS tools in Expression Web make it easy to create sophisticated styles and apply them to elements on your page. It can be great fun to play with the style tools because they instantly add color and visual interest to your design. However, understanding some basic concepts about CSS can keep your enjoyable endeavor from turning into frustration. You decide to take some time and learn about how Cascading Style Sheets work.

DETAILS

To use CSS effectively, it is important to understand:

- **What a CSS style rule is**

  CSS, as you know, stands for Cascading Style Sheets. As you've learned, a style sheet is a collection of style rules. A **style rule**, often referred to simply as a style, describes how a particular element or piece of content should be displayed.

- **What CSS can do**

  If you use only HTML to design Web pages, your design options are limited since HTML works best for describing document structure, not visual design. A good example is the current state of the TradeWinds pages. While they are structurally sound, they're not very visually exciting. With CSS, you can control almost every aspect of your site's visual design. You can create styles that dictate what text looks like, where images are displayed, how the pages are laid out, and more. You can even create styles that hide content and keep it from appearing on the page. Refer to Table D-2 for an overview of the CSS tools available in Expression Web.

- **How CSS style rules work**

  Style rules are written in the CSS language, which is different from HTML. A style rule has two parts, the selector and the declaration. A **selector** tells the browser what the style should apply to. CSS provides three basic types of selectors—IDs, elements, and classes. An ID selector can only be used once on a page and is usually used in conjunction with a <div> tag to style layout elements of a page. You learn more about element and class selectors later in this unit. The **declaration** part of the rule describes what properties you want to change and how you want to change them. Each declaration has a **property**, describing what to change, and a **value**, indicating how to change the property. For example, you want to change the background color to yellow. Figure D-11 shows a style rule within a style sheet.

QUICK TIP

When you set the CSS options in the Page Editor options in Unit B, you chose options that will prevent Expression Web from adding inline styles to the body tag or layout divs.

- **Options for placing style rules**

  The set of rules that guide the display of your pages is always known as a style sheet, whether it's written into the HTML file or is a separate file. As the Web designer, you must choose where to place your style sheet. You have three choices: you can create an external style sheet, you can create an internal style sheet, or you can create inline styles. The best option usually is to create an **external style sheet**, which is a separate file with a .css extension, and direct Expression Web to create the style rules in that file. Once that file is created and attached to all your HTML pages, you can use those styles in any page of the site. This also means that if you change a style in the external style sheet, the changes will be reflected in all your pages at once. This is one of the best features of CSS and can save you lots of time. See Figure D-12 for an example of an external style sheet. The second option, using an **internal style sheet**, is convenient because you create the rules directly within the HTML file, but it limits you to only being able to use the styles in that page. A third option is to create **inline styles** that are placed directly around content similar to HTML tags. Inline styles cannot be reused at all, even in the same page, but WYSIWYG editors such as Expression Web sometimes write inline styles and apply them when you use formatting tools in the program.

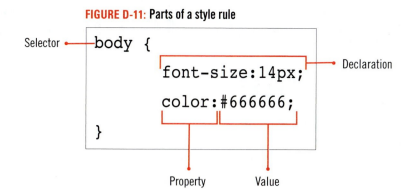

```
/* CSS layout */
#masthead {
}

#top_nav {
}

#container {
    position: relative;
    width: 100%;
}

#left_col {
    width: 200px;
    position: absolute;
    left: 0px;
    top: 0px;
}

#page_content {
    margin-left: 200px;
}

#footer {
}
body {
    font-family: Arial, Helvetica, sans-serif;
    font-size: 14px;
    color: #890120;
}
.highlight {
    font-weight: bold;
    background-color: #FFE9BB;
}
```

TABLE D-2: CSS tools available in Expression Web

tool	use to
Apply Styles panel	Apply, remove, modify, rename, and delete styles; attach or detach external Cascading Style Sheets (CSS); select all instances of a style; and go to the code that contains a style's rule set
Manage Styles panel	Perform all the functions of the Apply Styles panel; move styles between external and internal style sheets; and move the location of a style within a style sheet
CSS Properties panel	View all styles of current selection, the order of precedence of those styles, and all properties and values of the styles
Style toolbar	Apply, rename, and remove styles
Style Application toolbar	Control how styles are applied manually to page elements
CSS reports	View reports of style errors and styles that are in use on your page or site

Expression Web 3

Creating an Element-Based Style Rule

An **element-based style rule** uses an element selector to redefine the look of an HTML element. For example, you could write a rule that causes all paragraphs to be displayed with an indentation or all links to be displayed in bold.  You decide to create an element-based rule using the <li> or list item element as the selector, so that each list item displays with a square bullet instead of a round bullet in front of it.

TROUBLE
If you do not see the Apply Styles panel, click Panels on the menu bar, then click Reset Workspace Layout.

1. **Click the Turn on AutoHide button ▣ on the Toolbox panel**

    The Toolbox panel collapses and the Apply Styles panel expands, giving you more room to work in the panel. See Figure D-13. The Apply Styles panel provides access to all of the tools you need to create, modify, and apply styles. By default, styles are organized according to where they reside: styles available in attached external style sheets are listed first, and then styles available only on the current page are listed.

2. **If necessary, make the store page the active page, then click the New Style button on the Apply Styles panel**

    The New Style dialog box opens, where you can access every property for constructing a style rule. The properties are organized by categories, listed under Category. Clicking one displays all the properties for that category in a series of lists and text boxes.

3. **Click the Selector list arrow, then click li**

    The Selector list displays all HTML elements so you can choose the one for which you wish to create a style rule.

QUICK TIP
When you created your Web pages using Expression Web's CSS layout templates in Unit B, the program generated a style sheet for you and attached it to the page, and you named it twstyles.css.

4. **Click the Define in list arrow, then click Existing style sheet**

    The Define list lets you choose whether you want to define this style rule in an internal or external style sheet. If you didn't already have a style sheet attached to the page, you could create one here and attach it.

5. **Click the URL list arrow, then click twstyles.css**

6. **Click List in the Category list, click the list-style-type list arrow, then click square**

    Compare your screen to Figure D-14.

7. **Click OK**

    See Figure D-15. The list on the store page now displays a square rather than a round bullet in front of each item. The twstyles.css tab on the editing window indicates the file is open, with an asterisk beside the file name indicating that changes have been made. When you use any of the style tools to create rules that affect an external style sheet, Expression Web opens that file. No changes have been made to the HTML file, since the style was created in the external style sheet.

8. **Save your changes to all open pages**

    This saves changes to the CSS file and any open Web pages.

FIGURE D-13: Apply Styles panel

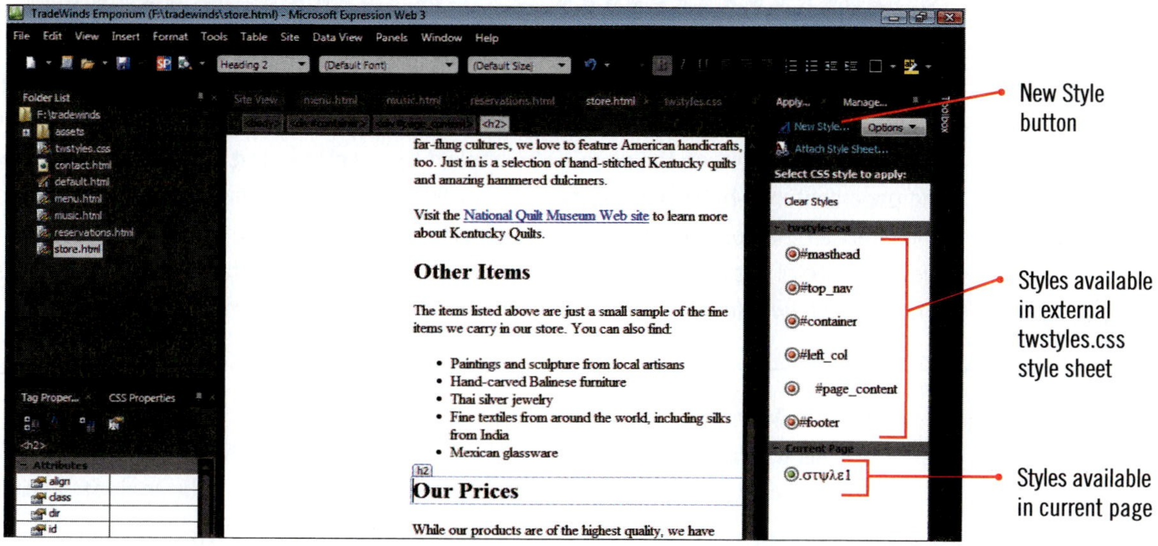

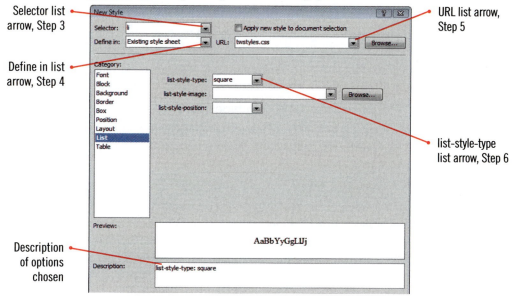

New Style button

Styles available in external twstyles.css style sheet

Styles available in current page

FIGURE D-14: New Style dialog box after choosing options

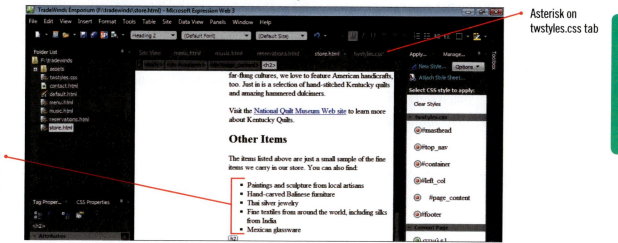

Selector list arrow, Step 3

URL list arrow, Step 5

Define in list arrow, Step 4

list-style-type list arrow, Step 6

Description of options chosen

FIGURE D-15: Editing window after creation of new list item style

Asterisk on twstyles.css tab

New style rule applied to list item

Expression Web 3

Modifying a Style Rule

Once you create a style rule, you can easily modify it. If the style rule is defined in an external style sheet, changes will be reflected in all attached Web pages. Style rules have **inheritance**, which means that a style applied to an element on the page is also applied to any elements it contains. The <body> tag surrounds all the page content—by creating a style rule for this element and placing the rule in an external style sheet, you affect all the content on every page of the site with one step.  You want to change the color, font, and size of the text on all pages. Expression Web already created a rule based on the body style when it created the twstyles.css file, so you decide to modify this rule to make your changes.

STEPS

TROUBLE

If the Manage Styles tab does not appear in the pane, click the Manage Styles button along the side.

1. **Click the Manage Styles tab in the Apply Styles panel**

   The panel title bar changes to display the name of the active tab, Manage Styles. Element-based rules appear here because they are shown only in the Manage Styles panel, not in the Apply Styles panel.

2. **In the list of styles right-click the body style, then click "Modify Style..."**

   The Modify Style dialog box opens. It includes the same options as the New Style dialog box, except that you cannot modify the location of the style sheet. You would not change the selector unless you wanted the rule to apply to a different element.

3. **Click the font-family list arrow, then click Arial, Helvetica, sans-serif**

   Expression Web includes a long list of available font families, but to ensure consistency across browsers, you should limit yourself to the first three options. In order for a font to appear in a visitor's browser, it must be installed on their computer. When choosing a font for a style rule, it's common practice to define not just one but an entire list of fonts. The visitor's computer will go down this list until they find one that is installed.

QUICK TIP

The default setting for text in browsers is 16 px, but if the default size looks too large, you can specify a smaller number such as 12 or 14.

4. **Click in the font-size text box, then type 14**

   The font-size units list box becomes active after you type a number into the font-size text box, with px selected as the default. The px stands for pixels. A **pixel** is the basic unit of measurement for anything displayed on a computer screen.

QUICK TIP

You can also choose a color by clicking the color swatch, clicking a color in the More Colors dialog box, then clicking OK. Expression Web will fill in the hex value for you.

5. **Click in the color text box, then type #41924B**

   Compare your screen to Figure D-16. The swatch beside the color text box turns green. The strange characters you typed are a **hex value** (short for hexidecimal code), a sequence of six numbers and/or letters used to define a specific color in CSS rules. In this case, you knew the hex value of the color you wanted, but you could also click the color list arrow to choose a color without knowing the hex value.

6. **Click OK**

   The dialog box closes and your changes are reflected in the page, as shown in Figure D-17. No changes were made to the store.html code, only to the external style sheet, so only the twstyles.css tab above the editing window displays an asterisk.

7. **Switch to each open page, using the tabs on the editing window**

   The change in the font face, color, and size reflects that the modified style has been applied to the <body> element on all pages. The <body> tag surrounds all the page content, so by creating a style rule for this element and placing the rule in an external style sheet, you affect all the content on every page of the site with one step. That's because style rules have **inheritance**, which means that a style applied to an element on the page is also applied to any elements it contains.

8. **Save your changes to all open pages**

FIGURE D-16: Modify Style dialog box

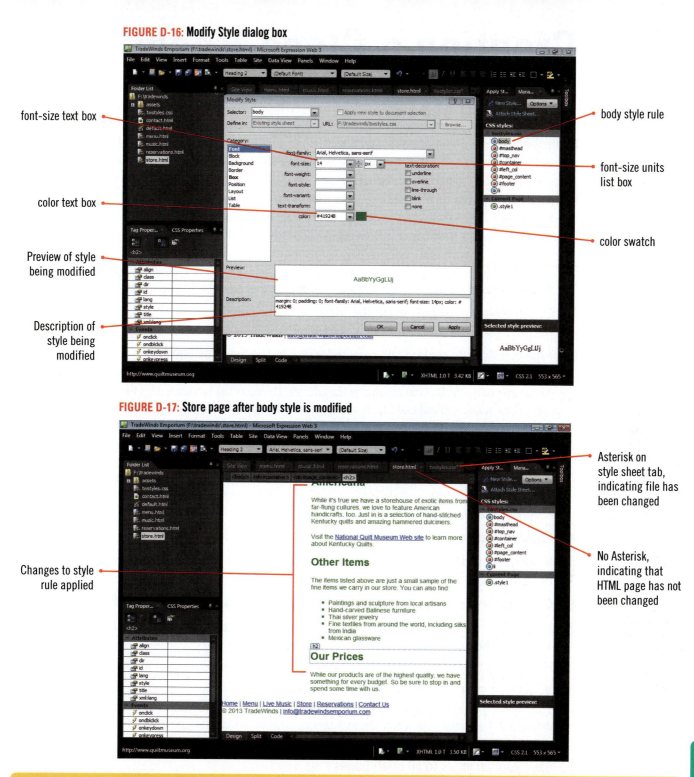

font-size text box

body style rule

color text box

font-size units list box

color swatch

Preview of style being modified

Description of style being modified

FIGURE D-17: Store page after body style is modified

Asterisk on style sheet tab, indicating file has been changed

Changes to style rule applied

No Asterisk, indicating that HTML page has not been changed

Taking control of your styles

Once you begin to create and apply your own styles in Expression Web, you should avoid using the Font, Font Size, Font Color, Highlight, Align Text Left, Center, and Align Text Right tools on the Common toolbar. If you use the toolbar options rather than creating and applying styles using the Apply Styles panel, Expression Web will make and apply a style for you and add the style rule to the HTML page. This can present several problems. First, Expression Web names the styles incrementally as .style1, .style2, etc. These aren't very descriptive names, and it becomes difficult to sort them out.

The second issue is that because Expression Web inserts the styles into the HTML document, you cannot use these styles on other pages in your site. Finally, because of the cascade, these applied styles can override any styles you place in the external style sheet later, causing frustration when the styles aren't acting as you expected. The CSS Properties panel can be helpful when trouble-shooting these issues as it shows all styles applied to a selection and the order of precedence.

Creating a Class-Based Style Rule

Element-based rules are unbeatable if you want an element to appear the same way on every page of a site. But what if you need a style that can be applied to a single instance of an element or only part of an element? Use a class-based style. A **class-based rule** is a style rule that uses a class selector. They can be created and applied to any selected content or element. Class-based styles must be manually applied to content.  Catalina wants to be able to highlight text in certain areas of the site with a subtle shade of yellow. You create a class-based style to display bold text against a light yellow background.

STEPS

1. **If necessary, make the store.html tab page active in the editing window**

2. **Click the New Style button on the Manage Styles panel**
   The New Style dialog box opens.

   > **QUICK TIP**
   > Be sure not to type over the period before the class name. If you do, retype the period. The style will not show up as an available style to use unless you start it with a period.

3. **Type highlight to replace the selected name in the Selector text box**
   Unlike an element-based style where you use an existing HTML element as the selector, for a class-based style you create your own class and use that as the selector. The new class is named .highlight. The period in front of the name is required and indicates that this is a class-based rule. When naming a class, do not use a number as the first character. It's also best to avoid using spaces, although they are allowed. You should choose class names based on meaning, not on appearance. For example, you plan to use this style to call attention to certain text on the site, so "highlight" is appropriate. "YellowBackground" would be less appropriate since it describes the intended appearance rather than the purpose of the class. There's a practical reason for this. If Catalina changes her mind and decides she wants to highlight text by putting a blue border around it instead of using a yellow background, the name of the class still makes sense.

4. **Click the Define in list arrow, then click Existing style sheet**

5. **If twstyles.css does not appear in the URL list, click the URL list arrow, then click twstyles.css**

6. **Click the font-weight list arrow, click bold, then compare your screen to Figure D-18**

   > **QUICK TIP**
   > Hex values are not case sensitive; typing either #FFE9BB or #ffe9bb results in the same shade of pale yellow.

7. **Click Background in the Category list, click in the background-color text box, type #FFE9BB, then compare your screen to Figure D-19**
   Notice that the Font category is in bold, indicating that style options have been selected in that category.

8. **Verify that your screen matches Figure D-19, then click OK**
   The New Style dialog box closes. In the Manage Styles panel, a red dot indicates an id-based style, a green dot indicates a class-based style, a blue dot indicates an element-based style, and a yellow dot indicates an inline style. A circle around the dot means that the style is used in the current page.

9. **Save your changes to all open pages**

Understanding the cascade in Cascading Style Sheets

Style rules are applied in a particular order, called a **cascade**. The cascading order is only important when two or more rules could possibly apply to an element. When troubleshooting styles in Expression Web, it's helpful to know that inline styles take precedence over internal styles, which take precedence over external styles, which take precedence over the browser default styles. The simplest way to avoid worrying about this is to be sure you put all your styles in the external style sheet for your site. This keeps conflicts to a minimum and makes it easier to fix any problems that might arise.

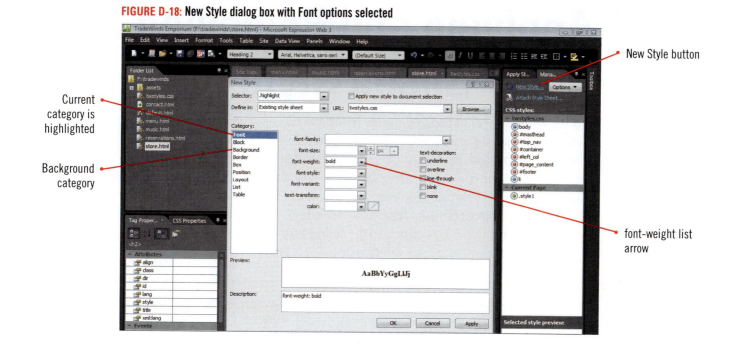

FIGURE D-18: New Style dialog box with Font options selected

Current category is highlighted

Background category

New Style button

font-weight list arrow

FIGURE D-19: Background category of New Style dialog box

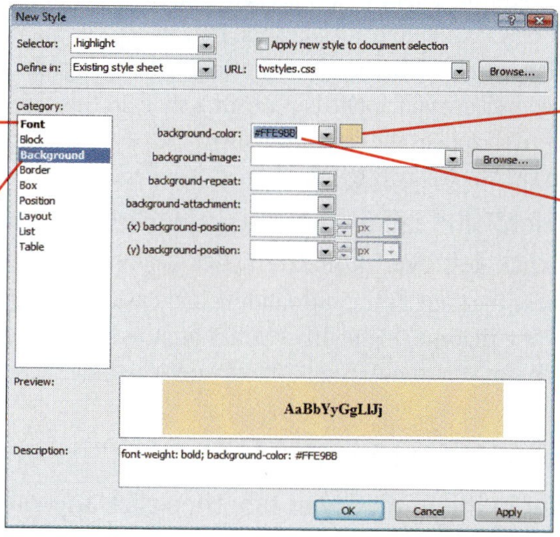

Bold indicates options have been set in this category

Current category

background-color swatch

background-color text box

Working with CSS font measurement units

The font-size units list box lets you specify relative sizing using keywords (such as small or x-large), ems, or percentages, or type a specific measurement, choosing from 10 different measurement units. Many measurement options are unreliable in the way they display fonts on different systems, so avoid using points (pt), picas (pc), inches (in), centimeters (cm), and millimeters (mm). In theory, choosing relative sizing is a great alternative because it allows your text size to be scalable rather than absolute. You could declare that, say, a first-level heading should be twice as large as the body text. In practice, though, you have to be quite skilled in CSS to make this work reliably. That leaves you with an absolute measurement, pixels, as the best option.

Applying and Removing a Class-Based Style Rule

In order for Web pages to display properly, HTML and CSS must work together. A style rule must be connected to an HTML tag as an attribute. You can apply a class-based style in two ways. The first is to select an element in Design view, then apply the class to an existing element, such as a paragraph. The class then applies to that single <p> element, and the style is only displayed on that element. The second way is to select content that is only part of an element (such as a sentence within a paragraph) and apply the style. When you select a piece of content rather than an element, Expression Web inserts a <span> tag around the content, so that the style is applied only to the desired text. You apply the class to some text on the Store page to call attention to TradeWind's wide range of product prices.

QUICK TIP
Clicking the visual aid tab selects the entire element, including the HTML tags, not just the text.

1. **Verify that store.html is the active page, click anywhere in the last paragraph, then click the visual aid tab**

   The paragraph element is selected.

2. **Click the Apply Styles tab on the Manage Styles panel, then point to .highlight**

   When you point to a style, a list arrow and ScreenTip appear. The ScreenTip displays the style rule as it is written in CSS language. Clicking the list arrow opens a menu of options for applying and modifying styles.

3. **Click .highlight to apply the style, then click anywhere inside the selected text**

   The text is now bold with a light yellow background, as shown in Figure D-20. The quick tag selector and the visual aid tab display <p.highlight>, indicating that the <p> element now has a .highlight class applied to it. The store.html tab has an asterisk on it, indicating that a change has been made to the page. The CSS file has not been changed because you applied an existing style. In this case, the changes are made to the page itself when Expression Web applies the class attribute to the paragraph tag. You decide that highlighting the entire paragraph is too visually distracting.

4. **Click the <p.highlight> tab on the visual aid, click the .highlight list arrow in the Apply Styles panel, click Remove Class, then click anywhere inside the selected text**

   The text now looks the same as the surrounding body text. The quick tag selector and the visual aid tab display <p>, indicating that the .highlight class has been removed. Notice that the class is still available in the Apply Styles panel for you to use. You have only detached the class from the element; you have not deleted the style rule.

5. **Select the text something for every budget**

6. **Click .highlight in the Apply Styles tab, then click anywhere inside the selection**

   Compare your screen to Figure D-21. The quick tag selector and the visual aid tab indicate that the text is now part of a <span> element with a .highlight class applied to it.

7. **Save all changes, close the tradewinds site, then exit Expression Web**

FIGURE D-20: Style highlight applied to <p> element

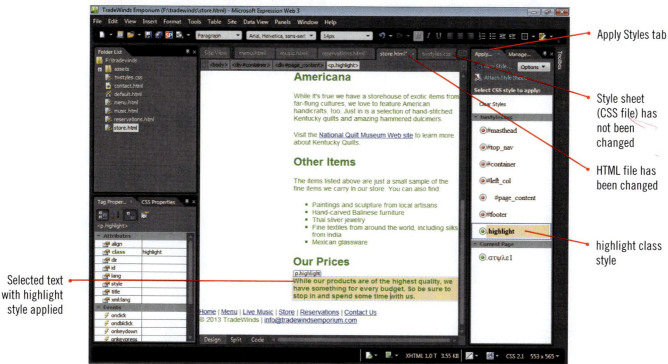

Apply Styles tab

Style sheet (CSS file) has not been changed

HTML file has been changed

highlight class style

Selected text with highlight style applied

FIGURE D-21: Style highlight applied to selected text

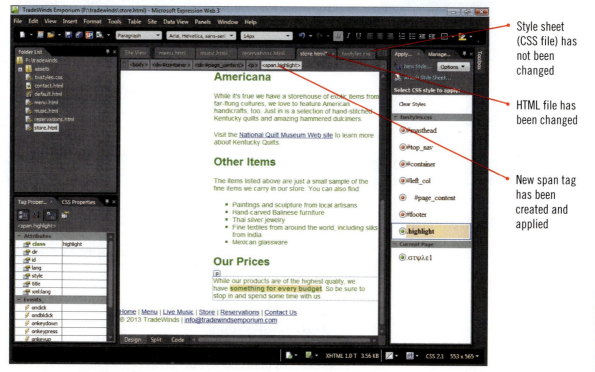

Style sheet (CSS file) has not been changed

HTML file has been changed

New span tag has been created and applied

Using multiple style sheets

You are not limited to using one style sheet on your site. For example, many sites now include a special style sheet that determines how a Web page will look when printed. These print style sheets often remove some of the design elements and format the text to make it more readable in print. Some sites also use a style sheet to serve up a different design to visitors using handheld devices. Multiple style sheets can also be used in conjunction with JavaScript code to enable visitors to display the site with a different layout or color scheme or, more important, to allow them to increase the text size to make it easier to read.

Practice

Concepts Review

For current SAM information including versions and content details, visit SAM Central (http://samcentral.course.com). If you have a SAM user profile, you may have access to hands-on instruction, practice, and assessment of the skills covered in this unit. Since we support various versions of SAM throughout the life of this text, you will want to check with your instructor for instructions and the correct URL/Web site to access those assignments.

Label each element in the Expression Web window shown in Figure D-22.

FIGURE D-22

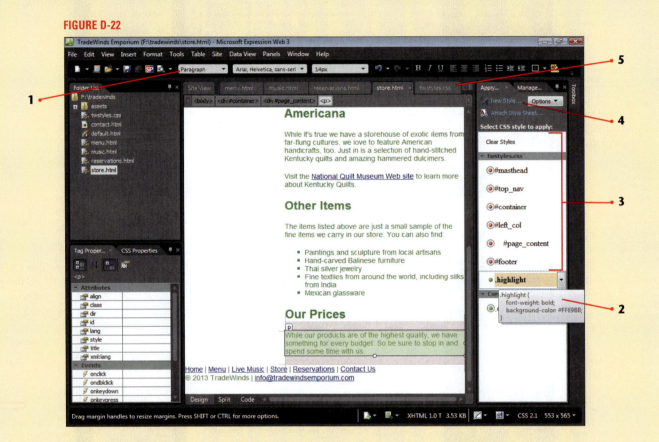

Match the HTML element with the statement that best describes when to use it.

6. `<p>`
7. `<br />`
8. `<h1>`
9. `<h2>`
10. `<ol>`
11. `<ul>`
12. `<span>`

a. Create an element so a class can be applied to it
b. Create a new paragraph
c. Create a first-level heading
d. Add a line break within a paragraph
e. Create a subheading
f. Create an unordered list of items
g. Create an ordered list of items

Select the best answer from the list of choices.

13. **Pressing [Shift][Enter] while in Design view inserts a(n):**
    a. <p> tag.
    c.
 tag.
    b. <li> tag.
    d. <span> tag.

14. **Placing your style rules in a CSS file is known as using:**
    a. An internal style sheet.
    c. An external style sheet.
    b. Inline styles.
    d. Semantic markup.

15. **If you want to create a style rule that you can apply to only a few paragraph elements in your site, you would use:**
    a. The <body> tag.
    c. An element selector.
    b. The <br /> tag.
    d. A class selector.

16. **A hex value is used to:**
    a. Remove an applied style.
    c. Determine the font size.
    b. Define a color in a style rule.
    d. Attach a style sheet to an HTML file.

17. **The combination of an opening HTML tag, content, and a closing HTML tag is called:**
    a. An element.
    c. An attribute.
    b. Inheritance.
    d. A style rule.

Skills Review

1. **Create paragraphs and line breaks.**
   a. Launch Expression Web, then open the careers Web site.
   b. Open the contact page.
   c. Click in front of the text **9283** at the bottom of the page, then switch to Split view.
   d. Create a paragraph break at the location of the insertion point.
   e. Undo your last action.
   f. Create a line break at the location of the insertion point.
   g. Create a line break in front of the word **Avon**.
   h. Create a line break in front of the text **548-555-1212**.
   i. Switch back to Design view, then save your changes to the page.

2. **Create headings.**
   a. Select the text **Contact Careers Guaranteed** at the top of the contact page.
   b. Using the Style list box, apply the <h1> tag to the selected text.
   c. Open the home page, then apply the <h1> tag to the text **Your Career. Guaranteed**.
   d. On the home page, apply the <h2> tag to the text **Why we're different**.
   e. On the home page, apply the <h2> tag to the text **Testimonial**.
   f. Open the about page, then apply the <h1> tag to the text **About Careers Guaranteed**.
   g. On the about page, apply the <h2> tag to the text **Our Management Team**.
   h. Open the services page, then apply the <h1> tag to the text **Careers Guaranteed Services**.
   i. On the services page, apply the <h2> tag to each line of text that begins **Help with**.
   j. Save all open pages.

3. **Create lists.**
   a. On the services page, select the text beginning with **Career exploration** and ending with **future earnings and potential**.
   b. Use the Style list box options to create an ordered list of the selected text.
   c. Use the Style list box options to change it to an unordered list.
   d. Create a new list item at the end of the list, then type **Online career library**.
   e. Save your changes to the page.

4. Create an element-based style rule.

    a. Open the New Style dialog box.

    b. Choose the li element as a selector, and define the rule in the cgstyles.css style sheet.

    c. In the List category, set the list-style-type to circle.

    d. Click the OK button to close the New Style dialog box.

    e. View the list on the services page to verify the change in the list items.

    f. Save all open pages.

5. Modify a style rule.

    a. On the Manage Styles tab, right-click the body style, then open the Modify Style dialog box.

    b. Change the font-family to **Arial, Helvetica, sans-serif**, and the color to **#333333**.

    c. Click OK to close the Modify Style dialog box.

    d. View at least one other page in the Web site to verify that the font face and color changed on all pages.

    e. Save all open pages.

6. Create a class-based style rule.

    a. Switch to the home page, then open the New Style dialog box.

    b. Type **testimonial** in the Selector text box. (*Hint*: Be careful not to type over the period.)

    c. Define the style in an existing style sheet (cgstyles.css).

    d. Switch to the Background category, then set the background-color to **#DEE7EF**.

    e. Click the OK button to close the New Style dialog box.

    f. Save your changes.

7. Apply and remove a class-based style rule.

    a. Click anywhere inside the word **Testimonial** on the home page, click the h2 tab on the visual aid to select it, then apply the testimonial style to the selected element.

    b. Click the visual aid tab to select the heading element you just applied the style to.

    c. Point to the testimonial style in the Apply Styles panel, click the list arrow, then remove the class.

    d. Click in the last paragraph of text, and click the visual aid tab to select the element.

    e. Apply the testimonial style by clicking the style in the Apply Styles panel, then click anywhere inside the testimonial paragraph.

    f. Compare your screen to Figure D-23, save all open pages, close the Web site, then exit Expression Web.

FIGURE D-23

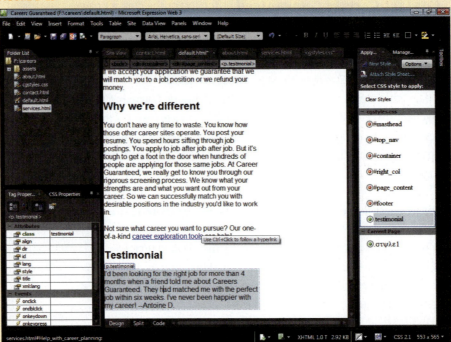

Independent Challenge 1

In this project, you continue your work on the ConnectUp Web site. Tiffany e-mailed you to ask about progress on the Web site. You decide your next step should be to mark up the text and create some styles for the site.

a. Launch Expression Web, then open the connectup Web site.

b. Open the contact page and add line breaks after each line of the address.

c. Select the text **Contact ConnectUp** and apply an <h1> tag.

d. Open the home page, then apply the <h1> tag to the text **ConnectUp to a Better Career and Life**.

e. Open the joinup page, then apply the <h1> tag to the text **Join Up with ConnectUp!**.

f. Open the faq page, then apply the <h1> tag to the text **Frequently Asked Questions about ConnectUp**. Apply the <h2> tag to the lines **Services**, **Pricing**, **Membership**, **Privacy**, and **About the Company**.

g. Select the four lines of text under the first answer, beginning with **friends** and ending with **neighborhood**, and create an unordered list.

h. Create a new style; use the body element as a selector and define it in the custyles.css external style sheet. Set the font-family as **Arial, Helvetica, sans-serif**. Click OK to close the New Style dialog box.

i. Modify the body style to make the font-color **#666666** and the font-size **14 px**. (*Hint*: You must use the Manage Styles pane to modify an element-based rule.)

j. In the custyles.css style sheet, create a class-based style rule named **.qa** that sets the font-color to **#488FDF** and the background-color to **#FBFB00**.

k. On the faq page, apply the qa style to the text **Q:** before each question and **A:** before each answer. (*Hint*: Be careful not to select the space after the colon.)

l. Modify the qa style to change the font-size to **16px** and the font-weight to **bold**.

m. Save changes to all open files, then preview the faq page in a browser.

n. Compare your screen to Figure D-24, save your work, close the Web site, then exit Expression Web.

FIGURE D-24

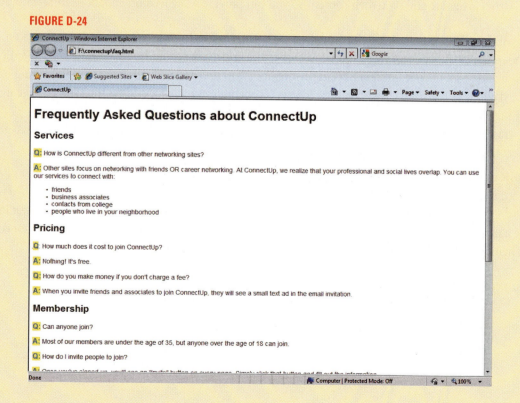

Expression Web 3

Independent Challenge 2

In this project, you continue your work on the Memories Restored Web site. You are ready to mark up your content, and then start creating some styles that will work with your design concept and color scheme.

a. Launch Expression Web, then open the memories Web site.

b. Go through each page and add <h1> and <h2> tags as appropriate. (*Hint*: On the contact page, you first need line breaks before the text **1579**, **Banff**, **T1L**, and **403-555-1212**.)

c. Mark up the services on the home page as an unordered list.

d. In the external style sheet, modify the body style by defining a font-family of **Arial, Helvetica, sans-serif**, a font-size of **12 px** and a font-color of **#663333**.

e. In the external style sheet, create a class-based style named **testimonialname**, then apply the style to each name on the testimonial page. You can choose how to style it, but include the color **#316A72** or **#CDE6EA**.

Advanced Challenge Exercise

- Open the tips page and create a class-based style named **.resources** in the external style sheet. Give the style a solid, thin, dark brown border.
- Apply the <h2> tag to the word **Resources**, then apply the .resources style to the h2 element.

f. Save your work, close the Web site, then exit Expression Web.

Independent Challenge 3

Note: This Independent Challenge requires an Internet connection.

The staff at Technology for All is most interested in developing a new graphical look for their new Web site. You, however, understand that the way the content is structured and styled is very important, too. You decide to research some sites you admire to see how they structure and style their content so you can provide some recommendations to Technology for All.

a. Visit at least three Web sites that you think are well-designed. Notice the way text is visually displayed on each site.

b. Use the View Source function of your browser to look at the underlying code. Try to identify any semantic markup. The page will include a lot of code but don't be intimidated or try to understand it all. Just focus on looking for the tags you learned about in this unit. (*Hint*: The View Source command is usually located on the View or Page menu; it might be called Page Source, Source, or something similar.)

c. Write a paragraph on each site that evaluates how readable the text is, how well-structured it is, and whether the content is easy to scan for structure.

Advanced Challenge Exercise

- For each site, identify one piece of text that is displayed as a heading. (For example, it's larger and a different color from the body text.) Find that text in the code in View Source, and note whether it is marked with HTML heading tags.
- Write a paragraph explaining the results of your research and discussing why the sites did or did not do a good job with marking up the content.

d. Add your name to the document, save it, and print it.

Real Life Independent Challenge

This assignment builds on the personal Web site you have worked on in previous units. In this project, you add structure and styles to the text on the pages.

- **a.** Review your text and add any necessary line breaks or paragraphs to complete the structure of the page.
- **b.** Apply appropriate HTML heading tags to the text headings and subheadings (if used) on your pages.
- **c.** Review your text and create lists where appropriate. Add content to create at least one list if necessary; it can be either an ordered or an unordered list.
- **d.** Create or modify at least one element-based rule in the external style sheet for your site that changes the look of your site's text in some way.
- **e.** Create at least one class-based style rule in the external style sheet, name it according to its function rather than its appearance, then apply the class-based style rule where appropriate.
- **f.** When you are finished, save changes to all pages, preview the site in a Web browser, then close the site and exit Expression Web.

Visual Workshop

Launch Expression Web, then open the ecotours Web site. Modify the home page and the external style sheet so that your screen matches Figure D-25. To accomplish this, you'll need to add text as necessary, structure the text, create an element-based style, and create and apply a class-based style. (*Hint*: The color used in the element-based style has the hex value #663300 and the color used in the class-based style has the hex value #FFCF88.) When you are finished, save your changes, close the Web site, then exit Expression Web.

FIGURE D-25

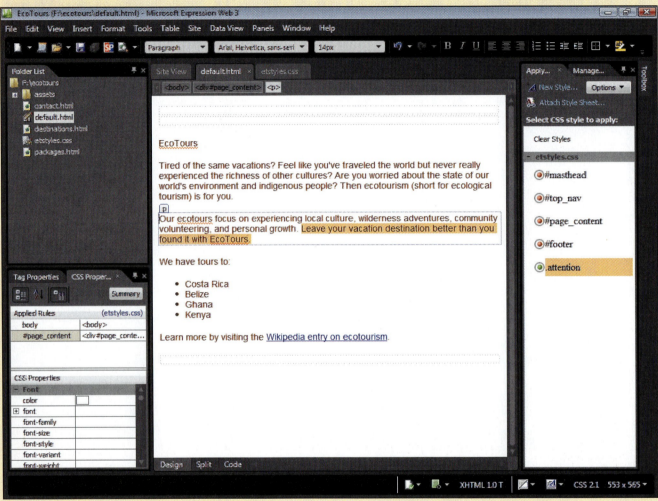

Working with Pictures

Using Expression Web, you can add pictures, also called **images** or **graphics**, to your Web pages. Pictures add visual interest to any Web site, helping to draw visitors into the site's content. For some types of sites, such as online stores, portfolios, and photo galleries, they are an essential part of the content. In Expression Web, you can resize and enhance pictures, adjust their margins and alignment, and create small pictures that link to larger ones. Now that you have created a solid foundation for the TradeWinds site and added all the text, you decide to add pictures to the site.

OBJECTIVES

Understand Web graphics

Insert a picture

Resize and resample a picture

Edit a picture

Set wrapping style and margins

Set Auto Thumbnail options

Create a thumbnail picture

Style a thumbnail picture

Understanding Web Graphics

Web graphics can be one of the most fun and yet most frustrating aspects of Web design. The possibilities for creativity are endless, but learning the terminology and tools involved in creating and editing images properly requires time and patience. Web graphics is an entire field unto itself; in fact, many sites are designed by one person or team who works on the code and another who creates the graphics. However, with a little education about digital graphics, you can be comfortable working with pictures in Expression Web.  You decide to learn more about Web graphics.

To work successfully with pictures in Expression Web, it's important to understand:

- **Image measurements**

  The size of an image can be measured in two ways: dimensions and file size. The **dimensions** of an image are its height and width, usually measured in pixels. Dimensions determine how large the picture looks on a screen. The **file size** of an image is measured in kilobytes (KB) and affects how long it takes the picture to display in a visitor's browser. In general, the larger an image's dimensions, the larger its file size. However, the file format and the amount of color and detail in the image also affect the file size.

- **Page download times**

  The **download time** of a page is the amount of time it takes the page to load into a browser. Download time is determined by two factors: the file size of the page and its referenced files (including image files), and the speed of the visitor's Internet connection. You have no influence over a visitor's Internet connection speed, but you can control the size of your Web page files. Keeping your pages lean is critical to a successful Web site. Research has shown that people will wait an average of eight seconds for a page to load before surfing away to a different site.

  The status bar in Expression Web shows the total file size for a page. See Figure E-1. It's a good idea to keep an eye on this as you're working to make sure your page size doesn't become too large. There is no ideal file size for a page, but as a rule of thumb, 50–100 KB is a safe range. A 100 KB page downloads in about 14 seconds on a 56k dial-up connection and in 2 seconds on a high-speed connection. You can keep the total page size down by using fewer images and using images that have smaller file sizes.

- **Image file formats**

  Digital images can be saved in dozens of different file formats, but only three of these, JPEG, GIF, and PNG, can be used for Web pages. The golden rule when saving images for the Web is to produce the best-looking image with the smallest possible file size. The format in which the file is saved affects both image quality and file size. The **JPEG** (pronounced jay-peg) format is best used for photographs and other images that contain many different colors, such as detailed artwork. The **GIF** (pronounced jif or gif) format is best used for images that are drawings, simple graphics, navigation buttons, or that contain large areas of solid colors. A GIF can also be animated and can have a transparent background color. The **PNG** (pronounced ping) format was created specifically for Web graphics. It produces high-quality images with small file sizes and is an alternative to the GIF format. Until recently, many browsers couldn't properly display PNG images, but that has changed and more designers are using the PNG format. See Figure E-2 for examples of a JPEG and a GIF.

FIGURE E-1: File size indicator on status bar

File size

FIGURE E-2: Examples of JPEG and GIF images

JPEG format is best for
photographs and paintings

GIF format is best for
images with fewer colors

Finding photographs for your site

If you're fortnate enough to be a talented photographer, you can shoot your own digital photos to use for your Web site. Or you could hire a professional photographer, but that can get expensive. It can be tempting to copy pictures off other Web sites, but unauthorized use violates copyright laws and leads to legal problems. A better option is to purchase stock photography, or to use photos that fall within the public domain. Stock photos are photos taken by professional photographers and then offered for sale to Web designers, graphic designers, and others who need images for Web sites, print advertisements, and other projects. Stock photography used to be very expensive, but now there are many Web sites that offer high-quality photos for reasonable prices. Public domain is work that is not protected by copyright law and is free to use and copy. To learn more about stock photography, enter the term "stock photography" in your favorite search engine and look through the listings. To learn more about public domain photos, visit a site such as www.pdphoto.org, or enter a term such as "public domain photos" in a search engine.

Inserting a Picture

A picture in a Web page is not embedded in the HTML file. Rather, the image remains a separate file and that file is referenced in the page's HTML code. When you insert a picture into a page, Expression Web inserts an <img> tag in the Web page code. The <img> tag contains the path to the image file as well as the height, width, and other attributes of the image. The Web browser then locates the image file and displays it in the page for the visitor.  Catalina has sent you a picture of a fountain in front of the TradeWinds Café that she would like to include on the home page.

STEPS

1. **Open the tradewinds Web site, then open the home page**

2. **Click just before the text Our guests experience, click Insert on the menu bar, point to Picture, then click From File**

TROUBLE

Make sure that a check mark appears in the Show this prompt when inserting images box.

3. **Navigate to the folder where you store your Data Files, click Fish Fountain.jpg, then click Insert**

   The Accessibility Properties dialog box opens, allowing you to set properties to improve the accessibility of your site. **Alternate text**, often referred to as alt text, is an attribute of the <img> tag that describes the image in words. Visitors who use screen reader software hear this text read aloud. Some people set their browsers to display alt text instead of images so pages load more quickly. A **long description** allows you to provide a more detailed description of the image, either by typing it in the box or by using the Browse button to link to an HTML file containing the description. This is necessary only for charts, graphs, and other data-intensive images. Neither of these properties is visible on the Web page; they are added to the code.

4. **Click in the Alternate text field, then type Fountain at TradeWinds**

QUICK TIP

You can move an image by clicking it, then dragging it to a new position on the page.

5. **Click OK, then click the Save button 🖬 on the Common toolbar**

   The Save Embedded Files dialog box opens. The picture you inserted is located outside the tradewinds root folder, so you can use this dialog box to save a copy of it in the root folder with your other Web site files. For more information on options available in this dialog box, see Table E-1. You want to save the image as prompted but the file name, Fish Fountain.jpg, contains spaces, which are not allowed in Web file names.

6. **Click Rename, type fishfountain.jpg, then press [Enter]**

   The new file name replaces the original name.

QUICK TIP

You can also move an image file by clicking the file name in the Folder List panel, then dragging it into the correct folder.

7. **Click Change Folder, click assets, click OK, then compare your screen to Figure E-3**

8. **Click OK again, then double-click the assets folder in the Folder List panel**

   Both the home page and image file are saved. The fishfountain.jpg file is now in the assets folder, as shown in Figure E-4. Notice that the file size of the page has increased to approximately 30 kilobytes.

TABLE E-1: Options in the Save Embedded Files dialog box

button	function
Rename	Rename the file before saving
Change Folder	Change the folder where the file is saved
Set Action	Allows you to choose an action based on what type of file you are saving; when saving a file you inserted from outside the root folder, allows you to leave the image in its original location
Picture File Type	Change the file type to GIF, JPEG, PNG-8, or PNG-24; you normally want to leave the image file type the same

FIGURE E-3: Save Embedded Files dialog box

Set to save to the assets folder

Change Folder button

Rename button

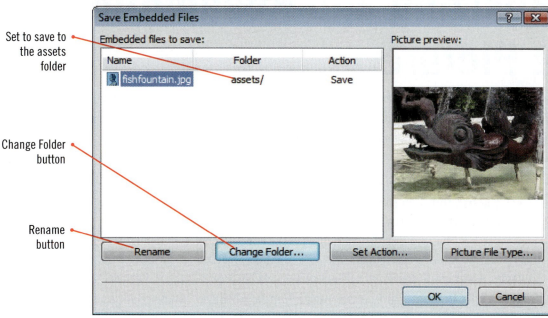

FIGURE E-4: Page and embedded files are saved

Saved image in assets folder

File size is larger

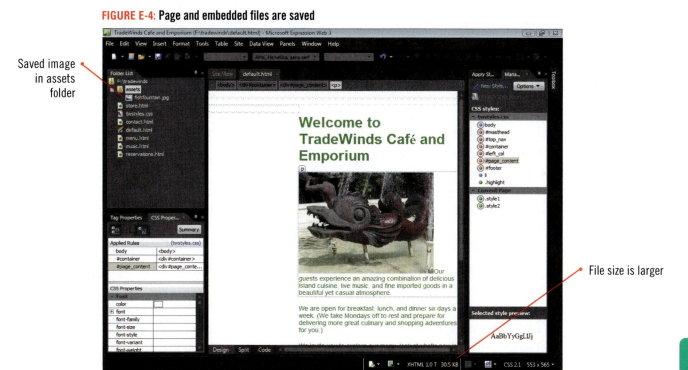

Writing meaningful alternate text

When creating alternate text, use as few words as possible to communicate the information the image conveys. For example, suppose you're using a photo of a baseball player in a story about his game-winning grand slam. Instead of using "David Ortiz" for the alt text, use something like "Ortiz rounds third base after hitting a grand slam."

Also, strive to keep the text to a minimum. Don't use unnecessary words like "picture" or "button." For example, alt text for a navigation button that says "Services" on it should read "Services," not "Services button." For a company logo, use the company name. And, if an image is purely decorative, such as a bullet or dividing line, it's acceptable not to use alternate text at all.

Working with Pictures

Expression Web 101

Expression Web 3

Resizing and Resampling a Picture

You can change the size of a picture in Expression Web by dragging the sides or a corner of the image until it's the right size. In general, reducing image dimensions works well but enlarging them can result in a significant loss of quality and a grainy or blurry appearance.  The fish fountain picture is so large that it overwhelms the text. You decide to make the picture smaller.

1. **Click the fish fountain picture to select it, then if necessary click the Tag Properties tab to to make it the active tab**

   See Figure E-5. The Tag Properties panel displays the image attributes, including the alternative text, height, file path, and width. Resize handles appear on the right side, bottom side, and bottom-right corner of the image. Clicking and dragging these handles allows you to change the size of the image.

2. **Point to the bottom-right corner resize handle until the cursor changes to** ⬊

3. **Press and hold [Shift], then drag the resize handle up and to the left**

   A ScreenTip appears showing the dimensions of the image in pixels. The first measurement is the width and the second is the height. You can watch the dimensions change on the ScreenTip so you know when to release the image. By holding [Shift] as you drag, the height and width change in the same proportion.

   > **QUICK TIP**
   > The image doesn't have to be exactly 225 pixels wide; anywhere between 220 and 230 pixels is fine.

4. **When the image is approximately 225 pixels wide, release the mouse button and [Shift]**

   The image appears smaller and the Picture Actions button appears below the picture, as shown in Figure E-6. The Picture Actions button provides the option of resizing or resampling the picture. When changing the size of an image in Expression Web, you can simply resize it or you can resample it. **Resizing** the picture means that Expression Web changes the height and width attributes in the <img> tag to make the image display differently on the page. The image dimensions themselves don't change, nor does the file size.

5. **Click the Picture Actions button list arrow** 🖼️ **, then click the Resample Picture to Match Size option button**

   The picture looks clearer. **Resampling** changes the actual dimensions and file size of the image, and removes extra pixels. It improves the clarity, so it's usually better than resizing alone. Resampling also decreases the download time.

6. **Click the Save button** 💾 **on the Common Toolbar**

   Because you have made changes to the image file, the Save Embedded Files dialog box opens, giving you options for saving the changes to the image file. You want to keep the original copy of the fish fountain just in case you need it later, so you decide to save the file with a different name.

   > **QUICK TIP**
   > If you don't want to keep an original image, just click OK; the edited image replaces the original image in the assets folder.

7. **Click Rename, type fishfountain_small.jpg, then click OK**

   Two image files are now in the assets folder. The file size has decreased to approximately 3 kilobytes, so the page will load more quickly in a visitor's browser.

8. **Preview your page in a browser, close the browser window, then return to Expression Web**

FIGURE E-5: Fish fountain picture selected

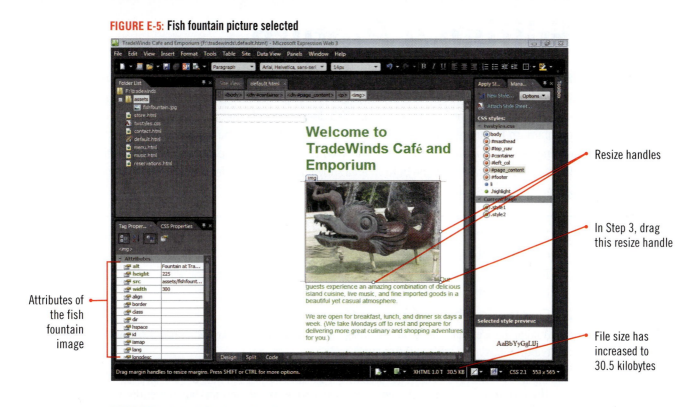

Attributes of the fish fountain image

Resize handles

In Step 3, drag this resize handle

File size has increased to 30.5 kilobytes

FIGURE E-6: Resized fish fountain picture

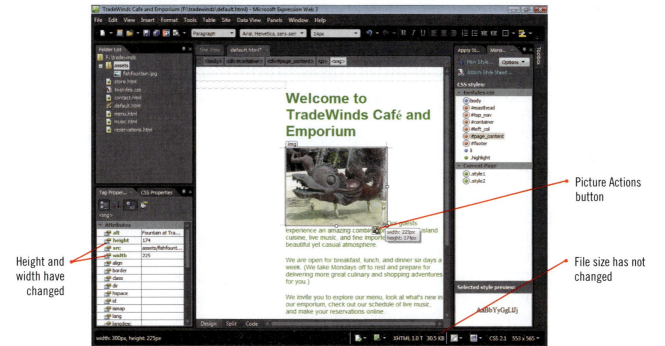

Height and width have changed

Picture Actions button

File size has not changed

Thinking in pixels

After spending your life thinking in inches or centimeters, it can be difficult to adjust to thinking in pixels. As you work more with pixel measurements, you will get better at knowing, for example, how large a 200x400 pixel image looks on the page. Until then, here are some tips to help you visualize:

• On most monitors, 75 pixels is about an inch and 30 pixels is about a centimeter.

• If you're not sure how wide an image should be, start at 200 pixels and adjust from there.

• Think of the measurement in relationship to your target screen resolution. If you're designing for a screen that's 1024 pixels wide, a picture that's 500 pixels wide takes up half the width of the screen.

Expression Web 3

Editing a Picture

Expression Web includes many image editing functions, available on the Pictures toolbar. These tools allow you to make simple changes to a picture, such as cropping or increasing contrast, without having to open it in a graphics editing program. Expression Web doesn't include the same capabilities as a full-blown graphics program, so for any significant changes in size, color, or tone, you'll want to edit the image in a graphics editing program, and then use Expression Web to insert it in the page.  You decide to edit the fish fountain picture to remove the bottom area showing the pipes under the fish. You also want to brighten the image, and flip it so the fish points to the right.

STEPS

1. **Right-click the fish fountain picture on the home page, then click Show Pictures Toolbar on the shortcut menu**

   The Pictures toolbar opens below the Common toolbar above the editing window. See Table E-2 for a description of the buttons on this toolbar.

2. **Click the Crop button ⊞ on the Pictures toolbar**

   A cropping area appears within the image, surrounded by eight crop handles. **Cropping** a picture trims or removes unwanted parts of the picture.

3. **Drag the crop handles until your cropping area matches Figure E-7, then press [Enter]**

   The picture is cropped so the pipes no longer show at the bottom, but the entire width of the fountain is visible.

4. **Click the More Brightness button ◑ on the Pictures toolbar four times**

   Each time you click the More Brightness button, the picture becomes brighter. You decide you've taken it a bit too far and would like to decrease the brightness.

5. **Click the Less Brightness button ◐ on the Pictures toolbar two times**

6. **Click the Flip Horizontal button ◭ on the Pictures toolbar, then compare your screen to Figure E-8**

   The fish fountain image is now cropped, brightened, and faces right instead of left. You are finished with the pictures toolbar and want to close it to free up space on your screen.

7. **Click View on the menu bar, point to Toolbars, then click Pictures**

   The Pictures toolbar closes.

8. **Save the page**

   The Save Embedded Files dialog box opens. The edits to the picture were made to the picture file itself, so you need to save the file.

9. **Click Rename, type fishfountain_edited.jpg to replace the highlighted text, then click OK**

   You now have three versions of the fish fountain image in the assets folder: the original image, the resized image, and the resized and edited image.

Using the Pictures toolbar

The Pictures toolbar is packed with simple image editing tools. Using the features on the toolbar, you can change a picture from color to grayscale, wash out the color on a picture, rotate pictures, create multiple hotspots on a single picture that link to different pages, or add a beveled edge to your picture. A bevel is an angled edge that adds a three-dimensional look to an image. It's worth spending some time experimenting with the tools on the Pictures toolbar to see how they can enhance your Web site graphics.

FIGURE E-7: Fish fountain picture with crop marks

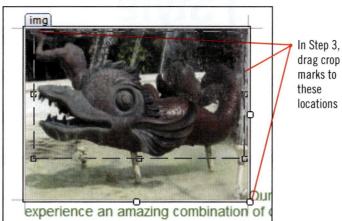

In Step 3, drag crop marks to these locations

FIGURE E-8: Cropped, brightened, and flipped picture

TABLE E-2: Buttons on the Pictures toolbar

button	use to...	button	use to...
Insert Picture From File	Insert a new picture or replace selected picture	More Brightness	Increase brightness of selected picture
Auto Thumbnail	Create a reduced-size version of selected picture and link it to a full-size version	Less Brightness	Decrease brightness of selected picture
Bring Forward	Set selected picture to display on top of surrounding content	Crop	Trim unwanted areas from selected picture
Send Backward	Set selected picture to display beneath surrounding content	Set Transparent Color	Make a specific color in selected picture transparent
Rotate Left 90°	Rotate selected picture 90° counterclockwise	Color	Make colors of selected picture grayscale or washed out
Rotate Right 90°	Rotate selected picture 90° clockwise	Bevel	Create an angled edge on selected picture
Flip Horizontal	Flip selected picture horizontally	Resample	Increase or decrease pixel dimensions and physical file size of selected picture
Flip Vertical	Flip selected picture vertically	Select Rectangular Hotspot Circular Hotspot Polygonal Hotspot Highlight Hotspots	Select and create hotspot areas in selected picture that can be linked to files or pages
More Contrast	Increase contrast of selected picture	Restore	Undo all actions on picture since you last saved the Web page
Less Contrast	Decrease contrast of selected picture		

Setting Wrapping Style and Margins

Controlling a picture's wrapping style and margins helps you ensure that pictures and text work together to create a harmonious, easy-to-read design. The **wrapping style** is the way in which a picture is positioned relative to surrounding text; for example, a left wrapping style means that text flows around the right side of the picture.  You want the image to appear on the left with text flowing on the right, and some white space around the image.

STEPS

QUICK TIP

You can use the General tab of the Picture Properties dialog box to add alt text to the selected image; sometimes this is more convenient than entering it when you insert the image.

1. **Double-click the fish fountain picture**

   The Picture Properties dialog box opens. In the General tab, which is in front by default, you can change the image's file path, alternate text, and long description, and add or edit a hyperlink from the image.

2. **Click the Appearance tab in the Picture Properties dialog box**

   In the Appearance tab, you can set the wrapping style; determine layout options such as alignment, border thickness, and margins; and change the size of the image. The default wrapping style, None, causes text to start at the bottom edge of the picture, instead of flowing around it. The other options are Left, which places the picture on the left side with text wrapping around it on the right, or Right, which places the picture on the right side with text wrapping around it on the left.

3. **Click Left under Wrapping style**

4. **Select the text in the Horizontal margin box, type 10, select the text in the Vertical margin box, type 10, then compare your screen to Figure E-9**

   If you wrap text around your image, you also want to create margins around your picture so the text doesn't flow to the edge of the picture. The horizontal margin controls the left and right margins, while the vertical margin controls the top and bottom margins. These settings determine how much white space is displayed between the picture and surrounding text.

QUICK TIP

Expression Web assigns a name to each automatically-created style in a page using the word style and the next available number.

5. **Click OK, then point to .style3 (or the style with the highest number) in the Apply Styles panel**

   Expression Web created a class-based style rule and applied it to the <img> tag to control the alignment and margins. The style rule declares that the picture should float to the left margin and should have a 10-pixel margin all around it. The img visual aid reflects the 10-pixel margins by showing a pink, diagonally striped area all around the image. You can change the margin by dragging on the edge of the visual aid. You decide you want the right margin to be larger than the left.

TROUBLE

If you accidentally drag the image resize handles, you change the image size; to correct this, click Edit on the menu bar, click Undo Resize, then try again.

6. **Click the right edge of the visual aid box until the pointer changes to ⇔, drag to the right until the ScreenTip reads margin-right: 25px, then release the mouse button**

   The right margin is now larger than the left, as shown in Figure E-10.

7. **Point to the style with the highest number in the Apply Styles panel**

   The style has been revised to reflect the change in the right margin.

8. **Save the page, preview it in a Web browser, close the browser, then return to Expression Web**

FIGURE E-9: Appearance tab of Picture Properties dialog box

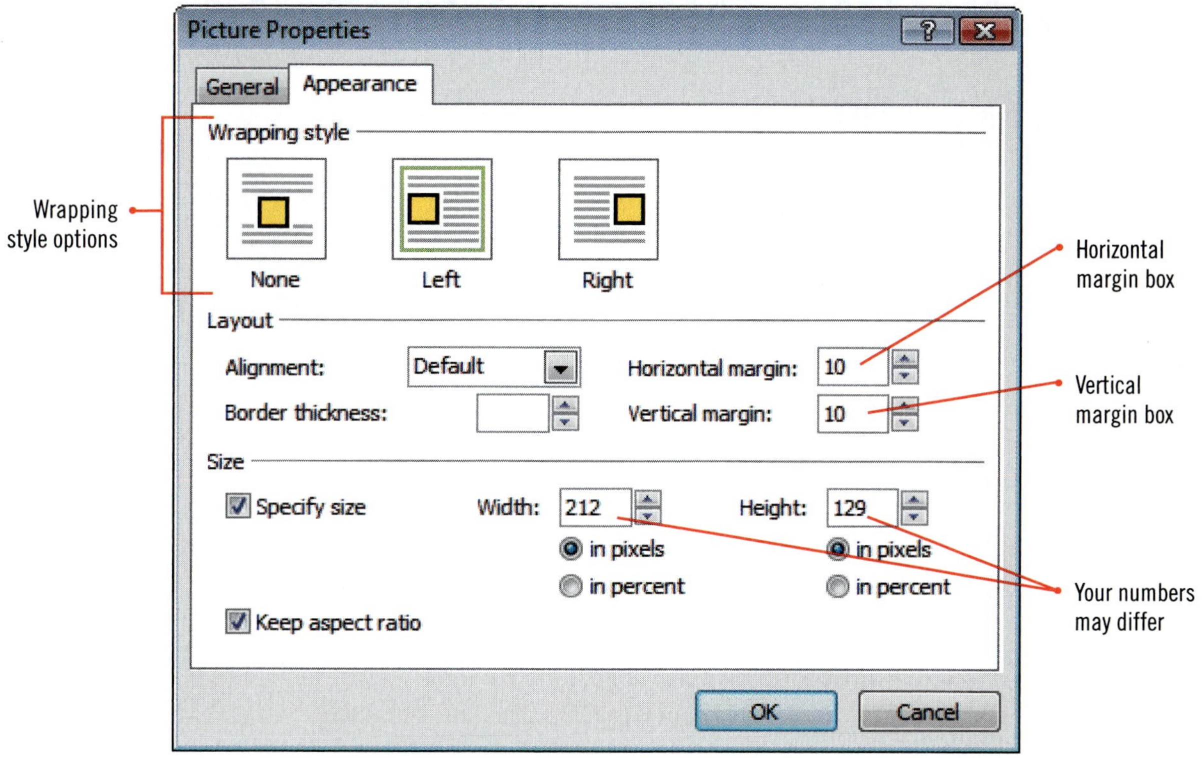

Wrapping style options → Wrapping style

None   Left   Right

Horizontal margin box

Vertical margin box

Layout
Alignment: Default   Horizontal margin: 10
Border thickness: Vertical margin: 10

Size
☑ Specify size   Width: 212   Height: 129
   ● in pixels   ● in pixels
   ○ in percent   ○ in percent
☑ Keep aspect ratio

Your numbers may differ

OK   Cancel

FIGURE E-10: Fish fountain picture after right margin is enlarged

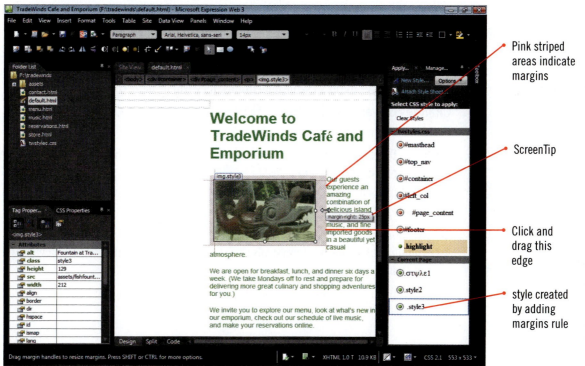

Pink striped areas indicate margins

ScreenTip

Click and drag this edge

style created by adding margins rule

Expression Web 3

Setting Auto Thumbnail Options

Sometimes you may want to display a series of smaller images and link them to a larger version of the same image. Using smaller images, called thumbnail pictures or **thumbnails**, saves space on the page and minimizes download time. Product galleries, sets of vacation pictures, and portfolios are all examples of pages that work well with thumbnail images. Expression Web includes an Auto Thumbnail tool that can help save time. It creates a thumbnail image and automatically links it to the larger image. Without this feature, you would have to resize the image in a graphics program and then use Expression Web to insert the thumbnail into the page and create a link to the larger image. You plan to include some thumbnail pictures on the TradeWinds site. You want thumbnail pictures to be no longer or wider than 150 pixels and you don't want them to include a border.

STEPS

1. **Click Tools on the menu bar, then click Page Editor Options**
    The Page Editor dialog box opens.

2. **Click the AutoThumbnail tab on the Page Editor Options dialog box**
    In the AutoThumbnail tab, you can set options that control the dimensions of the thumbnail, the size of the thumbnail's border, and whether a bevel is applied to the thumbnail. The default style for thumbnails creates images that are 100 pixels wide and have a 2-pixel border. If you want to create thumbnails with properties that differ from the default, you should change the Auto Thumbnail settings in the Page Editor options *before* you create the thumbnail.

3. **Click the Set list arrow**
    The Set options allow you to choose the dimensions of the width, the height, the longest side, or the shortest side.

    > **QUICK TIP**
    > You can change the value by selecting the value and then typing a new value, or by clicking the up and down arrows in the box.

4. **Click Longest side, then change the setting in the Pixels box to 150**
    The longest side of any thumbnail will not be longer than 150 pixels. Setting the longest or shortest side is useful if you have some images that are horizontal and some that are vertical; it ensures that while all thumbnails will not have the exact same dimensions, they will be more consistent in size.

5. **Change the value in the Border thickness Pixels box to 0**
    The thumbnail will not display a border.

6. **Click the Beveled edge check box to remove the check mark if necessary, then compare your screen to Figure E-11**
    The thumbnail will not display a bevel.

7. **Click OK**
    All new thumbnails you create in the Web site will be formatted with the new settings. When you change AutoThumbnail settings, all thumbnails you create afterward are affected, but previously created thumbnails will not change.

FIGURE E-11: AutoThumbnail tab of Page Editor Options dialog box

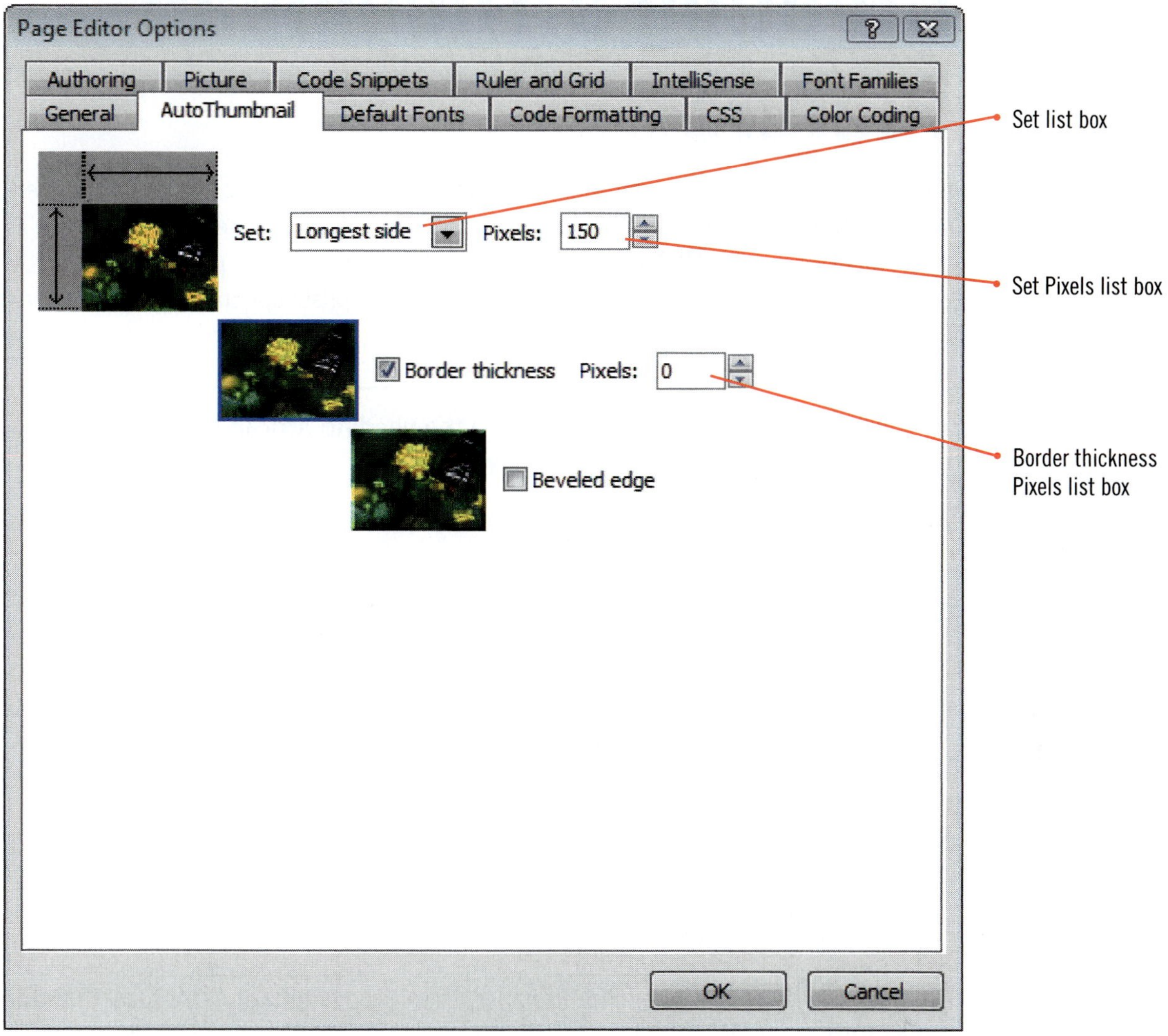

Maintaining a consistent graphical style

When deciding what graphics to use on your Web site, it's best to choose one style and stick with it. If you decide to use cartoon-like images, use them throughout the site. If you use photographs, don't mix them with illustrations. And if you use black-and-white photos, use them consistently rather than adding color images. Using a consistent style gives your site a polished and professional appearance.

Creating a Thumbnail Picture

After you have set the options for thumbnail pictures in a Web site, the next step is to insert the image into the page. You can then use the Auto Thumbnail command to create the thumbnail image as well as the link to the full-sized image.  Catalina has sent you a picture for the products page that you think would work best as a thumbnail. Now that you have set the appropriate options for your thumbnail image, you are ready to insert the image and create the thumbnail.

STEPS

1. **Open the store page, click just before the heading African Art, click Insert on the menu bar, point to Picture, then click From File**

2. **Navigate to the folder where you store your Data Files, click Elephant Sculpture.jpg, then click Insert**

QUICK TIP

If you want to make changes to an existing thumbnail, delete it, change the properties, then insert the picture again and re-create the thumbnail.

3. **Type African Elephant Carving in the Alternate text field, then click OK**
   The elephant sculpture picture is displayed in the page.

4. **Right-click the elephant sculpture picture, click Auto Thumbnail on the shortcut menu, then click anywhere on the page outside the picture**
   See Figure E-12. The picture is converted to a smaller thumbnail.

QUICK TIP

If you want to be able to see the entire file name, you can click the border between Name and Folder, then drag to the right to make the Name column wider.

5. **Save the page**
   The Save Embedded Files dialog box opens. Two files are listed. One is the thumbnail created by Expression Web and the other is the original elephant sculpture image. Depending on your screen size, you may not be able to see the entire file name of the image until you click the Rename button.

6. **Click the first file name, click Rename, then type elephant_sculpture_thumb.jpg**
   By default, Expression Web names the thumbnail image with the original file name plus "_small." Because the original file name had spaces in it, you needed to change the entire file name.

7. **Click the second file name, click Rename, then type elephant_sculpture.jpg**
   Compare your screen to Figure E-13.

8. **Click OK, preview your page in a browser, then click the elephant sculpture picture in the browser window**
   See Figure E-14. The thumbnail links directly to the large image. Because it links directly to the image and not to a Web page, nothing displays except the image.

9. **Close the browser window and return to Expression Web**

FIGURE E-12: Auto thumbnail of elephant sculpture

Auto thumbnail

FIGURE E-13: Renamed files in the Save Embedded Files dialog box

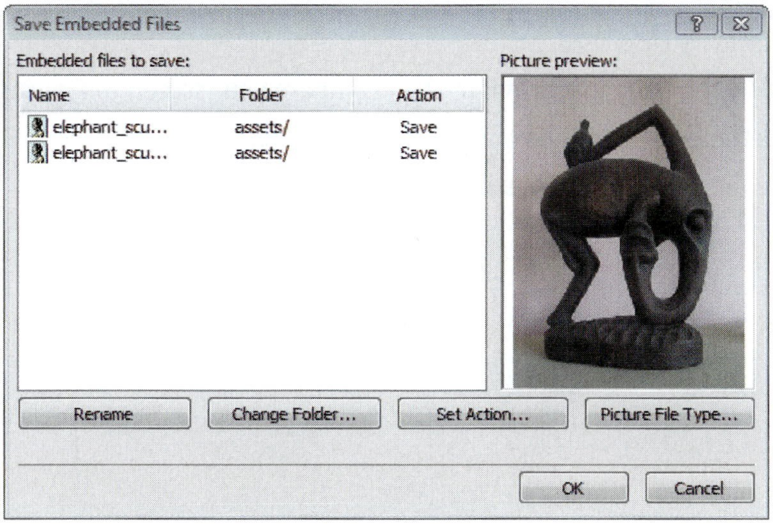

FIGURE E-14: Larger image linked to thumbnail

Styling a Thumbnail Picture

The AutoThumbnail settings in the Page Editor Options control the dimensions, border size, and beveled edges on the thumbnail. To change the wrapping styles, alignment, or margins, you use the Picture Properties options.  You are satisfied with the size of the thumbnail, but you want it to wrap to the left and have some white space around it.

STEPS

1. **Double-click the elephant sculpture thumbnail picture**

   The Picture Properties dialog box opens.

2. **Click the Appearance tab, click Left under Wrapping style, change the value in the Horizontal margin box to 10, change the value in the Vertical margin box to 10, then compare your screen to Figure E-15**

3. **Click OK**

   See Figure E-16. The tab on the thumbnail's visual aid indicates that a style, style 2, has been applied. The visual aid also shows the 10-pixel margins surrounding the image.

4. **Save your changes to the page**

   The Save Embedded Files dialog box does not open because you only made changes to the styles on the page, and not to the image itself.

5. **Preview the page in a browser, then compare your screen to Figure E-17**

6. **Close the browser window and return to Expression Web**

7. **Close the Web site, then exit Expression Web**

Understanding automatically generated styles

When you use toolbars or dialog boxes to change image or text properties, Expression Web usually generates a style rule in that page's internal style sheet and attaches it to the element. The styles are named incrementally (style1, style2, and so on). The styles appear in the Apply Styles and Manage Styles panels, allowing you to modify or delete the style properties if you wish. For example, if you choose to have Expression Web add a border when an auto thumbnail is created, a style is generated and applied to the thumbnail. You can then modify the style later to change the border color or size.

FIGURE E-15: Appearance tab of Picture Properties dialog box

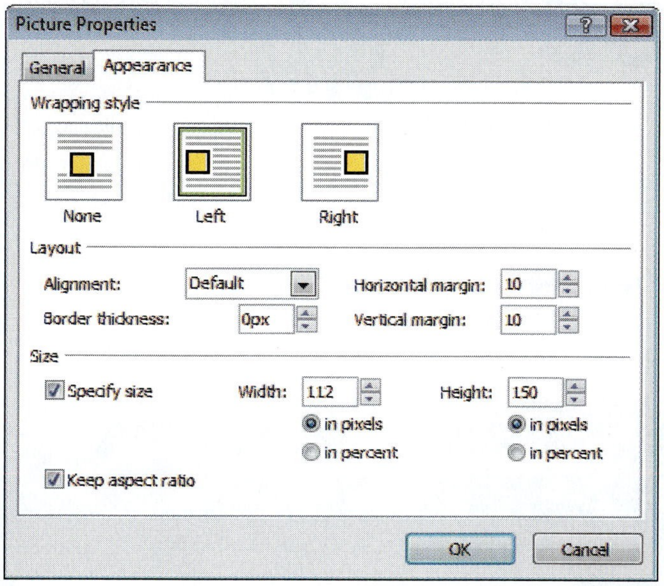

FIGURE E-16: Thumbnail picture with styles applied

FIGURE E-17: Store page displayed in browser

Practice

Concepts Review

For current SAM information including versions and content details, visit SAM Central (http://samcentral.course.com). If you have a SAM user profile, you may have access to hands-on instruction, practice, and assessment of the skills covered in this unit. Since we support various versions of SAM throughout the life of this text, you will want to check with your instructor for instructions and the correct URL/Web site to access those assignments.

Refer to Figure E-18 to answer the following questions:

FIGURE E-18

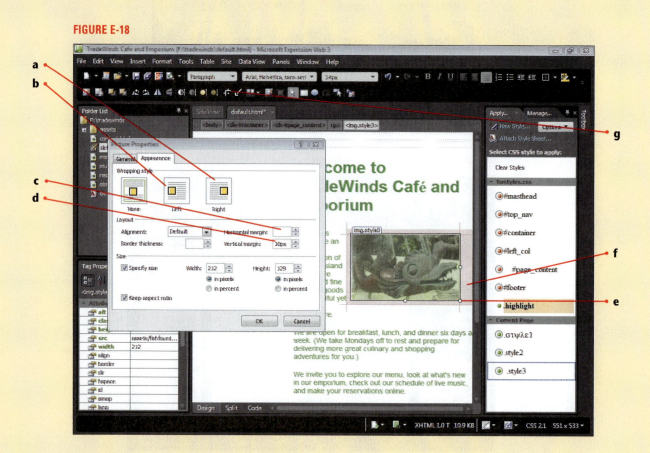

1. Which element do you click to crop a picture?
2. Which element do you drag to change the margin size?
3. Which element do you drag to change the image size?
4. Which element do you click to make the text wrap on the right of a picture?
5. Which element do you click to make the text wrap on the left of a picture?
6. Which element do you use to set the top and bottom margins of a picture?
7. Which element do you use to set the left and right margins of a picture?

Match each term with the statement that best describes it.

8. GIF
9. Resampling
10. JPEG
11. Resizing
12. PNG
13. Thumbnail

a. File format created specifically for Web graphics
b. File format best used for simple drawings and artwork with fewer colors
c. File format best used for photographs and detailed artwork
d. Changes the height and width attributes in the <img> tag but not the file dimensions
e. A small version of an image that links to a larger version of the image
f. Changes the dimensions and file size of an image, and removes extra pixels

Select the best answer from the list of choices.

14. **Which of the following controls the way text flows around a picture?**
    a. Margins
    c. Alignment
    b. Wrapping style
    d. Brightness

15. **When designing a Web page, you should in general strive to keep the file size within:**
    a. 500-1000 kilobytes.
    c. 1000-1500 kilobytes.
    b. 50-100 kilobytes.
    d. 5-10 kilobytes.

16. **Tools for cropping a picture and changing its brightness can be found on the:**
    a. Page Properties dialog box.
    c. Status bar.
    b. Apply Styles panel.
    d. Pictures toolbar.

17. **For which type of image is it acceptable to leave the Alternate text box empty?**
    a. Decorative image, such as a bullet
    c. Pictures accompanying text
    b. Company logo
    d. Navigation buttons

18. **Which of the following does not affect the download time of a Web page?**
    a. Number of images used on the page
    c. File size of images used on the page
    b. Speed of visitor's Internet connection
    d. Speed of the Web designer's Internet connection

19. **When resizing an image by dragging its resize handles, which key do you press to maintain the image's proportion while changing the width and height?**
    a. [Tab]
    c. [Ctrl]
    b. [Alt]
    d. [Shift]

20. **How can you change the margins around a picture?**
    a. By dragging the visual aid around the image
    c. In the Appearance tab of the Page Properties dialog box
    b. On the Pictures toolbar
    d. Both a and c are correct.

Skills Review

1. **Insert a picture.**
    a. Launch Expression Web, then open the careers Web site.
    b. Open the home page, then click before the word **Testimonial**.
    c. Open the Picture dialog box, navigate to where you store your Data Files, then insert **Testimonial Picture.jpg**.
    d. Add the following alternate text when prompted: **Antoine is a happy customer**.
    e. Save the page. When the Save Embedded Files dialog box opens, change the folder to assets and rename the file to **testimonial_antoine.jpg**. Click OK.
    f. Open the assets folder in the Folder List panel to verify that testimonial_antoine.jpg is in the folder.
    g. Preview your page in a browser, close the browser, then return to Expression Web.

2. **Resize and resample a picture.**
    a. Click the testimonial picture to select it.
    b. Use the bottom-right corner resize handle and the [Shift] key to resize the picture until the width is approximately 250 pixels. (*Hint*: You'll need to drag up and to the left.)
    c. Use the Picture Actions button to resample the picture.
    d. Save your changes. When the Save Embedded Files dialog box opens, rename the image file to **testimonial_antoine_small.jpg**. Click OK.
    e. Preview your page in a browser, close the browser, then return to Expression Web.

3. **Edit a picture.**
    a. Open the Pictures toolbar.
    b. Flip the picture horizontally.
    c. Close the Pictures toolbar.
    d. Save your changes. When the Save Embedded Files dialog box opens, rename the file to **testimonial_antoine_edited.jpg**. Click OK.

4. **Set wrapping style and margins.**

   a. Double-click the testimonial picture to open the Picture Properties dialog box.

   b. Use the Appearance tab to set the Wrapping style to Right and all margins to 15.

   c. Click OK to close the Picture Properties dialog box.

   d. Point to the .style2 rule in the Apply Styles panel and verify the style properties.

   e. Drag the left side of the image's visual aid to create a 40-pixel-wide left margin.

   f. Point to the .style2 rule in the Apply Styles panel and note the change in the size of the left margin.

   g. Save the page, preview in a browser, compare your screen to Figure E-19, then close the browser window and return to Expression Web.

5. **Set Auto Thumbnail options.**

   a. Open the Page Editor Options dialog box. On the AutoThumbnail tab, change the properties to a width of 75 pixels, a border of 0 pixels, and no beveled edge.

   b. Click OK to close the Page Editor Options dialog box.

6. **Create a thumbnail picture.**

   a. Open the contact page, then click just before the text **Careers Guaranteed** on the first line of the address.

   b. Open the Picture dialog box, navigate to where you store your Data Files, then insert Careers Map.jpg. Add the following alternate text when prompted: **Map of Careers Guaranteed office location**.

   c. Create an Auto Thumbnail from the map image.

   d. Save the page. When the Save Embedded Files dialog box opens, rename the first image file to **careers_map_thumb.jpg** and the second to **careers_map.jpg**.

   e. Preview the page in a browser, click the thumbnail image, then close the browser window and return to Expression Web.

7. **Style a thumbnail picture.**

   a. Double-click the map image.

   b. In the Appearance tab of the Picture Properties dialog box, set the Wrapping style to Left and the margins to 15 pixels each. When you are finished, close the dialog box.

   c. Save the page.

   d. Preview the contact page in your browser and compare it to Figure E-20.

   e. Close your Web browser, then exit Expression Web.

FIGURE E-19

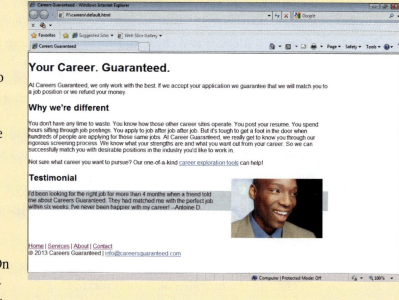

FIGURE E-20

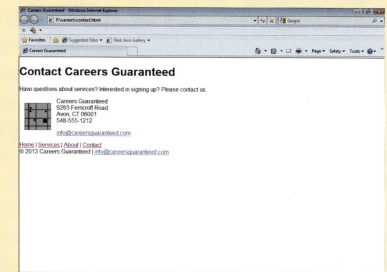

Independent Challenge 1

In this project, you continue your work on the ConnectUp Web site. Tiffany is happy with the text on the site but wants to see some progress on the visual design. You decide to add some images to the site in preparation for your next meeting with her.

a. Launch Expression Web, open the connectup Web site, then open the home page.

b. Click just before the text **You don't separate**, then insert the file Connected Badge.gif from the drive and folder where you store your Data Files. Add the Alternate text **Get Connected!**

c. Save the page, then save the image in the assets folder as **connected_badge.gif**. Preview the page in a browser, close the browser window, then return to Expression Web.

d. Use the [Shift] key to maintain proportions as you resize the image to approximately 150 pixels wide.

e. Resample the resized picture.

f. Save the page, then save the image in the assets folder as **connected_badge_small.gif**.

g. Open the Pictures toolbar, then use the Crop button to trim as much white space from around the button without trimming any of the green badge. When you are finished, close the Pictures toolbar.

h. Save the page, then save the image in the assets folder as **connected_badge_cropped.gif**.

i. Use the Picture Properties tools to set the Wrapping style of the image to Left and all margins to 25 pixels.

j. Drag the visual aid to decrease the top margin to approximately 10 pixels, then save the page.

k. Select the badge image, then drag it to move it right before the heading ConnectUp to a Better Career and Life.

l. Save your changes, preview the home page in the browser, then compare your screen to Figure E-21.

m. When you are finished, close the browser window, return to Expression Web, close the site, then exit Expression Web.

FIGURE E-21

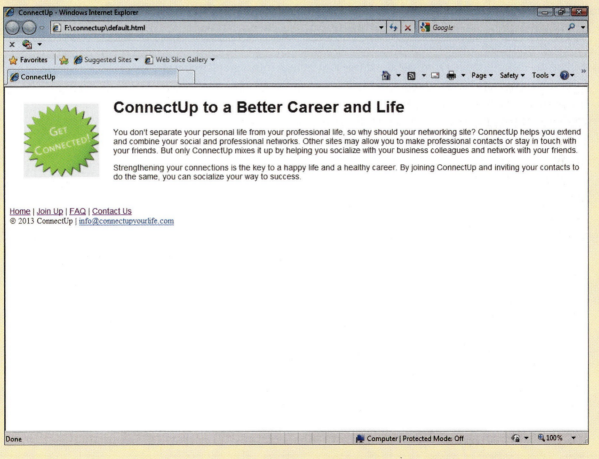

Independent Challenge 2

In this project, you continue your work on the Memories Restored Web site. You are ready to add some pictures that showcase the high-quality work of the photo restoration experts at Memories Restored.

a. Launch Expression Web, then open the memories Web site.

b. Open the home page, then choose a location anywhere in the page_content div that you think would be a good spot for an image that exemplifies the photo restoration done at Memories Restored. Click the desired location, then insert the picture Car Couple.jpg from the drive and folder where you store your Data Files. After you have inserted the image, use the Picture Properties dialog box to add appropriate alternate text.

c. Resize and edit the image as you'd like, using the Pictures toolbar.

d. Save the page, saving the image in the assets folder and renaming it appropriately.

e. Use the Picture Properties dialog box to adjust the margins and wrapping style as you'd like, then save the page.

f. Open the work page, click beneath the text **Example One**, then insert the Example One.jpg file. Repeat this process to insert Example Two.jpg under the text **Example Two**, and Example Three.jpg under the text **Example Three**. Add appropriate alternate text when prompted, or after completing the insertion using the Picture Properties dialog box.

g. Save your page, renaming the images appropriately and saving them within the assets folder.

h. Open the AutoThumbnail tab on the Page Editor options dialog box, and set the options as you'd like. (*Hint*: Because the images are so large, you might want to make these wider than normal thumbnails.)

i. Create an AutoThumbnail from each of the example images you inserted on the work page. Save your page and rename all images as you're saving. (*Hint*: If you're not happy with them, delete each one, go back and change the Page Editor options, reinsert the images, then re-create the AutoThumbnails.)

Advanced Challenge Exercise

- Open the tips page, click after the text **Photo Restoration Tips**, then insert the Tips Banner.jpg image, giving it appropriate alternate text when prompted.
- Use the Pictures toolbar to rotate the image and change it to a grayscale image.
- Save the page, and save the embedded image with an appropriate name.

j. Preview your page in a browser, click each thumbnail, close the browser windows, return to Expression Web, close the Web site, then exit Expression Web.

Independent Challenge 3

Note: This Independent Challenge requires an Internet connection.

Your client at Technology for All would like to use some photographs on the new Web site. The organization doesn't have any of their own photographs, and you don't have time to take photos yourself. You decide to look at some stock photography sites to see what your options are.

a. Go to your favorite search engine and enter **stock photography** as the search term.

b. Visit at least three of the sites that come up. At each site, search for images that would be suitable for Technology for All. Remember that the organization collects cast-off computers, repairs and upgrades them, and then donates the refurbished machines to low-income students.

c. Write a paragraph outlining what search terms you used while on the stock photography site to locate appropriate images.

d. Write a second paragraph describing at least five appropriate images you found for the site.

Advanced Challenge Exercise

■ Choose two similar images from two different sites and determine how much it would cost to purchase them. Assume that you plan to use the images on a Web site for at least five years at a size of at least 300×300 pixels. (*Hint*: You will have to look around the site for pricing information. You may have to add the images to a shopping cart to see the pricing, but you shouldn't need to enter any personal or payment information.)

■ Write a comparison of the costs for each image.

■ Write at least three sentences explaining whether you think any price difference between the images is justified and which image you would rather use, based on both appearance and price.

e. Add your name to the document, save it, and print it.

Real Life Independent Challenge

This assignment builds on the personal Web site you have worked on in previous units. In this project, you add pictures to your site.

a. Add at least three images to your site. You can use photographs you've taken, illustrations you've created, or other available graphics. Make sure that you own the copyright to the images or that they fall within the public domain.

b. Resize, resample, and/or move the images if necessary.

c. Make any edits to the pictures to improve their appearance, such as rotating them, changing the brightness or contrast, and so on.

d. Adjust the wrapping style and margins of each picture until you are pleased with the appearance of your pages.

e. Create at least one Auto Thumbnail and adjust the styles as you like.

f. Check the file size of each page in the status bar to make sure each of your pages has a reasonable download time. Document the file size of each page.

g. When you are finished, close the Web site, then exit Expression Web.

Visual Workshop

Launch Expression Web, then open the ecotours Web site. On the home page, insert the Rain Forest.jpg image from the drive and folder where you store your Data Files. Save the image, using an appropriate name, within the assets folder. Edit the image and properties as necessary so that your screen matches Figure E-22. (*Hint*: You'll need to add a border.) When you are finished, save your changes, close the Web site, then exit Expression Web.

FIGURE E-22

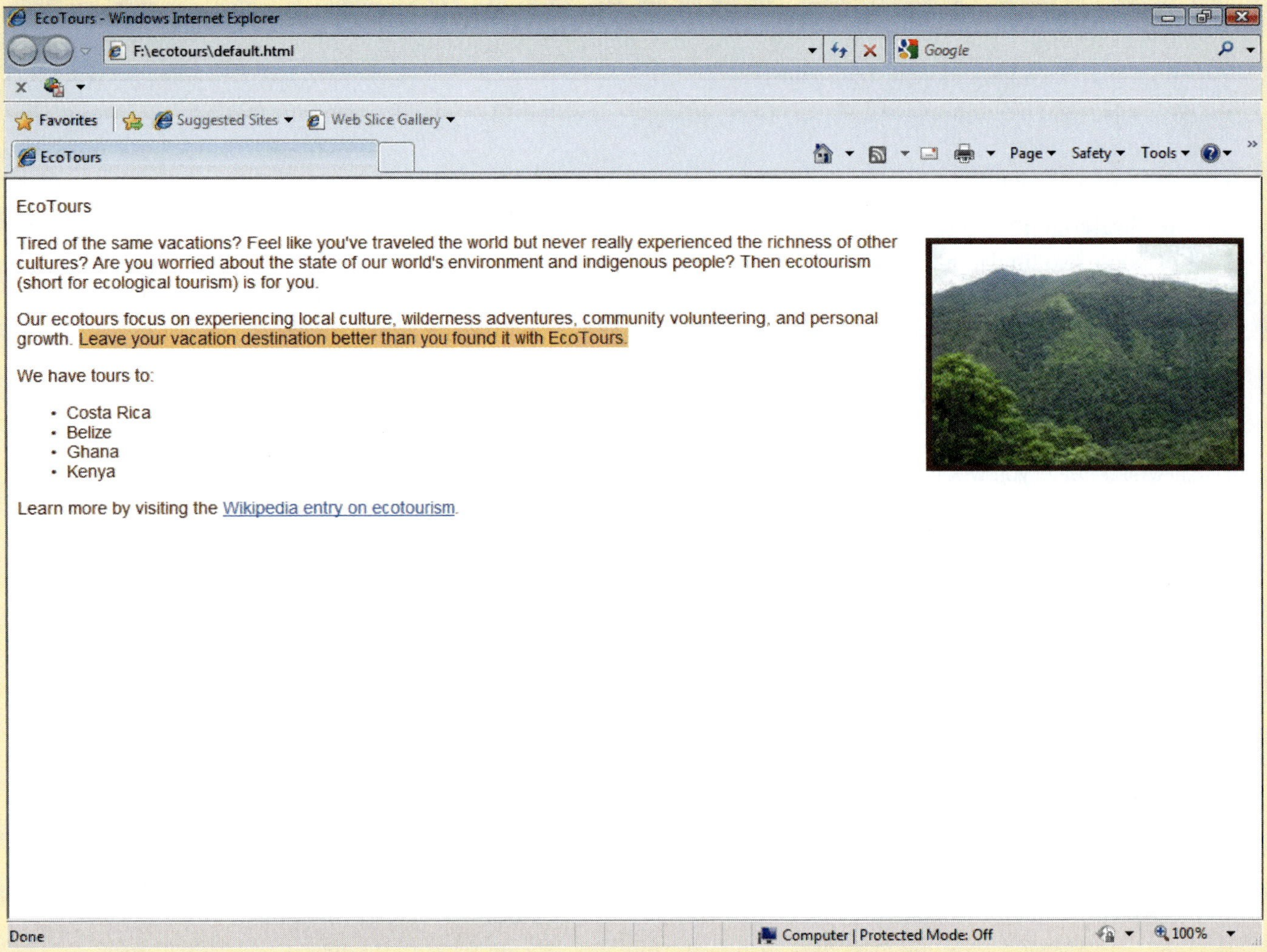

UNIT
F
Expression Web 3

Enhancing a Design with CSS

Paying attention to design details can make the difference between a site that is merely acceptable to visitors and one that truly captures their attention. Professionals accomplish this by adding background colors, background images, borders, and appropriate white space to page elements and headings in ways that create a pleasing and cohesive visual identity for the site. You're ready to add some polish to the TradeWinds Web site by creating styles for the layout elements and headings.

OBJECTIVES
Understand CSS layouts

Add background images

Set a background color using the Eyedropper

Set a background color using a swatch

Add a border

Add a font family

Style headings

Style the footer

Set padding and margins

Understanding CSS Layouts

To take full advantage of the formatting capabilities of CSS, you need to understand the model that under-lies it. In addition to understanding CSS principles, you should be familiar with the specific structure of the page you are designing. You decide to learn more about CSS layouts in general, and the TradeWinds page layout in particular.

Before you create styles for layout elements, it's important to understand:

- ### The CSS box model

  Familiar terms such as border and margin have particular rules and meanings in CSS. CSS presentation and layout is based on the **CSS box model**, which states that every element on a page is a rectangular box, including divs, images, headers, paragraphs, lists, and so on. Each box has one core component (the content area) and three optional components (borders, padding, and margins). The optional components do not appear unless specified in a style rule. Figure F-1 shows a diagram of the CSS box model.

  Understanding the order in which these components appear allows you to create style rules that work as intended. The **content area** is the innermost box, which contains the text, image, or other content. The **padding area** creates space between the content and the border. **Borders** enclose both the padding and content areas. The **margin** area creates space surrounding the other three components (borders, padding, and content). Margins can also be thought of as providing space between separate elements. For every element, you can apply different padding, border, and margin properties to each of the four sides of the box.

- ### CSS layouts in Expression Web

  When you create a Web page using one of Expression Web's CSS layouts, the new page is structured with the divs included in that layout, and the divs are placed according to the rules of the style sheet assigned to that page. The pages you created in Unit B for the TradeWinds site were based on the CSS layout Header, nav, 2 columns, footer—resulting in an HTML page with six divs arranged according to the style sheet for this layout.

  As you learned in Unit B, a div is an HTML container element that is often used for layout and position-ing. Divs are usually assigned an id attribute, which is a unique and specific name. Unlike a class attribute, an id can only be used once on a page. While class-based rules are indicated by a period before the selector name (.highlight, for example), id-based rules are indicated with "#" (#masthead, for example).

  You must understand the structure of your page in order to make intelligent decisions about how and where to apply styles. Refer to Figure F-2 to review the placement of the following divs in the TradeWinds Web pages:
  - masthead: used for the main header and branding area for the site
  - top_nav: can be used for horizontal navigation; the tradewinds design does not use this area
  - left_col: a left-hand column; the tradewinds design uses this for site navigation
  - page_content: an area to the right of the column that holds the site content, both images and text
  - container: a div that contains both the left_col and the page_content divs
  - footer: a div at the bottom of the page that holds text-based navigation and copyright notice

FIGURE F-1: The CSS box model

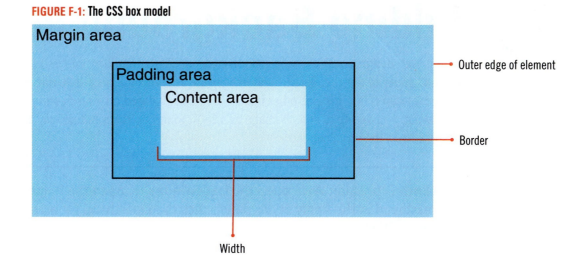

FIGURE F-2: Layout elements outlined on TradeWinds home page

Adding Background Images

Current Web design practices make extensive use of CSS background images to create a consistent look across all pages of the site. Background images are applied through a style rule instead of being directly inserted into an HTML page as other images are.  Based on your design plans for the TradeWinds page layout, you decide to add an image as a background on the masthead div and a second image as a background on the container div.

STEPS

1. **Launch Expression Web, open the tradewinds site, open the home page, point to #masthead in the Apply Styles panel, click the #masthead list arrow, then click Modify Style**

   The Modify Style dialog box opens. The #masthead style rule was created automatically when you created this page using one of Expression Web's prestructured CSS layouts in Unit B.

   QUICK TIP

   Expression Web uses the file path to your Data Files folder until you save the page and embedded images to your site's root folder.

2. **Click Background in the Category list, click the Browse button next to background-image, navigate to where you store your Data Files, click tw_header.gif, then click Open**

   The file path to the image in your data file folder appears in the background-image text box, and the image displays as the background in the preview box.

3. **Click the background-repeat list arrow, then click no-repeat**

   When you add the background-image property to a style rule, you can specify values for four properties. **Background-repeat** controls whether and how the image repeats across the element. **Background-attachment** controls whether the image scrolls with the element's content or stays fixed as the content scrolls over it. **(x) background-position** and **(y) background-position** control where the image is placed relative to the element's left edge and top edge, respectively. See Table F-1 for a description of each value. You want the TradeWinds header graphic to display only once. Boldly patterned and colored background images are best reserved for areas of the page that will not contain text, as they can make the text difficult to read.

   QUICK TIP

   Because you created a style rule in the external style sheet, this background image will show up on all pages that have the masthead div as part of their structure.

4. **Click Position in the Category list, type 197 in the height text box, then click OK**

   The masthead background image is now visible along the top of the page. Elements that don't contain content or have any specified dimensions collapse; they are not visible on the page. The background image is not considered content, because it's part of the style rule and not part of the HTML element. Specifying a height for the div that is the same height as the image prevents it from collapsing and allows the background image to be displayed.

5. **Point to #container in the Apply Styles panel, click the #container list arrow, then click Modify Style**

   QUICK TIP

   A limitation of background images is that they cannot include a link. If you want an image to appear on every page and include a link, you must insert the image in each page individually.

6. **Click Background in the Category list, click the Browse button next to background-image, navigate to the folder where you store your Data Files, click tw_bg.gif, click Open, click the background-repeat list arrow, click repeat-y, then click OK**

   See Figure F-3. Using the y-repeat method causes the image to repeat down the length of the element as needed to fill the space; it keeps the image file size small and allows you to fill the element without having to know its exact height.

7. **Click File on the menu bar, click Save All, click OK in the Save Embedded Files dialog box, preview your page in a browser, close the browser window and return to Expression Web**

   It's important to use the Save All command so that both the HTML file and the CSS file are saved to your site folder and all references to the images are maintained when you publish the site.

FIGURE F-3: Home page after background image added to #masthead and #container styles

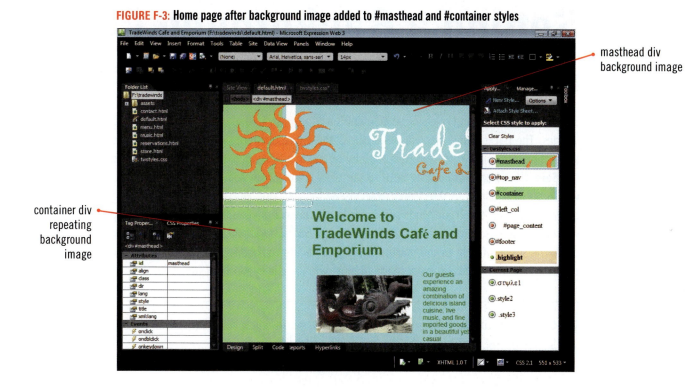

masthead div background image

container div repeating background image

TABLE F-1: Background image properties and values

property	value	what it does
background-repeat	no-repeat	Background image does not repeat
	repeat	Background image repeats vertically and horizontally; this is the default
	repeat-x	Background image repeats horizontally only
	repeat-y	Background image repeats vertically only
	inherit	Uses same background-repeat value as containing element
background-attachment	fixed	Background image is fixed to element and scrolls with the content
	scroll	Background image stays fixed and content scrolls over it
	inherit	Uses same background-attachment value as containing element
(x) background-position	center	Horizontally centers background image in element
	left	Positions background image on left edge of element
	right	Positions background image on right edge of element
	inherit	Uses same horizontal position for background image as containing element
	(value)	Allows specification of a pixel value to dictate the distance from left edge of element to left edge of background image
(y) background-position	bottom	Positions background image on bottom edge of element
	center	Vertically centers background image in element
	top	Positions background image on top edge of element
	value	Allows specification of a pixel value to dictate the distance from top edge of element to top edge of background image

Expression Web 3

Setting a Background Color Using the Eyedropper

Specifying a background color for an element is a handy way to add color to a page without adding additional images. The background color displays across the entire element, including the margins. You have already learned how to specify colors in style rules by typing in a hex value, but you can also choose a color by using the **Select tool** or **eyedropper tool** to sample a color. When you **sample** a color, you click the color anywhere on your screen to select that exact shade for your use.  Because the background color of the body element on the TradeWinds site is white, the areas between the elements on the page are white. On higher resolution screens, the right area of the page background will also be white. You want those areas to be the same shade of blue as the masthead, so you decide to modify the body style rule to change the background color. To match the exact shade of blue, you use the eyedropper tool.

STEPS

1. **Confirm that the home page is the active page, click the Manage Styles tab in the Apply Styles panel, right-click body, then click Modify Style**

   The Modify Style dialog box opens. Element-based styles such as the body style are not displayed in the Apply Styles panel, so to modify the body style you use the Manage Styles panel.

2. **Click Background in the Category list, then click the background-color color swatch ▧**

   The More Colors dialog box opens, as shown in Figure F-4. On the left are swatches of all the Web-safe colors. **Web-safe colors** are colors that display reliably on all computer monitors. They were more important in the early days of Web design than they are now, since most visitors' monitors now display millions of colors. Some designers still restrict their color choices to the Web-safe palette if they are designing for cell phones or handhelds, since these devices can display fewer colors than the typical computer monitor.

3. **Click Select**

   The cursor changes to an eyedropper 🖋, which you can use to select any color that is visible on the page.

> **TROUBLE**
> If the dialog boxes are in the way, click the Cancel button on the More Colors dialog box, drag and move the Modify Style dialog box out of the way, click the background-color color swatch, then click Select.

4. **Point to any blue area in the background image, as shown in Figure F-5**

> **QUICK TIP**
> If you wanted a lighter or darker shade of the selected color, you could click Custom and use the slider on the right to change the color.

5. **Click the blue area, then click OK**

   Compare your dialog box to Figure F-6. The hex code #9BDBEB appears in the background-color box, and the background-color swatch displays the blue color you sampled.

6. **Click OK**

   The Modify Style dialog box closes and the background color of the body element matches the blue container background. A white area still appears between the first and second column. You will fix that in a later lesson.

7. **Save changes to all open files, preview the home page in a browser, then use navigation links at the bottom of the pages to view all pages in the site**

   Because you modified the styles in an external style sheet, all pages display the new background color for the body element. A gap still appears below the masthead. You will fix that in a later lesson.

8. **Close the browser window, then return to Expression Web**

FIGURE F-4: More Colors dialog box

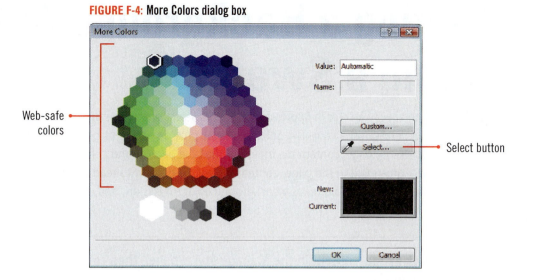

Web-safe colors

Select button

FIGURE F-5: Sampling a color with Eyedropper tool

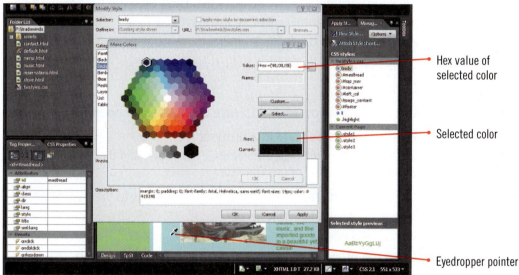

Hex value of selected color

Selected color

Eyedropper pointer

FIGURE F-6: Modify Style dialog box with sampled color as #body style background-color

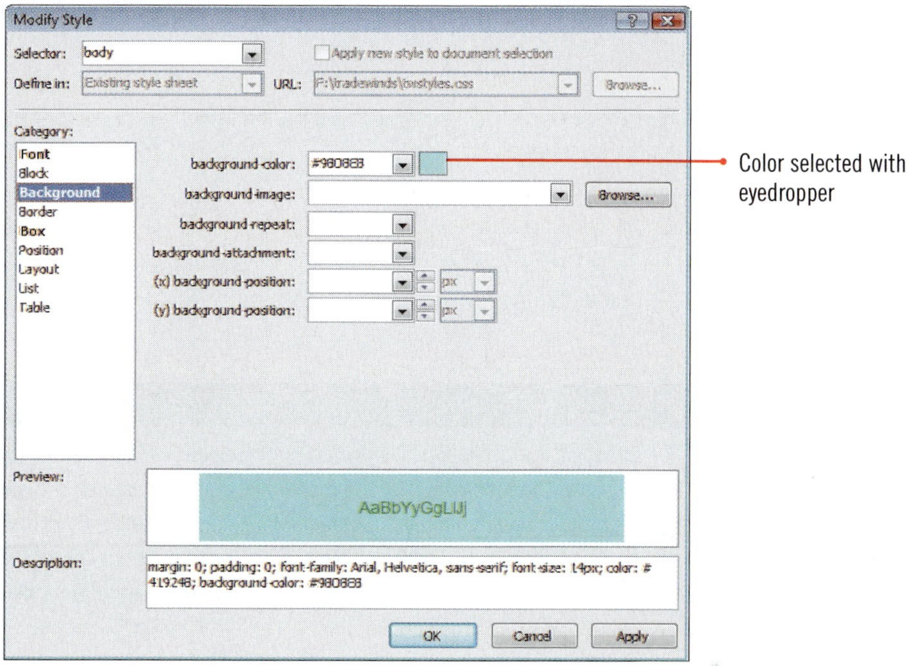

Color selected with eyedropper

Setting a Background Color Using a Swatch

Another way to specify a color in Expression Web is to select one of the predefined swatches that appear when you click a color list arrow. The color swatches provide access to basic colors such as red, yellow, and gray.  The page_content div inherited the blue background color from the body, You are concerned that the green text in the page_content div will be difficult to read on the blue background color. You think white would work better as a background color for this div, and decide to use a swatch to make this change.

STEPS

1. **Right-click #page_content in the Manage Styles panel, then click Modify Style**
   The Modify Style dialog box opens.

2. **Click Background in the Category list, then click the background-color list arrow**
   A palette of color swatches opens, as shown in Figure F-7.

> **QUICK TIP**
> These swatches work well for specifying basic black and white, but in most cases you want to choose a certain shade of, say, red rather than just using the generic swatch offered.

3. **Click the white color swatch (first row, second from the left)**
   The hex value for white, #FFFFFF, is displayed in the background-color text box.

4. **Click OK**

5. **Use the Save All command to save changes to all open files**

6. **Preview the home page in a browser**
   The background of the page_content div is now white, and the readability of the green text is improved, as shown in Figure F-8.

7. **Use navigation links at the bottom of the pages to view all pages in the site**
   Because you modified the styles in an external style sheet, all pages display the new background colors for the page_content div.

8. **Close the browser window and return to Expression Web**

Ensuring sufficient color contrast

When choosing a background color, be sure there is enough contrast, or perceived color difference, between an element's background color and any text that displays on the background. Visitors with poor eyesight might have difficulty reading dark text on a dark background or light text on a light background. Background and text that are too similar in color can also cause readability problems.

Several online tools allow you to check color contrast by providing the hex values for the desired text and the background colors; the tool then analyzes whether there is sufficient contrast between the two. Enter the term "color contrast tool" into your favorite search engine to learn more about available contrast-checking tools.

FIGURE F-7: Color swatches

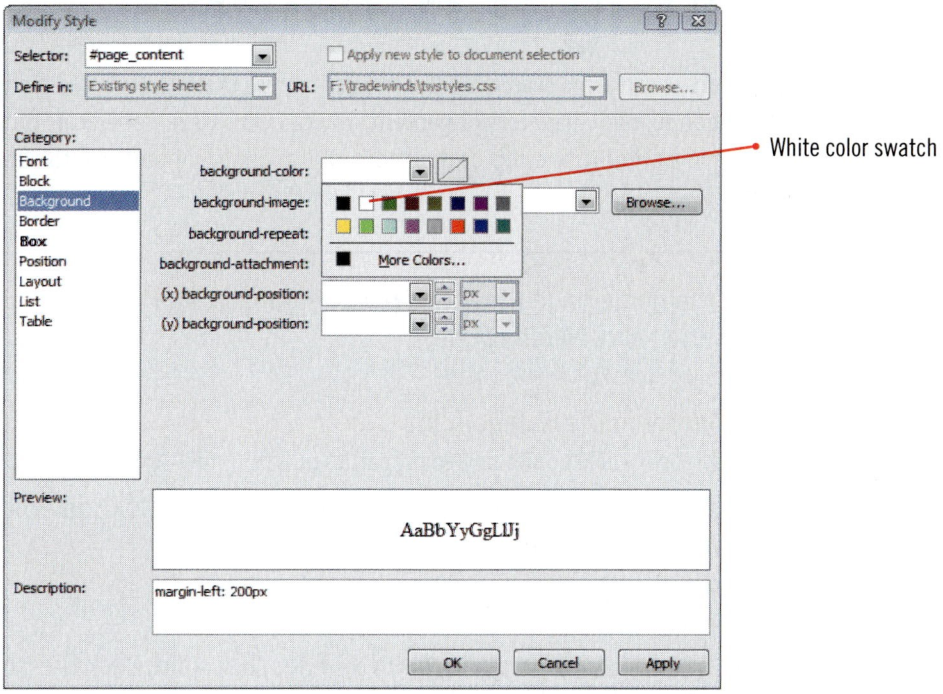

White color swatch

FIGURE F-8: Home page with background colors applied to body and page_content divs

Expression Web 3

Adding a Border

Colorful borders can serve several purposes. You can use them to enhance the visual design of a Web site, to draw attention to particular areas or content, and to act as visual separators on the page.  You decide to add a gold border to the top and bottom of the page_content div, to subtly set it off from the rest of the page.

STEPS

1. **Make the home page the active page, right-click #page_content in the Manage Styles panel, then click Modify Style**
   The Modify Style dialog box opens.

2. **Click Border in the Category list**
   You can specify three border-related properties in CSS: border-style, border-width, and border-color.

3. **Click the Same for all check boxes under border-style, border-width, and border-color to remove the check marks**
   Because you want to define only a top and bottom border, it's necessary to deselect the same-for-all check boxes.

QUICK TIP
If you don't specify a value for border-style, the border won't display, even if you set the border-color and border-width properties.

4. **Click the top list arrow under border-style, click solid, click the bottom list arrow under border-style, then click solid**
   For the border-style property you can choose from 11 different options, but not all of them are well-supported by current browsers.

5. **Click in the top text box under border-width, type 4, click in the bottom text box under border-width, then type 4**
   When specifying border-width, you can use keywords (thin, medium, or thick) or specify a value in pixels. It's best to choose a specific value rather than using keywords because different browsers interpret the keywords differently, which can cause your design to display differently than you intended.

6. **Click in the top text box under border-color, type #87E293, click in the bottom text box under border-color, type #87E293, then compare your screen to Figure F-9**
   A green color appears in the swatch beside top border-color and bottom border-color.

7. **Click OK**

8. **Save your changes to all open files, preview the home page in a browser, then compare your screen to Figure F-10**

9. **Use navigation links at the bottom of the pages to view all pages in the site, then return to the home page, leaving the browser window open**

FIGURE F-9: Completed Border options

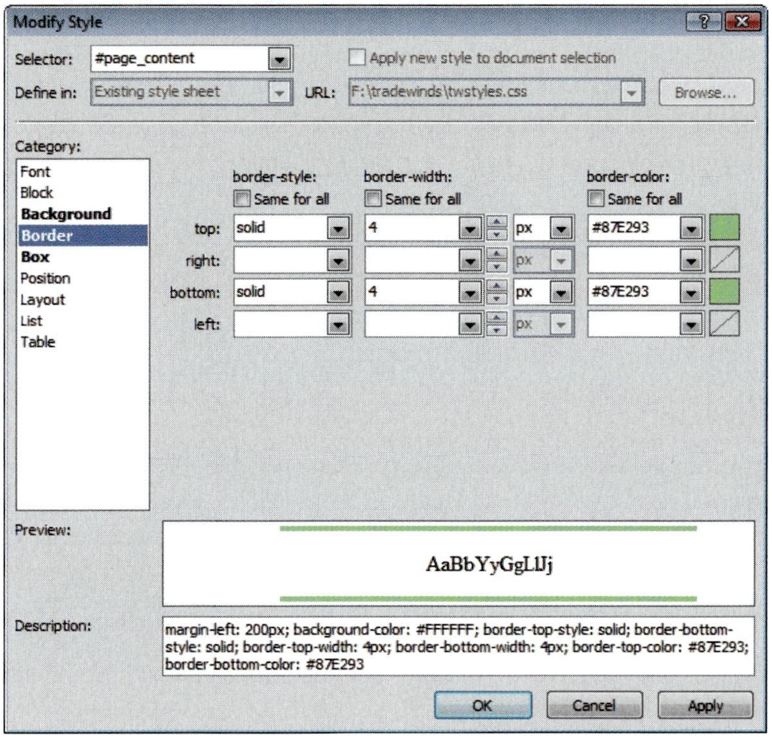

FIGURE F-10: Home page with border added to page_content div

Expression Web 3

Adding a Font Family

As you have learned, when writing a style rule you should specify a prioritized list of fonts, known as a **font family**, instead of a single font, in case the visitor's computer doesn't have a particular font installed. By default, Expression Web offers only three sets of font families. You can define your own sets of fonts, though, which will be available in the font-family lists when you create or modify a style. Catalina asks you to make the headings stand out more from the body text. You start by creating a new font family to use for the headings.

1. **Click Tools on the menu bar, click Page Editor Options, then click the Font Families tab**
   See Figure F-11.

2. **In the Select font family list, click (New Font Family) if necessary**
   The guidelines for creating a font-family list are as follows: Start with the font you prefer, then list Web-safe fonts for Windows and Mac systems, and then end with a generic font family. Although no font is guaranteed to be installed on a particular computer, **Web-safe fonts** are fonts likely to be available on Windows, Mac, and Linux-based computer systems. **Generic font families** are part of the CSS specification and are displayed if no other fonts in the list are available. Only three generic font families are consistently understood by browsers and therefore safe to use—serif, sans serif, and monospace. A **serif** font, such as Times New Roman, has visible strokes at the ends of the character. A **sans-serif** font, such as Arial, has no strokes at the end of the character. A **monospace** font, such as Courier, has equal space between the characters.

   > **QUICK TIP**
   > To quickly move to a different part of the list, type the first letter of the font name in the Add font text box.

3. **Scroll down in the Add font list, click Lucida Sans, then click Add**
   A new font family, consisting of Lucida Sans, is added to the Select font family list. This is your preferred font, so it will be used when available in any browser displaying your Web site.

4. **Scroll up in the Add font list, click Arial, then click Add**
   Arial appears after Lucida Sans in the Select font family list. Arial is a Web-safe font, and will be used on browsers where Lucida Sans is not available.

   > **QUICK TIP**
   > Be sure to add the fonts in the appropriate order; if you make a mistake, remove the font family and start over.

5. **In the Add font text box, type Helvetica, then click Add**
   Helvetica appears after Arial in the Select font family list; it will be used on browsers where neither Lucida Sans nor Arial is available. Only fonts installed on your computer appear in the Add font list. Because Helvetica is more common on Mac computers than on Windows computers, you need to type the font name rather than selecting it from the list.

6. **Scroll down in the Add font text box, click sans-serif, click Add, then compare your screen to Figure F-12**
   Sans-serif appears after Helvetica in the Select font family list.

7. **Click OK**
   The Page Editor Options dialog box closes. The new font family will be available when you create a style in this or any Web site on your computer. See Table F-2 for guidance on combining fonts in a font family.

Choosing fonts

In the printing world, conventional wisdom holds that serif fonts are better than sans-serif fonts for body text because they are easier to read. But recent research has shown conflicting results about which type of font affords the best onscreen readability, so feel free to use either. Try to limit your font usage to two font faces per design, though, to avoid visual overload. You can mix the two types, using sans serif for body type and serif for headings, or vice versa. You can also stick with the same font type for both body and heading text.

FIGURE F-11: Font Families tab in Page Editor Options dialog box

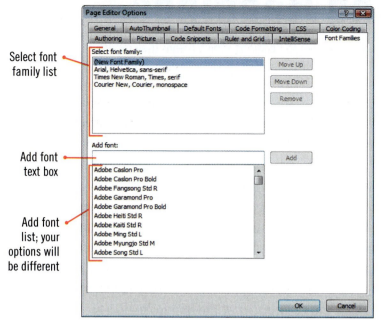

Select font family list

Add font text box

Add font list; your options will be different

FIGURE F-12: Completed font family

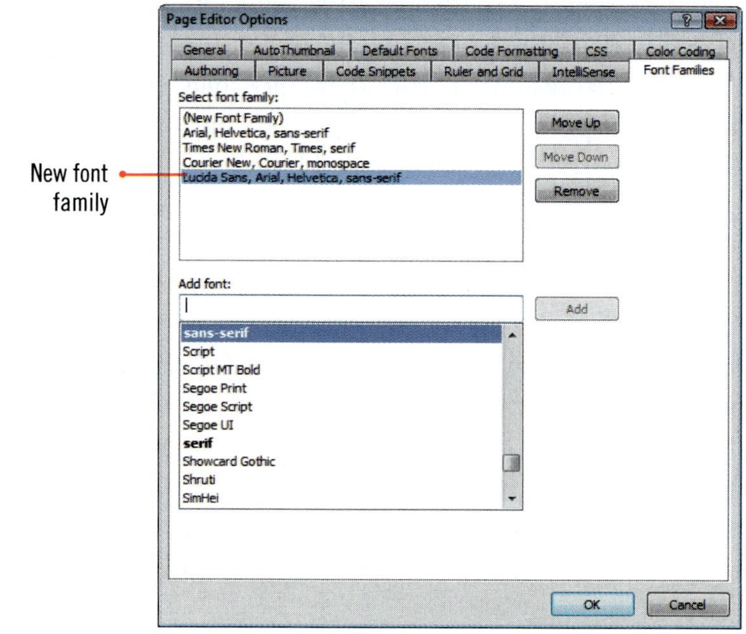

New font family

TABLE F-2: Suggested font family combinations

with this family type	pair these fonts		with these Web-safe fonts
Serif	Book Antiqua	Georgia	Times New Roman, Times, serif
	Bookman Old Style	Palatino	
	Century Schoolbook	Palatino Linotype	
	Garamond		
Sans-serif	**Arial Black**	Lucida Sans	Arial, Helvetica, sans-serif
	Avant Garde	Unicode	
	Century Gothic	Lucida Grand	
	Comic Sans MS	Tahoma	
	Geneva	Trebuchet MS	
	Impact	Verdana	
Monospace	Lucida Console		Courier New, Courier, Monospace

Enhancing a Design with CSS

Styling Headings

The CSS box model also applies to headings, which means they can have the same properties applied to them as other elements, such as borders, margins, padding, and background colors and images. Creating interesting styles for headings is a great way to make your site more readable and more visually pleasing. To make the headings in the TradeWinds site stand out more, you decide the first-level headings should be the same orange as the sun in the header, with a different font and a blue bottom border. You also want to remove the top margin to close the gap under the masthead. You want the second-level headings to be blue and smaller than the first-level headings, with no border.

STEPS

QUICK TIP

By default, browsers display HTML headings as bolder than paragraph text, with margins on the top and bottom and no border or background color or image; the displayed font size decreases as the heading level decreases.

1. Click the **New Style button** on the Manage Styles panel, click the **Selector list arrow**, click **h1**, click the **Define in list arrow**, click **Existing style sheet**, click the **URL list arrow**, then click **twstyles.css**

2. Click the **font-family list arrow**, click **Lucida Sans, Arial, Helvetica, sans-serif**, type **22** in the font-size box, click the **font-weight list arrow**, click **bold**, click the **font color swatch**, click **Select**, point the eyedropper at the **orange sun** on the page, click the mouse button, then click **OK**

3. Click **Border** in the Category list, then click the **Same for all check boxes** under **border-style**, **border-width**, and **border-color** to remove the check marks

4. Click the **bottom list arrow** under **border-style**, click **solid**, click in the **bottom text box** under **border-width**, type **1**, click in the **bottom text box** under **border-color**, type **#51A5BA**, then compare your screen to Figure F-13

5. Click **Box** in the Category list, click the **Same for all check box** next to **margin**, click in the **top text box** under **margin**, type **0**, then click **OK**

   This removes the default top margin of the h1 element, eliminating the gap between the masthead and page_content divs. You are ready to create the heading 2 style.

6. Click the **New Style button** on the Manage Styles panel, click the **Selector list arrow**, click **h2**, click the **Define in list arrow**, click **Existing style sheet**, click the **URL list arrow**, then click **twstyles.css** if necessary

7. Type **18** in the font-size box, click the **font-weight list arrow**, click **bold**, type **#51A5BA** in the color text box, compare your screen to Figure F-14, then click **OK**

8. Use the **Save All** command to save changes to all open files, preview the home page in a browser, then click the **Store link**

   See Figure F-15. The first- and second-level headings reflect the new style rules you created. The gap between the masthead and page_content div is also closed.

9. **Close the browser window and return to Expression Web**

FIGURE F-13: Border category for h1 style rule

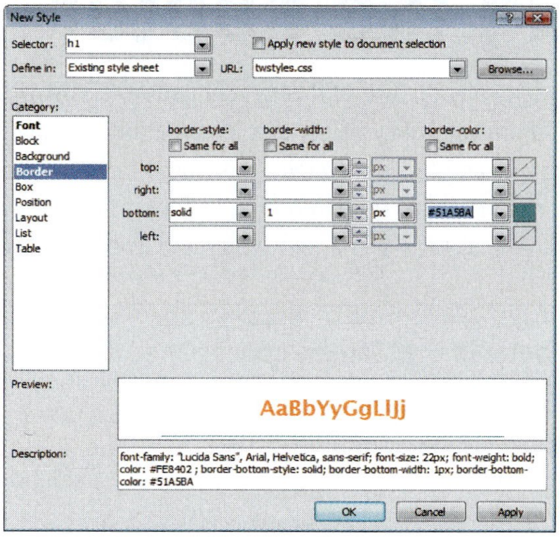

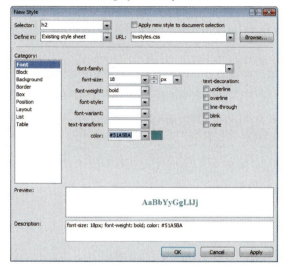

FIGURE F-14: Font category for h2 style rule

FIGURE F-15: Store page with new heading styles

First-level heading

Second-level headings

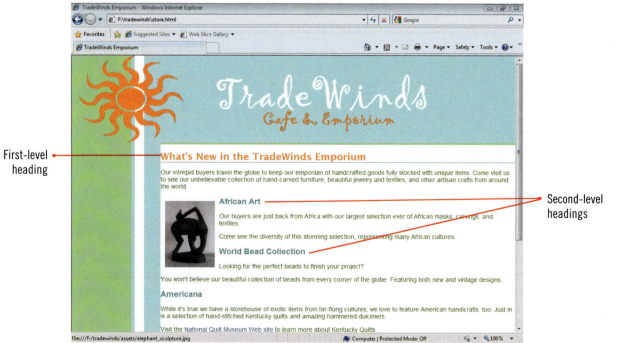

Styling the Footer

Web page footers generally feature text-only navigation, a copyright notice, and perhaps links to reference areas such as a privacy policy or contact information. Usually designers de-emphasize the footer by making the text smaller and less noticeable so it doesn't distract from other, more important content on the page.  You want the TradeWinds page footer to have a smaller font size and to have the text centered in the div. To make these changes, you need to modify the #footer style.

STEPS

1. **Right-click #footer in the Manage Styles panel, then click Modify Style**
   The Modify Style dialog box opens.

2. **Click in the font-size box, then type 10**
   While it's appropriate to make the footer font size small, a size below 10 pixels might be so small that it's unreadable.

3. **Click the font-weight list arrow, then click bold**
   See Figure F-16.

4. **Click Block in the Category list, click the text-align list arrow, then click center**
   See Figure F-17.

5. **Click OK, then scroll to the bottom of the page in the editing window**
   Figure F-18. The footer text now appears smaller and centered.

6. **Save changes to all open files, preview the home page in a browser, then use the bottom navigation to view the other site pages, leaving the browser window open**

Understanding semantic div ids

Unlike the list or paragraph element, the div element does not have a specific semantic meaning. However, divs are usually assigned an **id attribute**, which is a unique and specific name, and these id names are often semantic, reflecting the purpose of the div. When you use one of the CSS layouts in Expression Web, many of the divs have semantic ids, such as masthead, footer, or page_content, but some have non-semantic ids, such as left_col. You can feel free to use the divs for other purposes, though, such as using the masthead for horizontal navigation at the top of a page.

FIGURE F-16: Font category for #footer style

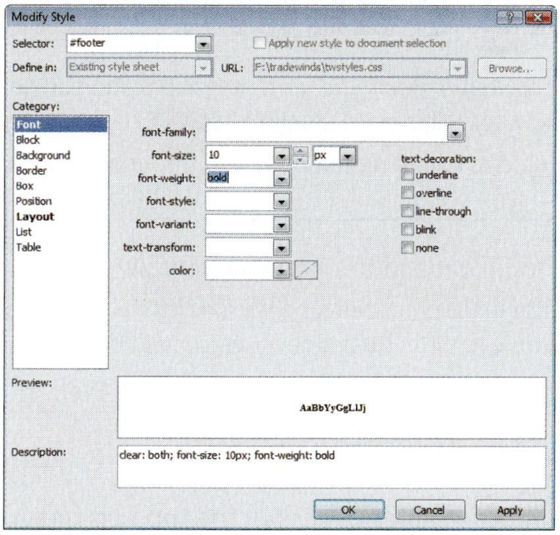

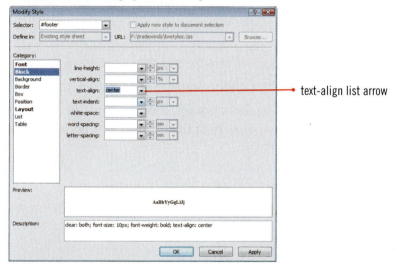

FIGURE F-17: Block category for #footer style

text-align list arrow

FIGURE F-18: Home page with modified #footer style

Footer text
is now
centered
and smaller

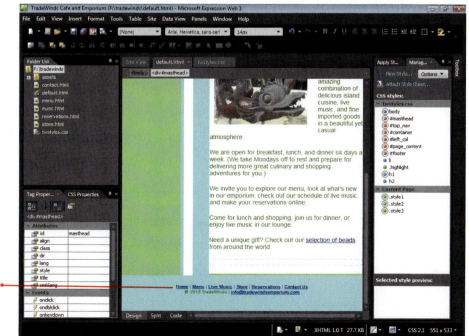

Enhancing a Design with CSS

Expression Web 3

Setting Padding and Margins

Adding white space to your pages in the form of margins and padding can improve the appearance of your design as well as the readability of the content. In reviewing the current TradeWinds page layout, you notice a few problems you think can be solved through specifying padding and margins.

STEPS

1. **Observe the home page in the browser window**
   Notice that the text in the page_content div is too close to the edge of the element. Notice also the text in the footer div is too close to the bottom of the page_content div.

2. **Close the browser window, return to Expression Web, right-click page_content on the Manage Styles panel, then click Modify Style**
   The Modify Style dialog box opens.

QUICK TIP
When the Same for all check box contains a check mark, all fields in the current setting change automatically when you enter a new value.

3. **Click Box on the Category list, click in the top text box under padding, type 15, then compare your screen to Figure F-19**
   You might notice the 200-pixel left margin setting; it was created when Expression Web generated the original style sheet for the page layout.

4. **Click OK**
   A 15-pixel padding surrounds the content and separates it from the edges of the page_content div.

5. **Right-click footer on the Manage Styles panel, then click Modify Style**

6. **Click Box on the Category list, click the Same for all check box next to margin to remove the check mark, type 20 in the top text box under margin, compare your screen to Figure F-20, then click OK**
   Because you only need to create space between the top of the text and the bottom of the page_content div, you only need to specify a top margin.

7. **Save changes to all open files, then preview the home page in a browser**
   Compare your screen to Figure 21.

8. **Use the bottom navigation to view the other site pages, close the browser window, return to Expression Web, close the tradewinds site, then exit Expression Web**

FIGURE F-19: Box category for #page_content style

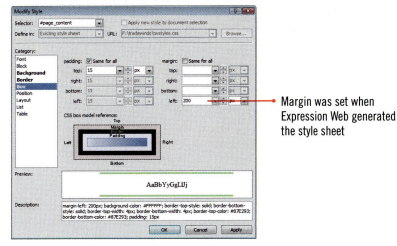

Margin was set when Expression Web generated the style sheet

FIGURE F-20: Modifying the Box category of #footer style

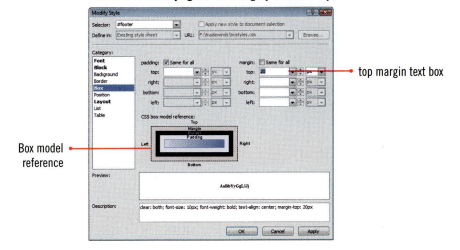

top margin text box

Box model reference

FIGURE F-21: Home page with modified padding and margins

Expression Web 3

Practice

SAM

For current SAM information including versions and content details, visit SAM Central (http://samcentral.course.com). If you have a SAM user profile, you may have access to hands-on instruction, practice, and assessment of the skills covered in this unit. Since we support various versions of SAM throughout the life of this text, you will want to check with your instructor for instructions and the correct URL/Web site to access those assignments.

Concepts Review

Label each element in the CSS box model diagram shown in Figure F-22.

FIGURE F-22

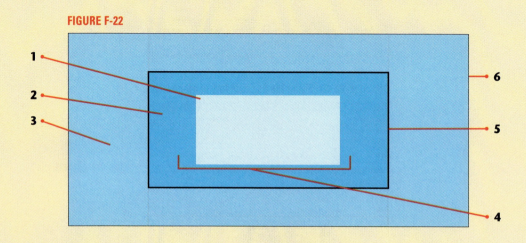

Match each term with the statement that best describes it.

7. (x) background-position
8. (y) background-position
9. sans-serif fonts
10. serif fonts
11. monospace fonts

a. Arial and Helvetica
b. Times and Times New Roman
c. Property that controls where a background image is placed relative to the element's top edge
d. Property that controls where a background image is placed relative to the element's left edge
e. Courier and Courier New

Select the best answer from the list of choices.

12. **Which property creates space between two different elements?**
    a. Background
    b. Padding
    c. Margin
    d. Border

13. **Which property creates space between an element's content and its border?**
    a. Background
    b. Padding
    c. Margin
    d. Border

14. **Which property allows you to specify that a background image stays fixed while the element's content scrolls?**
    a. background-attachment
    b. background-repeat
    c. background-color
    d. background-scroll

15. **Which value of the background-repeat property causes a background image to repeat horizontally across the page?**
    a. repeat-x
    b. repeat-y
    c. auto
    d. repeat-h

16. **How many background images can you add to an element?**
    a. One
    b. Two
    c. Three
    d. As many as you'd like

17. **What is an easy way to choose a basic color such as black or white?**
    a. Memorize the hex codes and type them in
    b. Use the color swatches
    c. Use the color wheel
    d. Use web-safe colors

18. **Which of the following is *not* a Web-safe font?**
    a. Courier
    b. Times New Roman
    c. Arial
    d. Copperplate Gothic

Skills Review

1. **Add background images.**
   a. Launch Expression Web, then open the careers site.
   b. Open the home page.
   c. Open the Modify Style dialog box for #masthead.
   d. In the Background category, specify **cg_logo.gif** (located in the drive and folder where you store your Data Files) as the background image, and set the background-repeat to **no-repeat**.
   e. In the Position category, set the height to **100 pixels**.
   f. Click OK to close the Modify Style dialog box.
   g. Use the Save All command to save your changes, confirm that you want to save embedded files, preview the home page in the browser, use navigation links at the bottom of the pages to view the other pages in the site, close the browser window, then return to Expression Web.

2. **Set a background color using the Eyedropper tool.**
   a. Using the Manage Styles panel, open the Modify Style dialog box for the body style.
   b. In the Background category, click the background-color swatch, then use the Select eyedropper to sample the blue color in the background of the header graphic. (*Hint*: You might need to cancel out of the dialog boxes to adjust the header graphic location, then reopen the necessary dialog boxes and/or drag the Modify Style dialog box to a different location.)
   c. Click OK to close the More Colors dialog box, then click OK to close the Modify Style dialog box.
   d. Use the Save All command to save your changes, preview the home page in the browser, use the bottom text links to view the other pages in the site, then close the browser window and return to Expression Web.

Skills Review (continued)

3. Set a background color using a swatch.

   a. Open the Modify Style dialog box for the #page_content style.

   b. In the Background category, click the background-color list arrow, then choose the white swatch from the palette.

   c. Click OK to close the Modify Style dialog box.

   d. Open the Modify Style dialog box for the #container style.

   e. In the Background category, click the background-color list arrow, then choose the white swatch from the palette.

   f. Click OK to close the Modify Style dialog box.

   g. Open the Modify Style dialog box for the #top_nav style.

   h. In the Background category, click the background-color list arrow, then choose the white swatch from the palette.

   i. Click OK to close the Modify Style dialog box.

   j. Use the Save All command to save your changes, preview the home page in the browser, use navigation links to view the other pages in the site, close the browser window, then return to Expression Web.

4. Add a border.

   a. Open the Modify Style dialog box for the #container style.

   b. Use the options in the Border category to create a solid border that is **2 pixels** wide with the color **#CE0000** on all four sides.

   c. Click OK to close the Modify Style dialog box.

   d. Use the Save All command to save your changes, preview the home page in the browser, use the navigation links at the bottom of the page to view the other pages in the site, close the browser window, then return to Expression Web.

5. Add a font family.

   a. Open the Page Editor Options dialog box, then switch to the Font Families tab if necessary.

   b. Select (New Font Family) in the Select font family list if necessary.

   c. Select **Georgia** in the Add font list, then add it to the font family.

   d. Select **Times New Roman** in the Add font list, then add it to the font family.

   e. Type **Times** in the Add font text box, then add it to the font family.

   f. Select **serif** in the Add font list, then add it to the font family.

   g. Click OK to close the Page Editor Options dialog box.

6. Style headings.

   a. Open the New Style dialog box, set the selector to h1, then create the style in the existing style sheet cgstyles.css.

   b. In the Font category, set the font-family to Georgia, Times New Roman, Times, serif; the font-size to **30 pixels**; the font-weight to bold; and the color to **#CE0000**.

   c. In the Border category, create only a bottom border with a border-style of dashed, a border-width of **2 pixels**, and a border-color of **#C0C0C0**.

   d. Click OK to close the New Style dialog box.

   e. Open the New Style dialog box, set the selector to **h2**, then create the style in the existing style sheet cgstyles.css.

   f. In the Font category, set the font-family to the Georgia, Times New Roman, Times, serif; the font-size to **20 pixels**; the font-weight to bold, and the color to **#CE0000**.

   g. Click OK to close the New Style dialog box.

   h. Use the Save All command to save your changes, preview the home page in a browser, then use the navigation links to view the other pages in the site.

7. Style the footer.

   a. Open the Modify Style dialog box for the #footer style.

   b. Use the options in the Font category to set the font-size to **12 pixels** and the color to **white**.

   c. Use the options in the Block category to set the text-align to center, then click OK to close the Modify Style dialog box.

   d. Use the Save All command to save your changes, preview the home page in the browser, use the navigation links to view the other pages in the site, close the browser window, then return to Expression Web.

Skills Review (continued)

8. Set padding and margins.

a. Open the Modify Style dialog box for the #page_content style.

b. Use the options in the Box category to set padding on all four sides to **20 pixels**.

c. Click OK to close the Modify Style dialog box.

d. Open the Modify Style dialog box for the #footer style.

e. Use the options in the Box category to set the top margin to 15 pixels.

f. Click OK to close the Modify Style dialog box.

g. Use the Save All command to save your changes then preview the home page in the browser.

h. Compare your home page to Figure F-23, close the browser window, return to Expression Web, close the site, then exit Expression Web.

FIGURE F-23

Your Career. Guaranteed.

At Careers Guaranteed, we only work with the best. If we accept your application we guarantee that we will match you to a job position or we refund your money.

Why we're different

You don't have any time to waste. You know how those other career sites operate. You post your resume. You spend hours sifting through job postings. You apply to job after job after job. But it's tough to get a foot in the door when hundreds of people are applying for those same jobs. At Career Guaranteed, we really get to know you through our rigorous screening process. We know what your strengths are and what you want out from your career. So we can successfully match you with desirable positions in the industry you'd like to work in.

Not sure what career you want to pursue? Our one-of-a-kind career exploration tools can help!

Testimonial

I'd been looking for the right job for more than 4 months when a friend told me about Careers Guaranteed. They had matched me with the perfect job within six weeks. I've never been happier with my career! --Antoine D.

Independent Challenge 1

In this project you continue your work on the ConnectUp Web site. Tiffany has sent you some ideas for the types of colors she wants to use—bright, eye-catching colors that will appeal to the site's target audience. You get to work incorporating her suggestions to the site by adding styles to the divs and headings. As part of your design, you are using the top_nav div as your header, and the masthead div for navigation.

a. Launch Expression Web, then open the connectup Web site.

b. Open the home page.

c. Modify the #top_nav style with the following properties: set the background-image to **cu_logo.jpg**, which can be found in the location where you store your Data Files. Set the background-repeat to **no repeat** and the height to **200 pixels**.

d. Modify the #page_content style to set background-color to **white** and create a border on the top and bottom only that is **solid**, **3 pixels wide**, and the color **#FFDF57**.

e. Modify the #top_nav style to use the Select eyedropper to set the background-color to the same color as the cu_logo.jpg background.

f. Modify the body style to set margins on all sides to **zero** and the background-color to **#488FDF**.

g. Modify the #page_content style to set padding on all sides to **25 pixels**.

h. Create a new font family containing **Trebuchet MS**, **Arial**, **Helvetica**, **sans-serif**, in that order.

i. Create a new h1 style in the custyles.css stylesheet with the following properties: set the font-family to **Trebuchet MS**, **Arial**, **Helvetica**, **sans-serif**; set the font-size to **32 pixels**; set the font-weight to bold; set the color to **#3399FF**; and set margins on the top, left, and right sides to **0** and on the bottom to **10 pixels**.

j. Create a new h2 style in the custyles.css stylesheet with the following properties: set the font-family to **Trebuchet MS**, **Arial**, **Helvetica**, **sans-serif**, set the font-size to **24 pixels**; and set the color to a shade of green sampled from the Get Connected! image.

FIGURE F-24

k. Modify the #footer style to set the font-size to **10 pixels**, the font color to **white**, the margins on all sides to **15 pixels**, and the text-align to **center**.

l. Use the Save All command to save your changes, preview the home page in a browser, then use the navigation links to view all pages.

m. Compare the upper portion of your faq page to Figure F-24, close the browser window, return to Expression Web, close the site, then exit Expression Web.

Independent Challenge 2

In this project you continue your work on the Memories Restored Web site. You are ready to add visual interest to the site through the use of background images, colors, borders, and heading styles.

a. Launch Expression Web, open the memories Web site, then open the home page.

b. Modify the #masthead style to add **mr_logo.gif** as the background image with the appropriate repeat. Set the height to **150 pixels**. Set the background color to match the background color of the mr_logo image.

c. Modify the body style to add **mr_bg.gif** as a repeating bg image.

d. Modify the #page_content div to add padding, borders, and a background color that makes the page text easy to read. You may need to experiment with different settings until you find a combination you like.

e. Modify the #footer div as you'd like.

f. Create a new font-family list using a beginning font of your choice, followed by a list of web-safe fonts, and the appropriate generic font family.

g. Create a style in the existing style sheet using h1 as a selector and using the font family you created. If you wish, change the size, color, border, or any other characteristics of the h1 style.

h. Create a style in the existing style sheet using h2 as a selector and using the font family you created. If you wish, change the size, color, border, or any other characteristics of the h2 heading.

Advanced Challenge Exercise

- Open the tips page.
- Modify the .resources style to create attractive spacing between the text and the border.
- Apply any other settings you'd like to change the appearance of the style.

i. Save your changes to all open files, preview the site in a browser, then use the navigation links to view all pages. When you are finished, close the browser, return to Expression Web, close the site, then exit Expression Web.

Independent Challenge 3

Note: This Independent Challenge requires an Internet connection.

As part of your research for the Technology for All redesign, you want to explore the ways that designers are creating the striking designs you've seen accomplished through CSS. The css Zen Garden site uses one HTML file paired with different style sheets to display the same content with radically different appearances. The designs are accomplished using the same techniques you learned in this unit—use of divs styled with background images, background colors, and borders, and creative heading styles. In addition, you will notice that many designers use advanced CSS to position the divs in different locations on the page, something you have not learned yet.

a. Visit www.csszengarden.com, then click through the available designs to find two that you like but that differ from each other in look or feel.

b. View the sample HTML file on the site to see what the unstyled content looks like.

c. Analyze the two designs by comparing the appearance and location of each content area on the two designs. Note the use of colors, images, borders, and fonts.

d. Write at least three paragraphs describing what CSS techniques you think the designers used to create the visual design of the sites.

Advanced Challenge Exercise

■ Using the same two designs, analyze what types of sites and audience the design would be appropriate for, and why.

■ Write one paragraph giving an example of the type of site and audience that would be best suited to each design.

e. Add your name to the document, save it, and print it.

Real Life Independent Challenge

This project builds on the personal Web site you have worked on in previous units. You're ready to enhance your design with background images, background colors, borders, margins, and paddings. You will also style your headings.

a. Open your site in Expression Web, then carefully review the pages, identifying each div that makes up the layout. On a piece of paper, write down any design issues you think could be solved by adding background images, background colors, borders, margins, or padding.

b. Add a background image to at least one element.

c. Add a background color to at least one element.

d. Add a border to at least one element.

e. Add margins and/or padding as desired to create white space around at least one element. (*Hint*: You may need to add both margins and padding , or just one of these attributes, to the element.)

f. Create a new font-family list, then use it to create a new heading style for either the h1 element, the h2 element, or both.

g. Save your changes to all open files, preview the site in a browser, then use the navigation links to view all pages. When you are finished, close the browser, return to Expression Web, close the site, then exit Expression Web.

Visual Workshop

Open the ecotours Web site in Expression Web. Modify the home page and the external style sheet so that your screen matches Figure F-25. To accomplish this, you need to add background colors, borders, and padding to different divs as necessary. (*Hint*: The colors used are #CCCCCC and #DABD83. The green color you need can be sampled from the photo on the page.) When you are finished, save your changes, close the Web site, then exit Expression Web.

FIGURE F-25

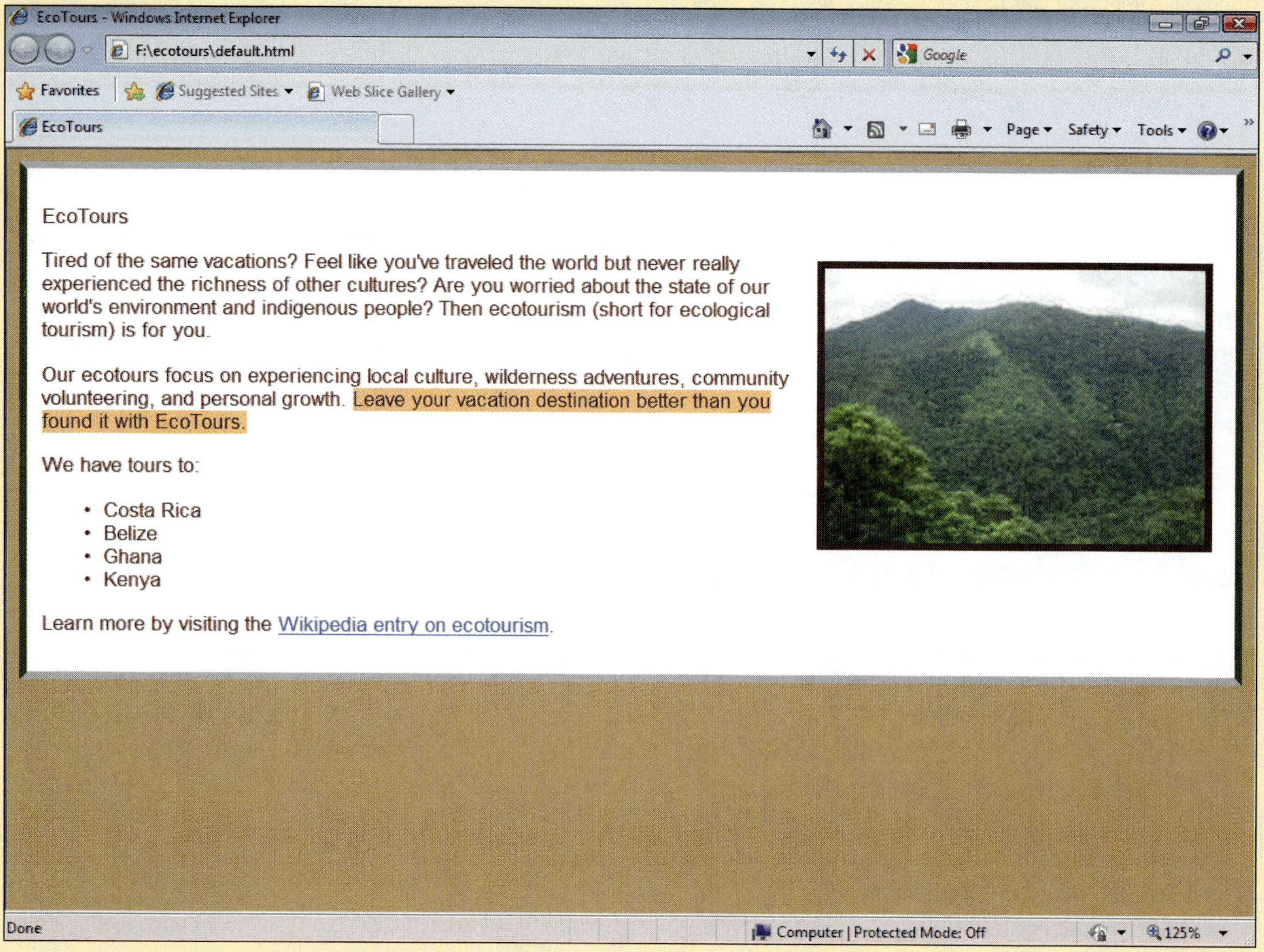

Designing Site Navigation

Navigation is an essential element of a successful site. No matter how compelling your site's design and content are, if the navigation is confusing, your visitors will not be able to find what they're seeking. That means they will get frustrated and leave your site. By creating a system of links that is clear and logical, you ensure that visitors can navigate from page to page easily. Content, graphics, and styles are all in place on the TradeWinds site. Now it is time to add the navigation and style the links so they complement the look of the site.

OBJECTIVES

Understand effective navigation

Create an interactive button

Edit an interactive button

Create a navigation bar

Add a navigation bar to site pages

Understand link styles

Create link styles

Understanding Effective Navigation

A site's navigation should both orient the visitor and provide clear options for where the visitor can go next. Creating an effective navigation system for a Web site can be fairly straightforward for a small site focused on one topic. However, as a site's complexity and diversity of content increase, it becomes more challenging to design navigation that is simple and easy to use. Knowing some basic principles can help you create a user-friendly navigation system for any size Web site. Before creating the navigation for the TradeWinds Web site, you decide to review some design principles.

To design effective navigation, it helps to understand:

- ### Guidelines for navigation

    Good navigation is consistent, clearly labeled, and reflects the needs of the site's audience. Visitors can easily feel disoriented on sites they are not familiar with, but links that are similar on every page can help to build their sense of familiarity and encourage them to explore the entire site. Navigation labels are usually short, so there's no room to be clever with the wording—keep it clear and succinct. Above all, navigation should be designed for the needs of your site's visitors.

- ### Types of navigation

    Global navigation is the navigation that appears consistently on each page, usually at the top or left side. It usually contains links to each top-level section in the site. **Local navigation** is the navigation that appears in a specific section of a site, and it tends to change from section to section. For example, a site that sells books, music, and movies might feature links to each of these major categories in the global navigation, which would appear the same on each page. The local navigation in each section would feature links to more specific subcategories, such as action and comedy in the movie section or pop and jazz in the music section. Local navigation isn't always necessary, but it's useful when there is so much content in a section that global navigation is inadequate. **Related navigation** usually appears within the content area and highlights content related to that page's information. For example, the page featuring a specific movie for sale might list movies by the same director in the related navigation. See Figure G-1 for an example of the three types of navigation.

- ### Navigation elements

    The elements that make up your navigation should be determined by the site's purpose, content, and target audience. For many years, most sites used graphics for navigation. In recent years, text links that are creatively styled with CSS have become popular. Pulldown menus, which feature list arrows that, when clicked, reveal a longer list of options, are convenient when space is at a premium and you have a long list of links to feature.

Architecting information

Did you know that there is an entire field devoted to the art and science of organizing and labeling Web content? **Information architects**, or **IAs** for short, are people whose job it is to create structures, navigation, and search systems for Web sites. IAs work as independent consultants or as part of in-house Web design teams within organizations. Working with an IA can be especially useful on complex sites that have thousands of pages of content or that deal with multiple audiences or topics. IAs understand how people look for information and are trained in specific research techniques that can help designers create and test site structures and navigation.

FIGURE G-1: The three types of navigation

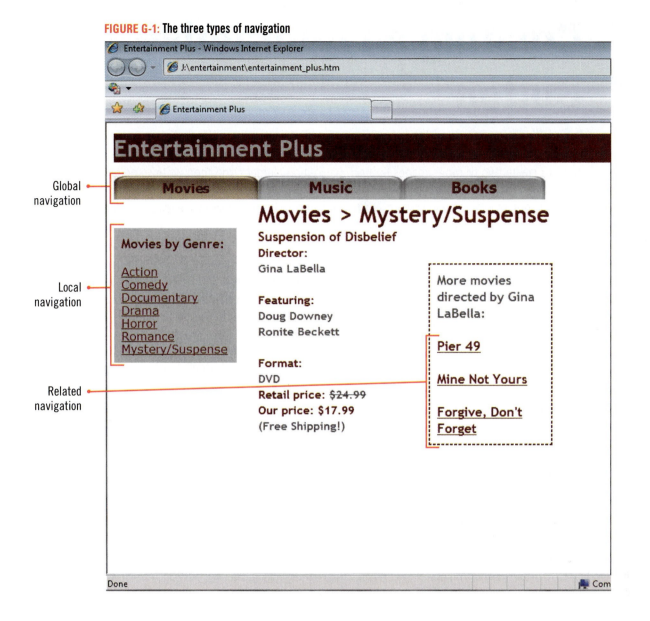

Global navigation

Local navigation

Related navigation

Expression Web 3

Learning how your visitors think

When designing a Web site that includes several pages, you might find that it pays to do some research before structuring your navigation. **Card sorting** is a technique you can use to involve actual or potential Web site visitors in this process. To perform a card sort, take a stack of index cards and on each card write the name of a topic, feature, or piece of content that is currently on your site or you are planning to have on your site. (Using about 25 cards works well for a small site. You may need more for a larger one.) Recruit 5 to 10 people who either use your site or are members of your site's target audience, and make an appointment with each. At each meeting, ask the person to read through the cards and to put cards they feel are related together into groups and to label each group. Record the results of each session on a spreadsheet. At the end of the process, review the information you gathered. Everyone thinks a bit differently, so you'll never have complete agreement, but look for trends that can help you decide how to group and label the content on the site.

Creating an Interactive Button

Interactive buttons, also known as **rollovers**, are navigation graphics that change appearance when a visitor interacts with them. The usual way to create this type of interactive image is to use a graphics program to create two or more images for each navigation element and then write some JavaScript code to control the change in appearance. But a much easier alternative is to use the predesigned interactive buttons included with Expression Web.  You decide to create interactive buttons and place them in the left column of the TradeWinds home page.

QUICK TIP
You can also link a button to an external Web page or an e-mail address.

1. **Launch Expression Web, open the tradewinds site, open the home page, click in the left_col div, click Insert on the menu bar, then click Interactive Button**

   The Interactive Buttons dialog box opens, as shown in Figure G-2. The dialog box includes three tabs—Button, Font, and Image—each of which allows you to control a different set of options for the button you are creating. When you click an option in the Buttons list, a preview of your choice appears in the Preview box. If you point to the Preview area, the image changes to a preview of the button's hover state.

2. **In the Buttons list click Braided Column 4, select the text in the Text field, press [Spacebar], then type Home**

   Inserting a space gives you some room between the left edge of the text and the right edge of the circular decoration on the button. The text " Home" will appear on the finished button.

3. **Click Browse next to the Link field**

   The Edit Hyperlink dialog box opens. From here you can choose any of your site files and Expression Web creates a link from the interactive button to the file.

TROUBLE
If you don't see default.htm listed, make sure that both Existing File or Web Page and Current Folder are selected.

4. **Click default.html (open), then click OK**

5. **Click the Font tab**

   The Font tab options allow you to change the font face, style, and size. Interactive buttons can have three different states: the **original state** (appears when a visitor is not interacting with the button), the **hover state** (appears when a visitor points to or hovers over the image), and the **pressed state** (appears while a visitor is clicking the button). You can choose different font colors for each of the three button states and set the vertical and horizontal alignment of the button text in relationship to its background graphic.

6. **Click Arial, Helvetica, sans-serif in the Font list, click Bold in the Font Style list, click 12 in the Size list, click the Horizontal Alignment list arrow, click Left, then compare your screen to Figure G-3**

TROUBLE
Make sure the assets folder is listed in the Folder column; if it isn't, click the Change Folder button, navigate to the assets folder, click the assets folder, then click OK.

7. **Click OK, then save your changes**

   The Save Embedded Files dialog box opens. Three image files are listed in the Embedded files to save list. Expression Web has created three versions of the Home button, one for each state. The program has also added to the page all the HTML and JavaScript code necessary for the buttons to function.

8. **Click OK, then preview the page in a browser; if a yellow bar appears at the top of the page, click it and click Allow Blocked Content, then click Yes**

   Compare your screen to Figure G-4.

9. **Point to the Home button, click the Home button, close the browser window, then return to Expression Web**

   The button changes when you point to it and changes again when you click on it.

FIGURE G-2: Button tab of Interactive Buttons dialog box

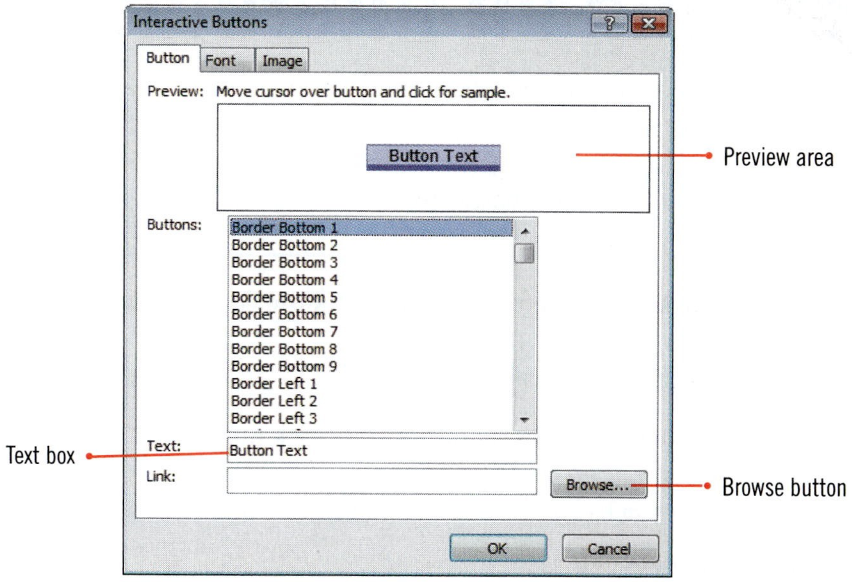

Preview area

Text box

Browse button

FIGURE G-3: Completed Font tab of Interacive Buttons dialog box

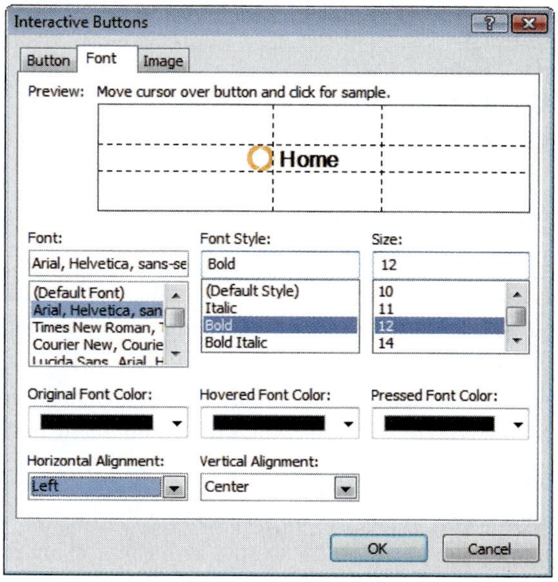

FIGURE G-4: Home page with interactive button added

Editing an Interactive Button

Once you create an interactive button, Expression Web makes it easy to edit it or change the formatting.  The navigation button you created is a good start, but you want the background color to blend with the background image on the page, and the font color to change when a visitor points to the button. You also want the button to be a bit larger.

1. **Double-click the Home button, then click the Font tab in the Interactive Buttons dialog box**

2. **Click the Original Font Color list arrow, then click the white color swatch**

You can also click More Colors to use the eyedropper or type in a specific hex code.

3. **Click the Hovered Font Color list arrow, click the orange color swatch in the Document Colors section, then compare your screen to Figure G-5**
This option determines the color the text will appear when a visitor points to the button.

4. **Click the Image tab**
See Figure G-6. The Image tab options allow you to change the height and width of the button. You can also control whether Expression Web creates a hovered and a pressed image. If you add a check mark to the Preload button images check box, Expression Web will generate code and add it to the page that causes the images for all states of the navigation images to load when the page loads. This prevents any delay between the time the visitor points to an image and the time the hover state of the image appears.

5. **Select the text in the Width box if necessary, then type 120**
Because the Maintain proportions check box is selected, the height changes to 24 pixels to make the height larger in proportion to the increased width.

6. **Click the Make the button a GIF image and use a transparent background option button, then compare your screen to Figure G-7**
The preview area changes to show a checkerboard pattern. This indicates that the image will have a transparent background, so that it blends into the background color on which it is placed. The effect of this option varies slightly, depending on the button style. On some styles, including this one, this option makes the entire button background transparent; on other styles it changes only the white space around the button, such as that surrounding the rounded corners of a capsule-style button.

7. **Click OK, then save your changes**
The Save Embedded Files dialog box opens, showing the file names of three images. Expression Web has created three new images to replace the existing home button images.

If you see a yellow bar at the top of the page, click the bar, click Allow Blocked Content, then click Yes.

8. **Click OK in the Saved Embedded Files dialog box, preview the page in a browser, point to the Home button, click the Home button, close the browser window, then return to Expression Web**

FIGURE G-5: Completed Font tab of Interactive Buttons dialog box

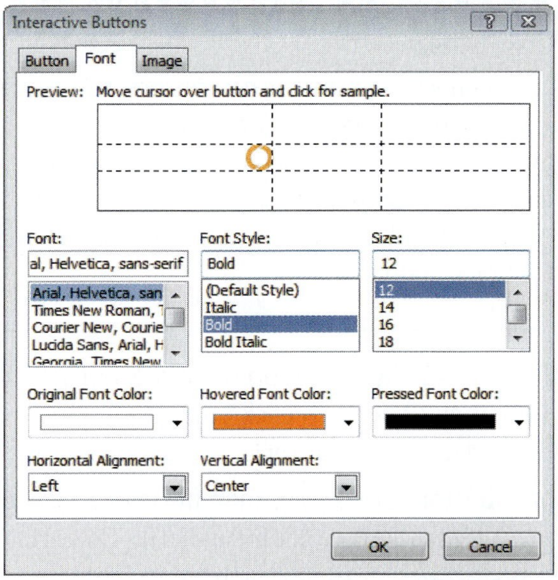

FIGURE G-6: Image tab of Interactive Buttons dialog box

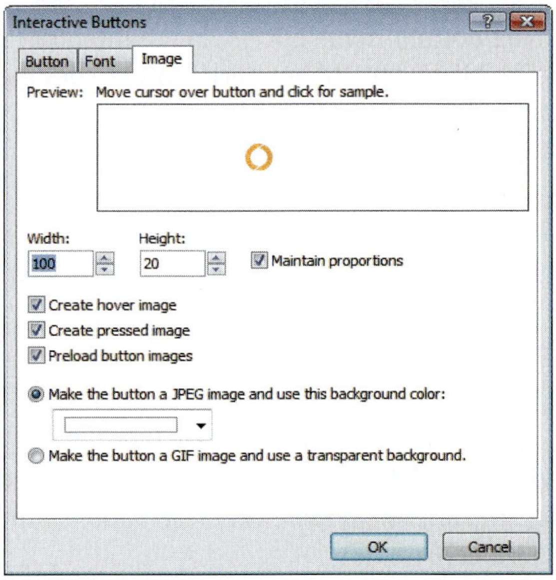

FIGURE G-7: Image tab of Interactive Buttons dialog box with transparent GIF option selected

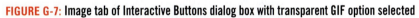

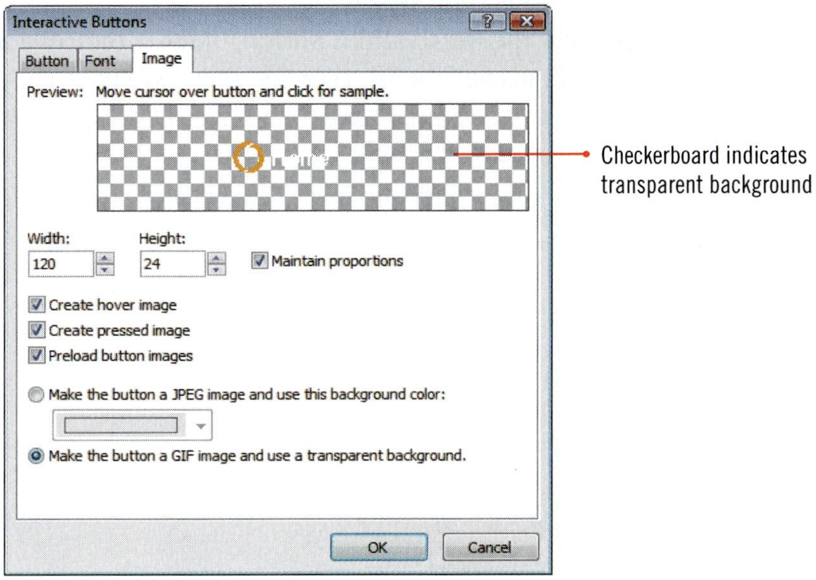

Checkerboard indicates
transparent background

Creating a Navigation Bar

A set of related navigation links, whether text or images, is known as a **navigation bar**. Maintaining a consistent look among the buttons in a navigation bar makes a Web site easier to navigate and your design more cohesive. Once you have created one interactive button that you like, the easiest way to create the others is to copy and paste the original button and then change the text and link. Using this technique, all the buttons look similar. To finish the navigation bar on the home page, you create and modify several copies of the Home button.

1. **Click the <div#left_col> list arrow on the quick tag selector bar, click Select Tag Contents, click Edit on the menu bar, then click Copy**

   The home button and related code are copied to the Windows Clipboard.

2. **Click the Home button, press [→], then press [Shift][Enter]**

   This inserts a <br /> tag and creates a line break after the Home button, as shown in Figure G-8.

3. **Click Edit on the menu bar, then click Paste**

   A second Home button is in place on the new line under the original Home button.

   > **TROUBLE**
   > Make sure you don't select the space in front of the text, just the text itself.

4. **Double-click the bottom Home button, in the Interactive Buttons dialog box select Home in the Text field, type Menu, click Browse, click menu.html, click OK, then click OK again**

   You have created a second navigation button that reads " Menu" and links to the menu page. See Figure G-9.

5. **Click to the right of the Menu button, click [Shift][Enter], click Edit on the menu bar, click Paste, double-click the bottom Home button, select Home in the Text field, type Store, click Browse, click store.html, click OK, then click OK again**

   > **QUICK TIP**
   > When you create an interactive button, Expression Web also uses the button text as the alternate text attribute.

6. **Click to the right of the Store button, click [Shift][Enter], click Edit on the menu bar, click Paste, double-click the bottom Home button, replace the text in the Text field with Music, click Browse, double-click music.html, then click OK**

7. **Click to the right of the Music button, click [Shift][Enter], click Edit on the menu bar, click Paste, double-click the bottom Home button, replace the text in the Text field with Reservations, click Browse, double-click reservations.html, click OK, then compare your screen to Figure G-10**

   The navigation bar is almost complete, but the text on the Reservations button appears cut off because the word is too long to fit the button size.

8. **Double-click the Reservations button, in the Interactive Buttons dialog box click the Font tab, click 11 in the Size list, click OK, then save your changes**

   The Embedded Files dialog box opens with 12 files listed. Expression Web has created three versions for each of the four navigation buttons.

   > **TROUBLE**
   > Remember that if you see a yellow bar at the top of the page, click the bar, click Allow Blocked Content, then click Yes.

9. **Click OK, preview the page in a browser, point to the Store button, click the Store button, close the browser window, then return to Expression Web**

FIGURE G-8: Interactive button placed on home page

New line created after Home button

FIGURE G-9: Home page with Home and Menu buttons placed

FIGURE G-10: Home page with navigation bar in place

Text on Reservations button is too long to fit

Designing Site Navigation

Adding a Navigation Bar to Site Pages

Each page on a Web site should include a global navigation bar, which should be consistent from page to page so that visitors can easily navigate. Once you have created a global navigation bar on one page, it is a simple matter of copying and pasting to add it to each page of the site. **You add the navigation bar from the TradeWinds home page to the other pages.

STEPS

QUICK TIP
Using the Select Tag Contents option ensures that you only select the navigation bar and not the containing div.

1. **Click anywhere in the left_col div, point to <div#left_col> on the quick tag selector bar, click the <div#left_col> list arrow, then click Select Tag Contents**
   Selecting the content of the left_col div selects all the interactive buttons and their corresponding code.

2. **Click Edit on the menu bar, then click Copy**
   The buttons and corresponding code are copied to the Windows Clipboard.

3. **Open the store page**

QUICK TIP
Instead of using the Edit menu, you can right-click where you would like to paste and then choose Paste from the shortcut menu.

4. **Click in the left_col div, click Edit on the menu bar, then click Paste**
   See Figure G-11. The entire navigation bar and all links are now incorporated into the store page.

5. **Open the contact page, then repeat Step 4**

6. **Open the menu page, then repeat Step 4**

7. **Open the music page, repeat Step 4, open the reservations page, then repeat Step 4**

8. **Save changes to all files, click OK each time the Save Embedded Files dialog box opens, then preview the reservations page in a browser**
   Compare your screen to Figure G-12.

9. **Use the links in the navigation bar to view all the pages in the site, then close the browser and return to Expression Web**

Choosing fonts for navigation buttons

Using graphics, such as interactive buttons, instead of text for navigation affords you much more flexibility in your font choices. Because Expression Web actually creates an image of the text, you are not limited to using Web-safe fonts. When creating interactive buttons, you can safely choose any font that appears in your font list. When choosing the font face, size, and color, make sure that the text is large enough to read and that it has enough contrast with the background color to be legible.

FIGURE G-11: Navigation bar pasted into store page

FIGURE G-12: Previewing the reservations page in a browser

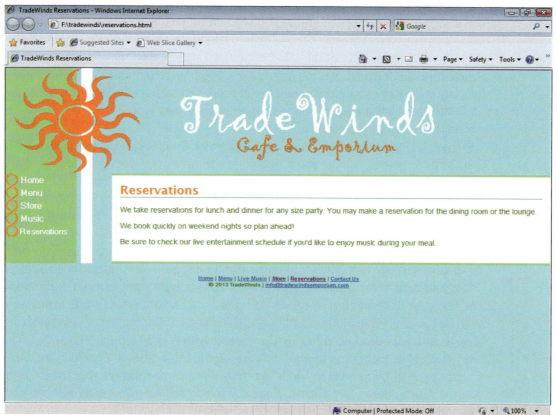

...erstanding Link Styles

...early days of the World Wide Web, all linked text looked the same—it was blue and underlined ...every Web site. This consistency made it instantly stand out to visitors as a clickable link. Today, thanks to CSS, designers have much more control over how links appear—they can be blue or not, underlined or not, and formatted almost any way you wish. But with this control comes a responsibility to create link styles that clearly indicate to a visitor that the link is clickable. Before styling the links on the TradeWinds site, you want to know more about the concepts and principles behind this area of Web design.

To understand link styles, you should be familiar with the following terms and guidelines:

- **Link states**

  So far you have learned about using classes, elements, and ids as selectors for creating style rules. Links can be styled by using the <a> or anchor tag as the selector, but links are unique in that you also have the option of attaching a pseudo-class to the tag. A **pseudo-class** defines properties for a particular state of the element. Links have four commonly used pseudoclass selectors:

  - **a:link** indicates the normal, unvisited state of a link
  - **a:visited** indicates that the link has been clicked in the visitor's browser and is present in the browser's history
  - **a:hover** indicates that the visitor's cursor is pointing to the link
  - **a:active** indicates that the link has been clicked but not released

- **Guidelines for creating link styles**

  Creating an a:active style is optional. It's best to create a style rule for at least the a:link, a:visited, and a:hover states so that each state looks different to visitors. The a:active state is seen for such a brief period (only during the actual click on the link) that creating a style for this state is not usually critical.

  Leave links underlined. You can remove underlines from your links by modifying the text-decoration property in CSS, but it's advisable to leave the underline on your links. Underlined text is almost universally understood to be a clickable link, and using underlines will make your site more user-friendly. See Table G-1 for available text-decoration options.

  Differentiate between visited and unvisited links. Creating different styles for visited and unvisited links helps visitors keep track of which areas of the site they have visited. By default, normal links are blue and underlined and visited links are purple and underlined, as shown in Figure G-13. But you can choose different formatting. In general, it's best to create styles that make unvisited links more noticeable and visited links less so. This can be accomplished through using a brighter color for unvisited links and a more subtle or less saturated color for visited links.

  Experiment with hover styles and colors. Creating a slightly more dramatic style for the hover state is an effective way to provide feedback to visitors that the link is indeed clickable. For example, you can add a background color for the hover state so the link appears to be highlighted, or use an overline to add emphasis. Feel free to use link colors that coordinate with your design; however, avoid purple to indicate normal links and blue to indicate visited links, since this reverses the normal color conventions and could confuse visitors.

  Create link pseudo-class styles in the correct order. In a Web page, link pseudo-class styles are applied according to the order in which they are listed in the style sheet. Expression Web writes style rules in the style sheet in the order in which you create them, so always create your styles rules in this order: a:link, a:visited, a:hover, and a:active. A popular way to remember this order is to think of the phrase LoVe—HA (**L**ink, **V**isited, **H**over, **A**ctive).

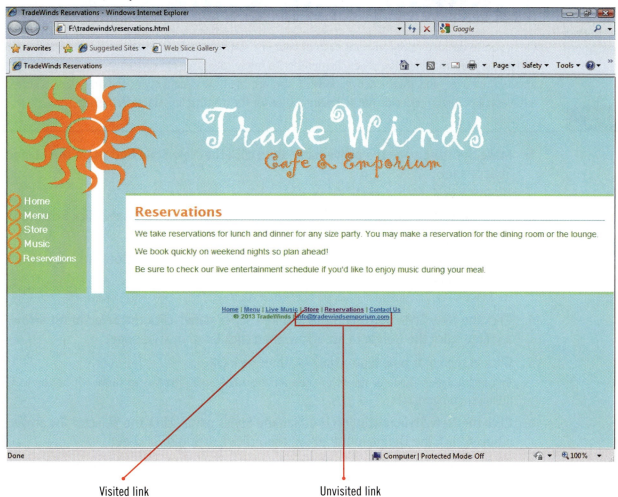

Visited link   Unvisited link

TABLE G-1: Available text-decoration options

value	effect
underline	Displays a line under the text
overline	Displays a line above the text
line-through	Displays a line through the center of the text
blink	Displays text as blinking; not well-supported by browsers
none	Displays text with none of the preceding decorations; use when styling links to remove the default underline

Using more than one set of link styles on a site

Sites commonly need to include more than one set of link styles. For example, the designer may want the navigation text links to look different from the text links that are within the site's content. CSS makes this simple to accomplish through the use of descendent selectors. **Descendent selectors** define properties for all instances of an element that occur within a defined container. For example, if you want all links contained in the footer div to have a different style from other links on the site, create a new style and in the Selector box type #footer a:link, define it in your external style sheet, then choose your options. This will create a normal link style that only applies to links contained within your footer div. Create styles for the other states in the same manner by using #footer a:visited, #footer a:hover, and #footer a:active as the selectors. You can also use the same principle with any div and any element. For example, you could use the selector #masthead h1 to define a style that only applies to h1 elements that are within the masthead div.

Creating Link Styles

Once you've decided how you want each of your link states to look, you can use the New Style button in Expression Web to create the styles. Remember to follow the LoVe-HA order when creating them: a:link, a:visited, a:hover, and then a:active.  You are ready to create styles for the a:link, a:visited, and a:hover link states. You decide not to create a style for the a:active link states in this site.

1. Make the store page the active page, then click the New Style button on the Manage Styles panel
   The New Style dialog box opens.

2. Click the Selector list arrow, click a:link, click the Define in list arrow, click Existing style sheet, click the URL list arrow, then click twstyles.css

3. Click in the color box, type #28AACA, then click OK, then scroll down to the bottom of the store page
   See Figure G-14. The unvisited links are now a blue color.

4. Click the New Style button on the Manage Styles panel, click the Selector list arrow, click a:visited, click the Define in list arrow, then click Existing style sheet

5. Click in the color box, type #18677A, then click OK
   By using a darker shade of the color used for the a:link style, the visited links will not be as visually prominent on the page.

6. Click the New Style button on the Manage Styles panel, click the Selector list arrow, click a:hover, click the Define in list arrow, then click Existing style sheet

7. Click in the color box, type #FE8402, click the overline check box under text-decoration, click the underline check box under text-decoration, compare your screen to Figure G-15, then click OK

8. Save changes to all files, preview the store page in the browser as shown in Figure G-16, point to the National Quilt Museum Web site link, close the browser window, return to Expression Web, close the tradewinds site, then exit Expression Web

Rearranging your styles

You can see the order of your styles by looking at either the Manage Styles or Apply Styles panel. The styles are listed in the order in which they appear in the style sheet. If your link styles get out of the proper LoVe-HA order, open the Manage Styles panel, click the name of the style you want to move, then drag it to the correct location in the list.

FIGURE G-14: Store page with new link styles displayed

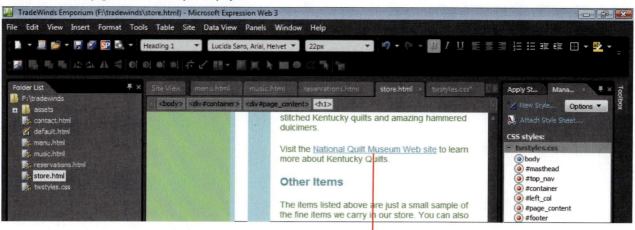

Unvisited link

FIGURE G-15: New Style dialog box for a:hover style

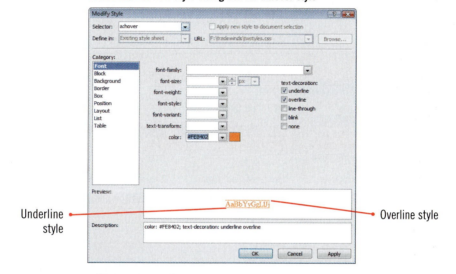

Underline style

Overline style

FIGURE G-16: Store page in browser with link styles

a:link style

Expression Web 3

Practice

SAM

Concepts Review

For current SAM information including versions and content details, visit SAM Central (http://samcentral.course.com). If you have a SAM user profile, you may have access to hands-on instruction, practice, and assessment of the skills covered in this unit. Since we support various versions of SAM throughout the life of this text, you will want to check with your instructor for instructions and the correct URL/Web site to access those assignments.

Refer to Figure G-17 to answer the following questions:

FIGURE G-17

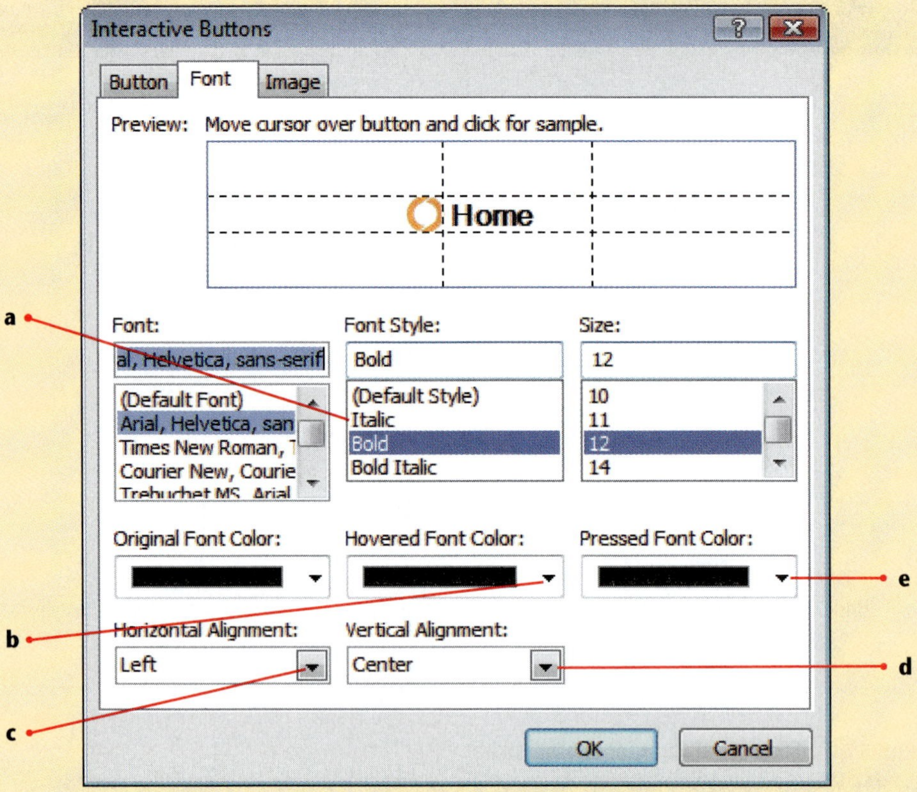

1. Which element would you click to change the color of the text when a visitor points to the button?
2. Which element would you click to change the color of the text when a visitor clicks a button?
3. Which element would you select to make the text align to the right edge of the button?
4. Which element would you select from to italicize the text on a button?
5. Which element would you click to make the text align to the bottom edge of the button?

Match each link state with the order in which it should appear in the style sheet.

6. **a:link**
7. **a:hover**
8. **a:visited**
9. **a:active**

a. First
b. Second
c. Third
d. Fourth

Select the best answer from the list of choices.

10. **The default style for a visited link is:**
    a. Purple and underlined.
    b. Blue and underlined.
    c. Purple and bold.
    d. Blue and bold.

11. **Which type of navigation area features links that are related to a particular section of a site?**
    a. Global navigation
    b. Local navigation
    c. Utility navigation
    d. Site map navigation

12. **Compared to normal unvisited links, visited links should be:**
    a. More noticeable.
    b. Less noticeable.
    c. Underlined.
    d. Overlined.

13. **A person who specializes in structuring and organizing content and navigation is called a(n):**
    a. Structuralist.
    b. Organizational designer.
    c. Navigation specialist.
    d. Information architect.

14. **Which link state occurs when a visitor points to a link?**
    a. a:active
    b. a:visited
    c. a:unvisited
    d. a:hover

15. **Which type of navigation features links to each top-level section in the entire site?**
    a. Global navigation
    b. Local navigation
    c. Utility navigation
    d. Site map navigation

16. **The default style for a normal link that has not yet been visited is:**
    a. Purple and underlined.
    b. Blue and underlined.
    c. Purple and bold.
    d. Blue and bold.

17. **The technique of card sorting can be used to:**
    a. Involve your audience in organizing your site content.
    b. Create effective link styles.
    c. Edit interactive buttons.
    d. Design navigation graphics.

18. **If the visitor has clicked a link and the link is present in the visitor's history, which pseudoclass style is displayed?**
    a. a:link
    b. a:hover
    c. a:active
    d. a:visited

19. **The acronym LoVe-HA is used to help remember the order in which:**
    a. Interactive buttons should be copied and pasted.
    b. Navigation bars should be created.
    c. Link pseudoclass styles should appear in a Web site's style sheet.
    d. Navigation should appear on a page.

20. **Another term for interactive button is:**
    a. Pressed button.
    b. Rollover.
    c. Graphic.
    d. Link.

Skills Review

1. **Create an interactive button.**
   a. Launch Expression Web, then open the careers site.
   b. Open the home page.
   c. Click in the top_nav div, click Insert on the menu bar, then click Interactive Button.
   d. On the Button tab of the Interactive Buttons dialog box, choose Chain Column 1, replace the text with **Home**, then use the Browse button next to the Link field to link it to the home page.
   e. Click OK to close the Interactive Buttons dialog box.
   f. Save your changes, then click OK when the Save Embedded Files dialog box appears.

2. **Edit an interactive button.**
   a. Double-click the Home button.
   b. On the Font tab, set the font size to **14**.
   c. Using the swatches in the Document Colors section, set the Hovered Font Color to **red** and the Pressed Font Color to **medium (not dark) blue**.
   d. On the Image tab, set the width to **150 pixels** while maintaining the proportions.
   e. Click OK to close the Interactive Buttons dialog box.
   f. Save your changes, preview the home page in a browser, point to the Home button, click the Home button, close the browser, then return to Expression Web.

3. **Create a navigation bar.**
   a. Select the Home button, click Edit on the menu bar, then click Copy.
   b. With the Home button selected, press **[→]**, click Edit on the menu bar, then click Paste.
   c. Double-click the second Home button, then edit the properties so the text reads **Services** and the button links to the services page.
   d. Click to the right of the Services button, click Edit on the menu bar, then click Paste.
   e. Double-click the second Home button, then edit the properties so the text reads **About Us** and the button links to the about page.
   f. Click to the right of the About Us button, click Edit on the menu bar, then click Paste.
   g. Double-click the second Home button, then edit the properties so the text reads **Contact Us** and the button links to the contact page.
   h. Save all the pages, click the Change Folder button in the Save Embedded Files dialog box that opens, navigate to the assets folder, click assets, click OK, then click OK again.
   i. Preview the home page in a browser, click the Services button in the navigation bar, then close the browser window and return to Expression Web.

4. **Add a navigation bar to site pages.**
   a. Click inside the top_nav div, click the <div#top_nav> list arrow on the quick tag selector bar, then click Select Tag Contents.
   b. Copy the tag contents to the Clipboard.
   c. Open the services page.
   d. Click in the top_nav div, click Edit on the menu bar, then click Paste.
   e. Open the about page, then paste the contents of the Clipboard to the top_nav div.
   f. Open the contact page, then paste the contents of the Clipboard to the top_nav div.
   g. Save all pages, preview the services page in a browser, close the browser, then return to Expression Web.

Skills Review (continued)

5. Create link styles.

    a. Open the New Style dialog box.

    b. Choose **a:link** as the selector and define the style in the **cgstyles.css** style sheet. Set the color to **#CE0000**, then click OK to close the New Style dialog box.

    c. Open the New Style dialog box, choose **a:visited** as the selector, and define the style in the **cgstyles.css** style sheet. Set the color to **#002980**, then click OK to close the New Style dialog box.

    d. Open the New Style dialog box, choose **a:hover** as the selector, and define the style in the **cgstyles.css** style sheet. Switch to the Background category, set the background-color to **#FFFFCC**, then click OK to close the New Style dialog box.

    e. Save all pages, preview the home page in a browser, point to the career exploration tools link, then compare your screen to Figure G-18.

    f. Close the browser, return to Expression Web, close the careers site, then exit Expression Web.

FIGURE G-18

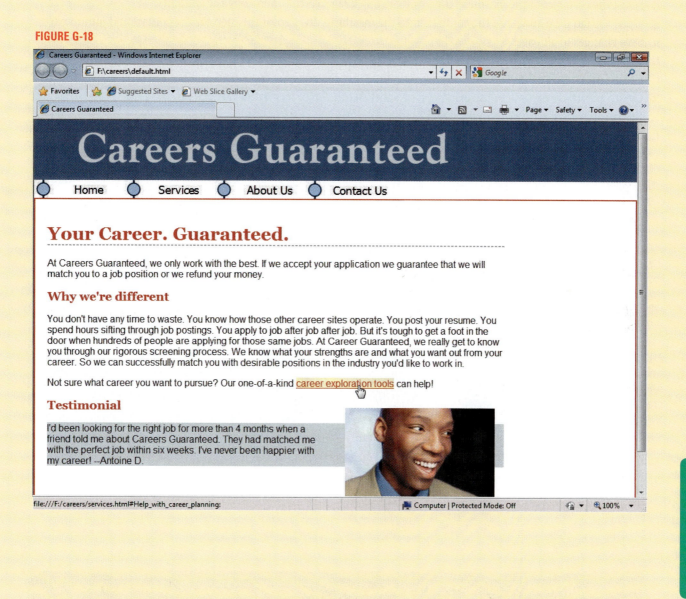

Independent Challenge 1

In this project, you continue your work on the ConnectUp Web site. Tiffany likes your design so far, but she would like to see some visual elements that really make the site pop. You decide to create a yellow tabbed navigation bar.

a. Launch Expression Web, then open the connectup Web site.

b. Open the home page.

c. Click in the masthead div and insert an interactive button with the following properties: the Glass Tab 4 button type, text that reads **Home**, a link to the **default.html page**, and font settings of **Trebuchet MS**, **bold**, **size 14**. Using the swatches in the Document Colors section, set the **Original Font Color** to **blue** and the **Hovered Font Color** to **green**. On the Image tab, select the option to create a GIF with a transparent background.

d. Select the Home button and copy it. Click to the right of the Home button and paste it. Modify this button to read **F.A.Q.**, and to link it to the faq page.

e. Click to the right of the F.A.Q. button and paste. Modify this button to read **JoinUp**, and link it to the join up page.

f. Select the contents of the masthead div using the quick tag selector, then copy the contents.

g. Open the faq page and paste the contents into the masthead div. Repeat this step for the contact and joinup pages.

h. Save changes to all pages.

i. Create an **a:link** style in the existing style sheet. Set the color to **#85C016** and the **font-weight** to **bold**.

j. Create an **a:visited** style in the existing style sheet. Set the color to **#666666** and the **font-weight** to **bold**.

k. Create an **a:hover** style in the existing style sheet. Set the color to **#488FDF**, the **font-weight** to **bold**, and the **background color** to **#FFDF57**.

l. Save the changes to all pages, preview the contact page in a browser, and compare your screen to Figure G-19. Use the navigation tabs to click through to the other pages, close the browser, return to Expression Web, close the site, then exit Expression Web.

FIGURE G-19

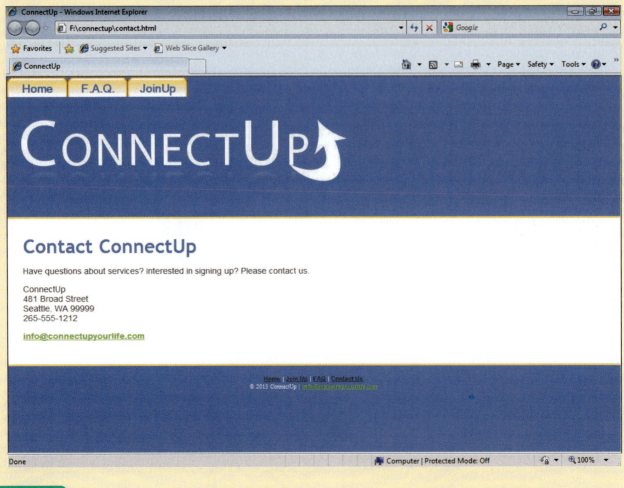

Independent Challenge 2

In this project, you continue your work on the Memories Restored Web site. You are ready to add a navigation bar to the site and create styles for the links.

- **a.** Launch Expression Web, then open the memories Web site.
- **b.** Taking note of the shapes and colors used in the Memories Restored Web site, insert an interactive button in the left_col div that complements the site's design. The button should have the text Home on it and link to the home page.
- **c.** Edit the button as necessary until you are satisfied. You may even need to delete the button and start over again a few times until you find a design you like.
- **d.** Copy, paste, and modify the finished button as necessary to create a navigation bar that links to all the site pages except the contact page.
- **e.** Add the navigation bar to all site pages, including the contact page.
- **f.** Save changes to all pages.
- **g.** Create link styles for a:link, a:visited, and a:active in the external style sheet, using settings that you think complement the overall site. Figure G-20 shows an example of one possible design; your project will differ.

Advanced Challenge Exercise

- ■ Create a style for a:hover.
- ■ Use the Manage Styles panel to move this style to the correct position in the style sheet.

- **h.** Save your changes to all open files, preview the site in a browser, then use the links in the navigation bar to view all pages. When you are finished, close the browser, return to Expression Web, close the site, then exit Expression Web.

FIGURE G-20

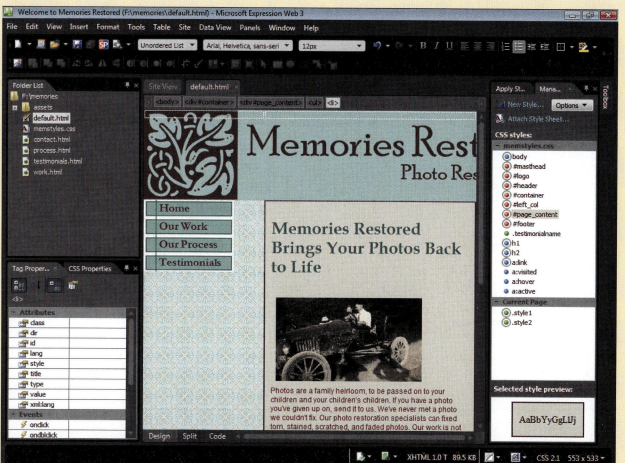

Expression Web 3

Independent Challenge 3

This Independent Challenge requires an Internet connection.

You've been attending some meetings at Technology for All related to the Web site redesign. The discussions have been difficult because several people have strong but conflicting opinions on how the navigation should be structured and how the content should be organized and labeled. Over coffee, a friend tells you about usability.gov, a Web site that features research-based guidelines on many aspects of Web site design. You decide to review the materials at usability.gov to see if perhaps the guidelines could be helpful in resolving some of the design arguments that have been brewing among the staff.

a. Visit the usability.gov Web site, then navigate to the Guidelines section, as shown in Figure G-21.

b. Read at least two chapters that interest you.

c. Write at least three paragraphs explaining what you learned from the guidelines and how such guidelines could be helpful in assisting Web design teams in making decisions.

Advanced Challenge Exercise

■ Familiarize yourself with the research behind these guidelines by reviewing the Strength of Evidence scale (the higher the number, the stronger the evidence) and the references for two of the guidelines you read about.

■ Write a paragraph explaining in what situations, if any, it would be appropriate to ignore these two guidelines in favor of relying on your own instincts in designing a site.

d. Add your name to the document, save it, and print it.

FIGURE G-21

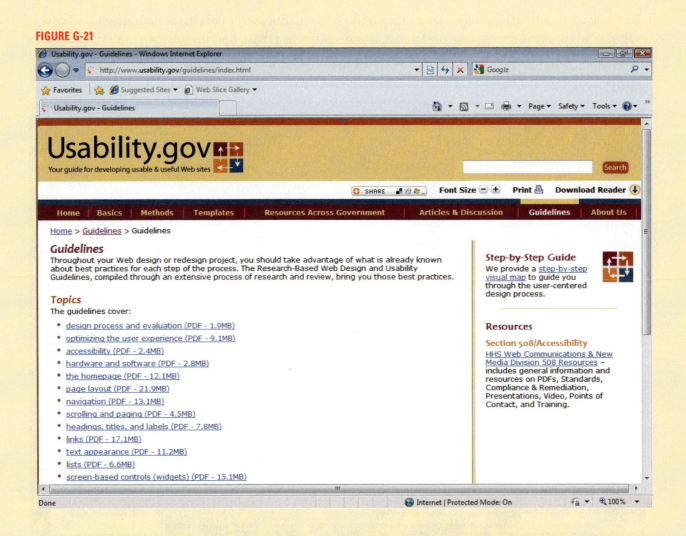

Real Life Independent Challenge

This assignment builds on the personal Web site you have worked on in previous units. In this project, you add a navigation bar to each page in your site and create link styles.

    a. Use the interactive button feature in Expression Web to create one interactive button for your site. Choose fonts, colors, and sizes that complement your site.

    b. Edit the button as necessary until you are satisfied with the design.

    c. Use this button to build a navigation bar, and then add the navigation bar to each page in your site.

    d. Create styles for the following link states in your external style sheet: a:link, a:visited, a:hover, and a:active.

    e. Save your changes to all open files, preview the site in a browser, then use the navigation links to view all pages. When you are finished, close the browser, return to Expression Web, close the site, then exit Expression Web.

Visual Workshop

Launch Expression Web, then open the ecotours Web site. Modify the home page and the external style sheet so that your screen matches Figure G-22. To accomplish this, you need to add interactive buttons and create an a:link style. (*Hint*: The text on the buttons is a dark brown and the link text is a dark green; you can choose which dark brown and green you would like to use as long as it is similar to the figure.) When you are finished, save your changes, close the Web site, then exit Expression Web.

FIGURE G-22

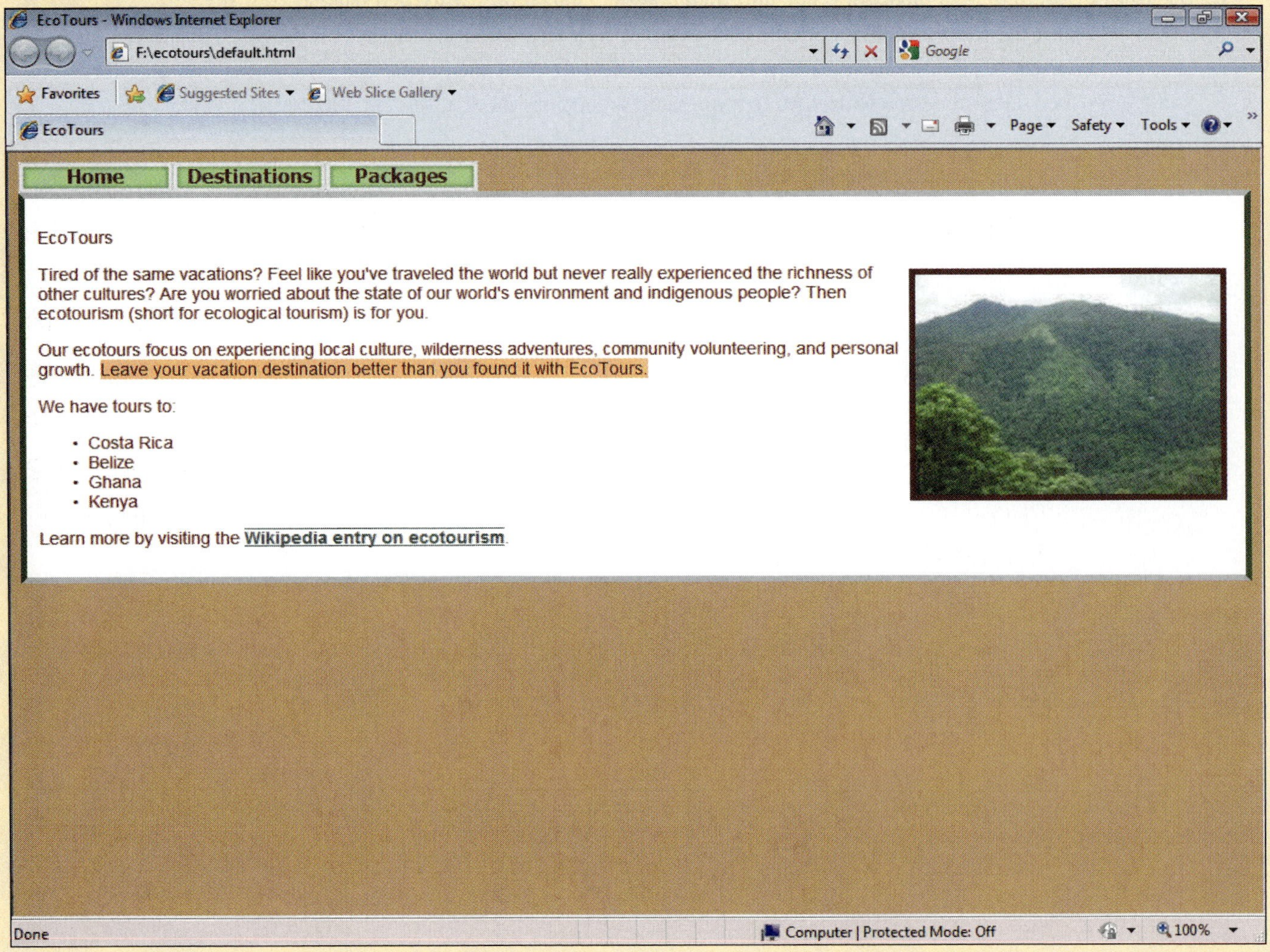

Testing and Publishing Your Web Site

Expression Web makes it easy to **publish** your Web site, placing a copy of the site files on a Web server so that people can visit it. Before you publish, you should test your site by viewing it in as many different browsers as possible, at different screen resolutions, and if possible on both Windows and Mac computers. In addition, check the spelling and grammar of all content. Once you've completed these steps, you're ready to use Expression Web reports to assist you in testing other features of the site, such as hyperlinks, accessibility, and page titles.  You prepare the TradeWinds site for publication and learn to use the publishing feature in Expression Web to publish the site.

OBJECTIVES

Verify hyperlinks

View and edit page titles

Understand accessibility

Test accessibility

Understand connection types

Set up and connect to a publishing destination

Publish a Web site

Verifying Hyperlinks

Expression Web includes a variety of reports to assist you in testing important features of the site, such as hyperlinks, accessibility, and page titles. As part of your preparation for publishing the TradeWinds site, you verify the external hyperlinks on the site.

STEPS

1. **Launch Expression Web, then open the tradewinds site**

   The Site View tab opens in Folders view.

2. **Click the Site View tab if necessary, then click the Reports View button at the bottom of the Site View tab**

   The Site Summary report appears, as shown in Figure H-1. From here, you can link to more detailed reports. See Table H-1 for a list of these reports and the information provided by each. The Unverified hyperlinks report shows a count of 1, indicating that there is one unverified hyperlink in the site.

   Verifying links means to check them to be sure they are working correctly. It's also a good idea to verify external hyperlinks on an ongoing basis, in case the page you have linked to is moved or removed. You must have an active Internet connection to be able to verify links.

> **QUICK TIP**
> It's a good idea to verify external hyperlinks on an ongoing basis, in case the page you have linked to is moved or removed.

3. **Click the Unverified hyperlinks link**

   As shown in Figure H-2, the Reports View dialog box opens, asking if you would like to verify hyperlinks. Behind the dialog box, you can see that the unverified hyperlink is the link to the National Quilt Museum.

> **QUICK TIP**
> If you need to fix a hyperlink, right-click the hyperlink in the report, choose Edit Hyperlink, then enter the correct URL in the Edit Hyperlink dialog box.

4. **Click Yes**

   The results are displayed in the Site View tab, as shown in Figure H-3. To verify a hyperlink, Expression Web visits the URL to make sure it is valid. If the hyperlink is not working, the word "broken" appears beside it in the report.

5. **Click the Hyperlinks list arrow, then click Site Summary**

   You return to the Site Summary report. The Count column of the Unverified hyperlinks report now indicates that there are no unverified hyperlinks in the site.

TABLE H-1: Reports available in Reports view

report name	lists...	report name	lists...
All files	Every file in the site	Unverified hyperlinks	Hyperlinks that have not been checked to see if they are valid, working links
Pictures	Number and size of picture files in the site	Broken hyperlinks	Hyperlinks that have been checked and were found to not be valid, working links
Unlinked files	Files that are not linked to any other pages; these can often be deleted	External hyperlinks	Links to Web pages outside of current site
Linked files	Number and size of files in the site that are linked to the home page	Internal hyperlinks	Links to Web pages within current site
Slow pages	Pages that take longer than 30 seconds to download at a connection speed of 56.6 Kbps	Style Sheet Links	Links to style sheets in the current site
Older files	Files that have not changed in the past 72 days	Dynamic Web Templates	All files that are associated with a Dynamic Web Template
Recently added files	Files added to site in the past 30 days	Master Pages	All files that are associated with an ASP.NET Master Page
Hyperlinks	All hyperlinks in the site, both internal and external		

FIGURE H-1: Reports view in Site View tab

Unverified
hyperlinks
link

Number of
unverified
hyperlinks

Reports View
button

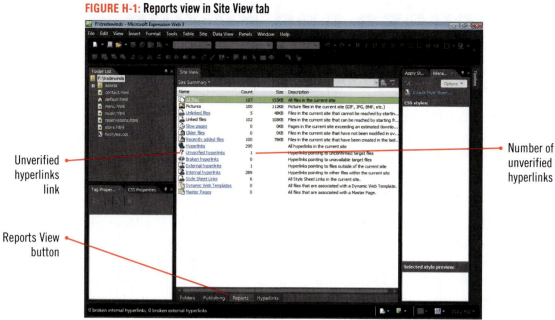

FIGURE H-2: Confirming hyperlink verification

Hyperlinks
list arrow

Unverified
hyperlink

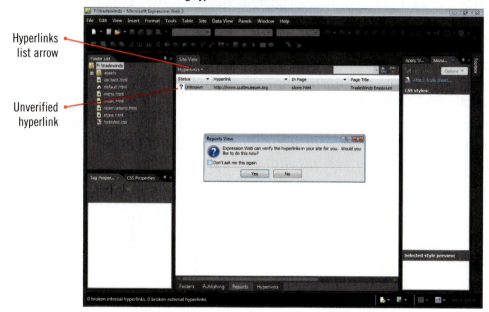

FIGURE H-3: Verified hyperlink

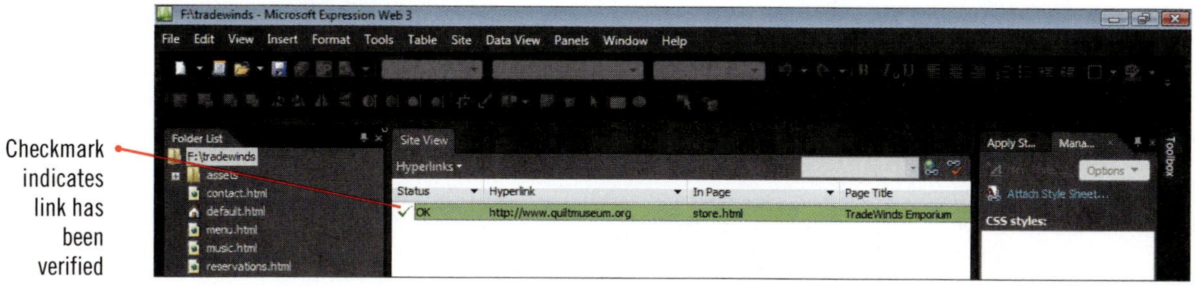

Checkmark
indicates
link has
been
verified

Viewing and Editing Page Titles

Expression Web offers several ways to view and edit the title of a Web page. Working in Hyperlinks view provides a helpful graphical display of each page's title as well as quick access for editing the title.  You decide to use Hyperlinks view to view each page's title in the TradeWinds site to see if any titles need to be edited.

STEPS

TROUBLE

If Hyperlinks view does not show links to and from the home page, click Site, click Recalculate Hyperlinks, then click Yes.

1. **Click the Hyperlinks View button at the bottom of the Site View tab, then click default.html in the Folder List task pane**
   The Hyperlinks view of the Site View tab is displayed with the home page in the center, as shown in Figure H-4. This view shows how the pages in the site are linked to the selected file—in this case, the home page.

2. **Right-click in any blank area of the Site View tab, then click Show Page Titles**
   See Figure H-5. The title of the page, rather than the file name, is now displayed. You see that the menu and music page titles need to be changed.

3. **Right-click in any blank area of the Site View tab, then click Show Page Titles**
   Show Page Titles is now deselected, and Hyperlinks view once again displays the file name of each page.

QUICK TIP

Remember that page titles show up in search engine results, in the browser's title bar, and as the title when a visitor adds the page to bookmarks or favorites.

4. **In the Site View tab, right-click menu.html, click Properties, type TradeWinds Menu in the Title box to replace the highlighted text, then click OK**
   The title changes to TradeWinds Menu.

5. **In the Site View tab, right-click music.html, click Properties, click in the Title box at the end of the text and press [Backspace] on your keyboard 8 times to remove the text You ca, then click OK**

6. **Right-click in any blank area of the Site View tab, click Show Page Titles, compare your screen to Figure H-6, right-click in any blank area of the Site View tab, then click Show Page Titles again to turn off this setting**

FIGURE H-4: Hyperlinks view with home page selected

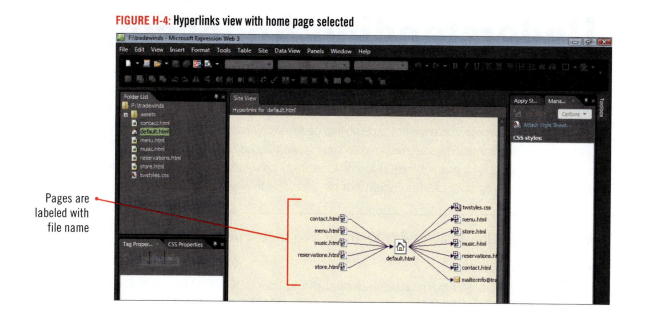

Pages are labeled with file name

FIGURE H-5: Hyperlinks view showing page titles

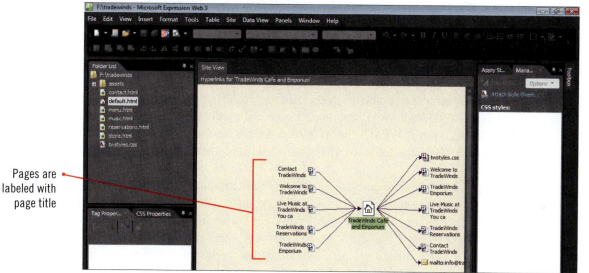

Pages are labeled with page title

FIGURE H-6: Hyperlinks view showing new page titles

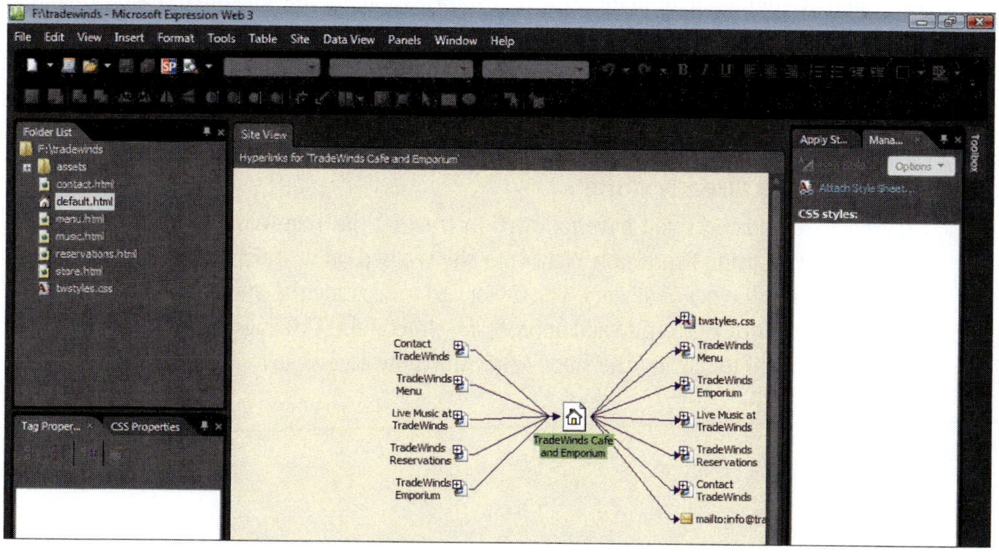

Understanding Accessibility

An **accessible Web site** is one that is usable by all visitors, including those with disabilities or those using devices such as cell phones to access the site. It makes good business sense to design your site to be accessible to anyone who wants to visit. It could also help you avoid legal problems. Several lawsuits have been filed against companies whose sites were not accessible to people with disabilities. In many countries, including the United States, government sites are required to comply with accessibility guidelines. Catalina has a sister who is legally blind, so she is very aware of accessibility concerns. You decide to learn more about Web site accessibility so you can make the TradeWinds site accessible to all visitors.

DETAILS

In order to develop an accessible Web site, you should be familiar with:

- **Types of disabilities**

  Disabilities fall into four major categories. **Visual disabilities** include legal blindness, low vision, and color blindness. **Hearing disabilities** include deafness and hearing loss. People with **motor disabilities** have a condition that may affect their ability to use a standard-issue mouse and/or keyboard to navigate a site. **Cognitive disabilities** include learning disabilities, memory impairments, and intellectual impairments. People with disabilities usually use assistive technologies to help them use a computer and navigate the Internet. **Assistive technologies** are software or devices that help people with disabilities to perform functions they otherwise would not be able to perform. See Table H-2 for examples of these assistive devices as well as accommodations recommended for people with different disabilities.

- **Guidelines for accessibility**

  Expression Web generates accessibility reports based on two different sets of guidelines:
  - The W3C (World Wide Web Consortium) has created a set of international Web Content Accessibility Guidelines, known as **WCAG**. The WCAG are based on research, expert opinion, and observations of people with disabilities using the Web. The WCAG guidelines are grouped into three sets of priority levels.
  - Priority 1: A Web content developer *must* satisfy this checkpoint. Otherwise, one or more groups will find it impossible to access information in the document. Satisfying this checkpoint is a basic requirement for some groups to be able to use Web documents. See Figure H-7 for a partial checklist of Priority 1 Guidelines.
  - Priority 2: A Web content developer *should* satisfy this checkpoint. Otherwise, one or more groups will find it difficult to access information in the document. Satisfying this checkpoint will remove significant barriers to accessing Web documents.
  - Priority 3: A Web content developer *may* address this checkpoint. Otherwise, one or more groups will find it somewhat difficult to access information in the document. Satisfying this checkpoint will improve access to Web documents.
  - In addition to the international WCAG guidelines, most countries have developed their own accessibility requirements. The U.S. federal government has issued guidelines in Section 508 of the Rehabilitation Act. These are often referred to simply as **Section 508 guidelines**.

- **What you've already done**

  Several of the practices you have followed in creating the TradeWinds site also help make it accessible. For starters, just by using Expression Web, your site is based on well-written, standards-compliant code that will be readable by all types of devices. The use of CSS to separate the presentation of the pages from the content, the use of semantic markup to add appropriate structural HTML tags, and the use of alternate text for images have contributed to making the TradeWinds site more accessible to all visitors.

FIGURE H-7: WCAG Web site

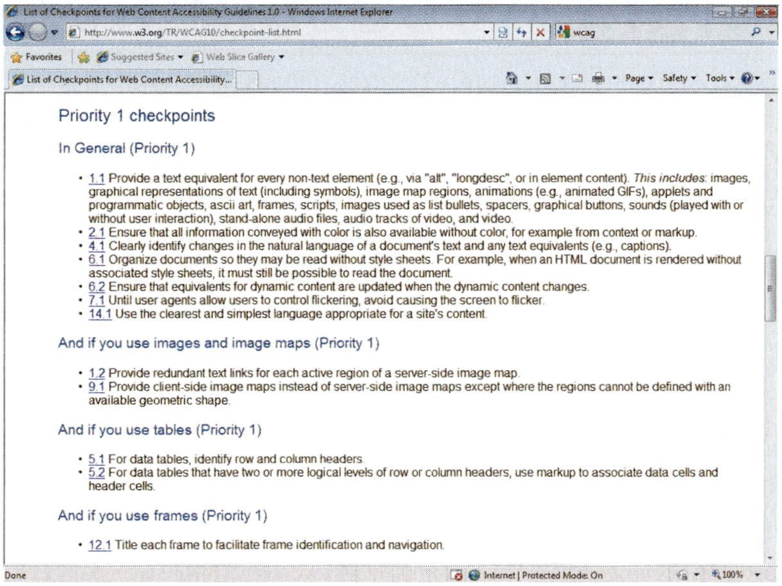

TABLE H-2: Assistive technologies and accommodations that help people with disabilities use computers

type of disability	available assistive technology	recommended accommodations
Visual	Screen magnifier software, screen reader software	• Provide alternate text for images • Ensure that link text is understandable out of context • Avoid using frames • Do not rely on color alone to convey meaning • Provide a means for users to skip links
Hearing	None usually needed	• Provide captions for audio and video
Motor	Mouth stick, head wand, breath-activated switches, voice-activated software, adaptive keyboards, eye-tracking software	• Ensure site is navigable via keyboard only without use of mouse
Cognitive	None	• Ensure content is clearly written • Provide clear and helpful error messages • Use white space, headings, subheadings, and bulleted lists to structure content
Seizure	None	• Avoid animations, graphics, or movies that strobe, flicker, or flash; these can induce seizures

Being visible to search engines

Designing a site to be standards-compliant also makes your site more visible to search engines. However, ensuring that your pages rank near the top of search results takes more work. Each search engine uses its own **algorithm** or method of deciding which pages show up, say, on page one rather than page three when you search for "chocolate chip cookie recipes." The algorithms used by search engines are a closely guarded secret. These algorithms are very sophisticated and change frequently. They take into account factors such as the number of times the search term shows up in your content, where the search term occurs on your page, and how many other reputable sites link to your site. Search terms that are included in the title tag and in linked text usually cause a page to rank higher. Search engines drive a considerable amount of traffic to Web sites, so **search engine optimization**, the business of adjusting a Web site so it ranks higher than competing sites on search engine pages, has become a thriving industry. Companies pay thousands of dollars to firms that can tweak their Web site's code and content in such a way that the site is displayed on the first page of results on popular search engines.

Testing and Publishing Your Web Site

Testing Accessibility

In Expression Web, you can generate accessibility reports that provide details of potential violations of the WCAG or Section 508 guidelines. Some accessibility issues may require additional research in order to be resolved, so Expression Web also provides a way for you to learn more about accessibility while viewing the report. You can also generate a formatted HTML version of the report, which you can save and/or print for reference. You can generate accessibility reports for a single page, multiple pages, or an entire site. ▰▰▰ You decide to check the TradeWinds contact page for any accessibility issues; you will check the rest of the pages in the site later. You want to print an accessibility report for Catalina, so that all potential issues can be resolved.

STEPS

1. **Click the Folders View button on the bottom of the Site View tab, then click contact.html in the Site View tab to select it**

2. **Click Tools on the menu bar, then click Accessibility Reports**

   The Accessibility Checker dialog box opens. Here you can choose which pages to include in the report, which guidelines to include, and whether to include errors (serious issues which definitely need to be fixed), warnings (issues which should be fixed), or a manual checklist (a list of issues which can't be checked automatically; you can use this to manually check your site for any accessibility problems).

> **QUICK TIP**
> To ensure the best results when testing for accessibility, run a report on one page at a time rather than testing the entire site at once.

3. **Verify or select options in the Accessibility Checker dialog box so that your screen matches Figure H-8, then click Check**

   The Accessibility task pane opens at the bottom of the Site View tab with the report results listed, as shown in Figure H-9. Each line lists the page and file name where the error or warning was found, the line of code that resulted in the error, the issue type (error or warning), the specific WCAG or Section 508 checkpoint to which the warning or error refers, and a summary of the problem. You may have to scroll left to right to see all the information. If you point to a line in the report, a ScreenTip will display the summary of the problem.

4. **Right-click the second line of the report, then click Learn More, as shown in Figure H-10**

   A browser window opens and displays the guideline on the WCAG Web site that corresponds to that issue. This information can be helpful in deciding how to address the issue.

5. **Click the Techniques for checkpoint 6.1 link**

   This detailed page provides more information about how to fix this particular problem.

6. **Close the browser window, then return to Expression Web**

7. **Click the Generate HTML Report button 🖹**

   Expression Web generates and displays an HTML version of the report. You can use this report to research and check off each issue as it is resolved.

8. **Click File on the menu bar, point to Print, click Print on the Print submenu, then click OK**

   A copy of the report is printed.

9. **Click the Close Window button ⊠ on the Accessibility task pane, click the Close Window button on the Accessibility Report.html tab, then click No when prompted to save**

   The task pane closes and the accessibility report closes.

FIGURE H-8: Accessibility Checker dialog box

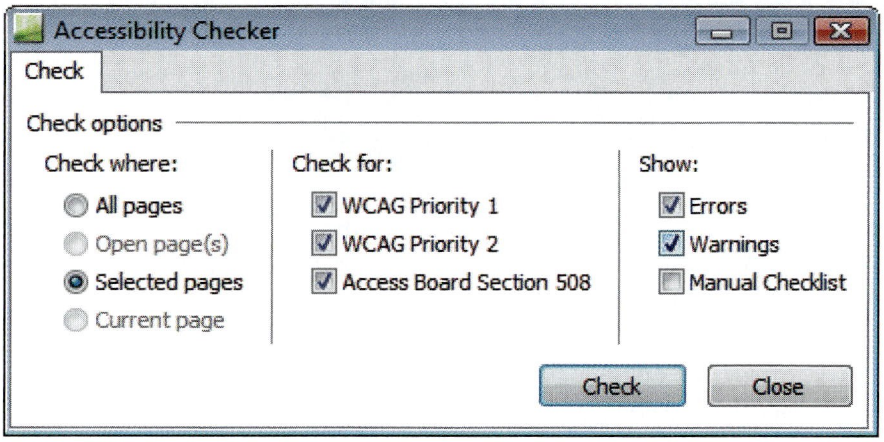

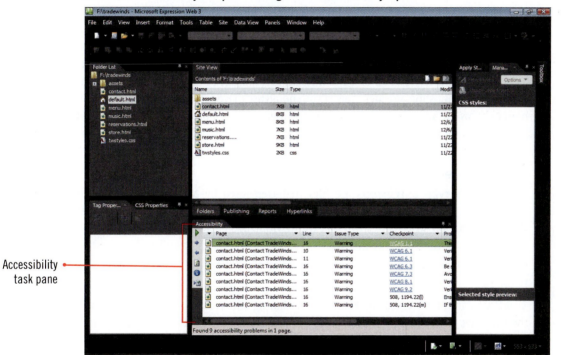

FIGURE H-9: Accessibility task pane showing results of Accessibility report

Accessibility task pane

Found 9 accessibility problems in 1 page.

FIGURE H-10: Shortcut menu

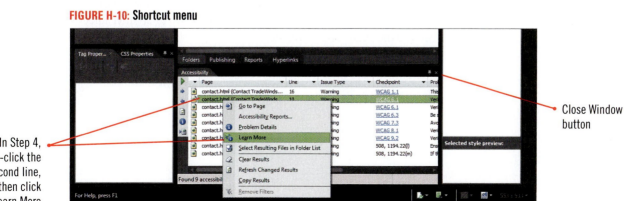

In Step 4, right-click the second line, then click Learn More

Close Window button

Understanding Connection Types

Before you can publish your site, you must have space available on a server, along with an account, so that you can access the space to log in and add files to it. The server that stores your Web site files is known as a **Web server**. Your Internet Service Provider (ISP) might include Web hosting space with your Internet service account; alternatively, you can purchase space from a Web hosting company. **Web hosting companies** provide server space for a monthly or annual fee. As part of publishing your site, you need to choose which connection type to use. The **connection type** controls the way your computer interacts with the Web server to transmit your files. Expression Web supports six different connection types to Web servers, as shown in Figure H-11. To find out which type of connection you need to use for publishing and to gather your account details, check with your Web hosting provider. ▰▰▰ To decide what type of connection type to use for TradeWinds, you review the options available in Expression Web.

DETAILS

Expression Web supports the following connection types for publishing a Web site:

QUICK TIP

Most Web servers are configured to only support one connection type.

- **FTP, SFTP, and FTPS**

  FTP, or File Transfer Protocol, is by far the most common method used to transfer files from a source site to a publishing destination. **SFTP** and **FTPS** are more secure methods of transferring files via FTP. You need to check with your hosting provider to see if you should use FTP, SFTP, or FTPS. To use any of these methods, you need to know the address to publish to and the user name and password for your account. In addition, you need to know the file path to the directory in which you plan to publish your files. You can usually find these details in the support or help section of your hosting provider's Web site.

- **FrontPage Server Extensions**

  FrontPage Server Extensions are files that were used by Microsoft's legacy Web design program, FrontPage, to facilitate publishing and to support interactive Web features. FrontPage Server Extensions should be used only when converting an existing FrontPage site to Expression Web. If you use this method to publish, you first need to verify that your server has the extensions installed. To publish your files, you need to know the address to publish to and the user name and password for your account.

- **WebDAV**

  WebDAV stands for Web-based Distributed Authoring and Versioning. WebDAV allows groups to work on the same files by providing workflow and collaboration features such as file check-in and check-out and versioning of files (to facilitate evolving drafts of a document). This method is not very common, so you should check with your hosting provider to see if it is supported. To publish files to WebDAV, you need to know the address to publish to, and the user name and password for your account.

- **File System**

  The **File System** option allows you to publish a copy of your site to a folder on the same computer or same network. Consider using this option to publish a copy of your site to another folder for backup purposes before you publish it to the publishing destination.

FIGURE H-11: Connection Settings dialog box

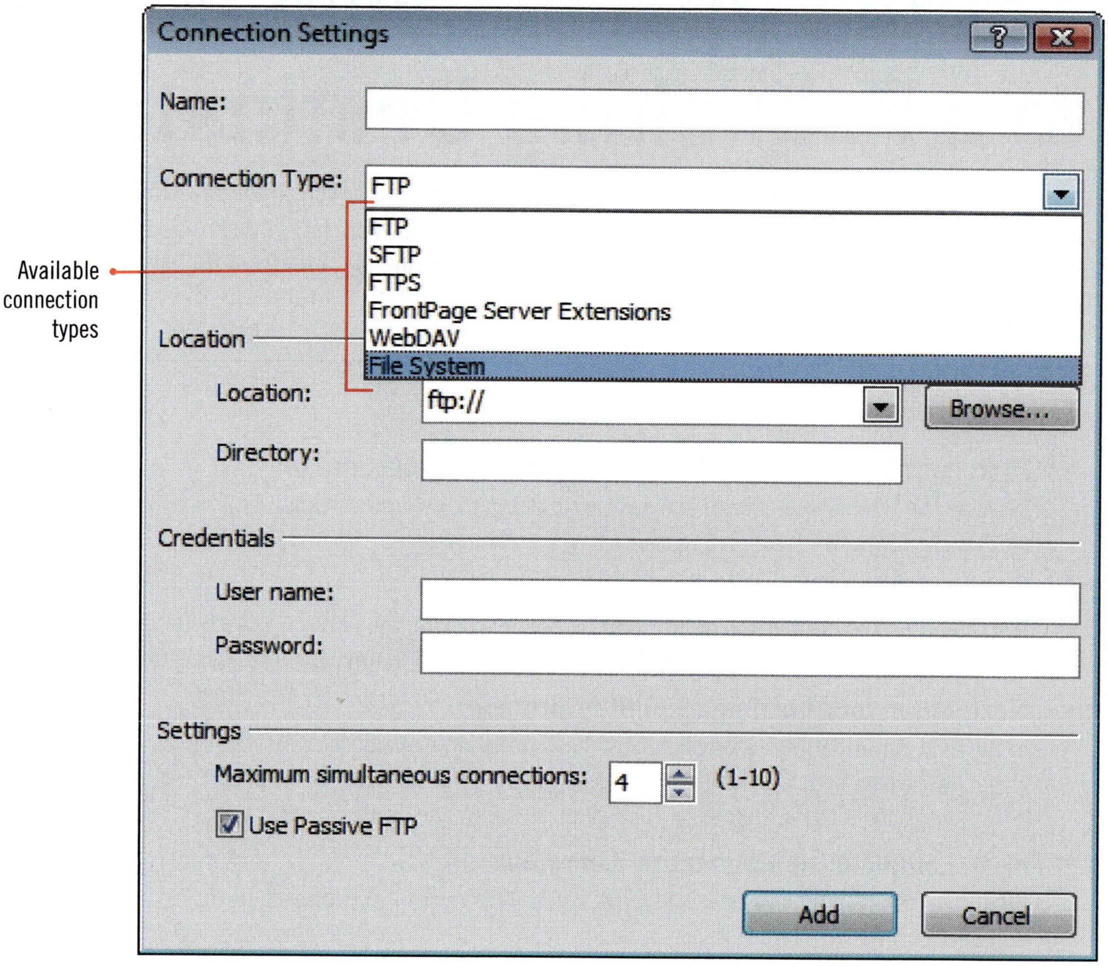

Choosing a hosting provider

With hundreds of Web hosting providers from which to choose, selecting a provider can be overwhelming. If you know people who are involved in creating or running Web sites, it can be helpful to ask which provider they recommend. You also need to be sure the provider and service package meet your needs. The following questions can assist you in selecting a provider:

- Does the provider offer Windows or Unix servers? If you are using any of the ASP.NET tools in Expression Web, you need a Windows server that is running ASP.NET.
- Does the service include access to traffic statistics for your site?
- How many e-mail accounts are included?
- Does the provider offer domain registration services to assist you in securing a domain name?
- How is support provided? By telephone, Internet chat, or e-mail only?
- Does the provider back up their clients' Web site files? If so, how often and how can you access the backup if needed?

- How is the provider's reliability? Don't settle for a company that has less than 95% uptime. **Uptime** is the time during which the servers are running and available.
- How much storage space is included in the packages? To select the package that's right for you, you need to know how much storage space you require. One way to check this is to navigate to your root folder in Windows Explorer, right-click the root folder, click Properties, then note the size of the folder.
- How much bandwidth do you need? Hosting packages usually include a maximum amount of traffic or bandwidth that is allowed to your site each month. Talk to your provider for assistance in determining how much bandwidth you are likely to need.
- What is the pricing structure, and is a contract required?

Setting Up and Connecting to a Publishing Destination

A **publishing destination** is the server space where you post your Web site files. Before you can publish your Web site, you must set up your publishing destination to tell Expression Web where to place the Web site files. In preparation for publishing the TradeWinds site files, you learn the process for setting up a publishing destination and then connecting to it.

DETAILS

To set up a publishing destination:

- **First, gather information about your publishing destination**

  Based on the Web hosting service you have arranged, gather your connection type, account information, and other account details for easy reference.

- **Next, open the Connection Settings dialog box**

  You can access the Connection Settings dialog box by clicking the Publishing View button at the bottom of the Site View tab, then clicking the Add a publishing destination link, as shown in Figure H-12.

- **Next, enter your hosting account information**

  In the Connection Settings dialog box, give your connection a name, choose your server type, then fill in the information requested. The information needed will vary depending on the publishing method you choose, but it always includes the address to publish to. When you are finished, click Add.

- **Next, complete the Connect to dialog box**

  When the completed Connection Settings dialog box closes, the Connect to dialog box opens with the username and password filled in, as shown in Figure H-13. Clicking OK completes the connection.

- **Finally, verify that you are connected**

  Once you are connected to your publishing destination, the view changes. In this view, two sets of files are listed: on the left side of the window are the files on your source site (your computer); on the right side are the files posted to your publishing destination (your Web server). See Figure H-14. The publishing destination area will likely be blank if you have not yet published any files. If you see any files on the publishing destination, don't remove them without first checking with your hosting company. The files might be necessary for your site to function. If you have already published your site at least once, you will see the files that are currently on your publishing destination listed on the right. The status area provides information about what is currently happening in the publishing process or about the most recent publishing session.

> **TROUBLE**
> If Expression Web is not able to connect successfully, an error message appears; if this happens, first check that you entered the information correctly, and then contact your hosting provider for help.

Testing your pages using SuperPreview

One of the most frustrating aspects of designing a Web site is ensuring that it looks the same or similar in all popular browsers. That's because browsers can display the same HTML and CSS code differently. In the past, thoroughly testing a design for browser compatibility involved either installing multiple browsers on your computer and viewing the site in each, or paying for a service to take snapshots of what the pages looked like in different browsers. Now there is a third option. SuperPreview is a new feature in Expression Web that allows you to quickly compare what a page looks like in different browsers. You can view side-by-side displays of each page as it would look in two different browsers. Moving the mouse around the display highlights differences in the way elements are placed on the page. SuperPreview gives you a fast and easy way to visually pinpoint differences in the way browsers display your design.

FIGURE H-12: Publishing view

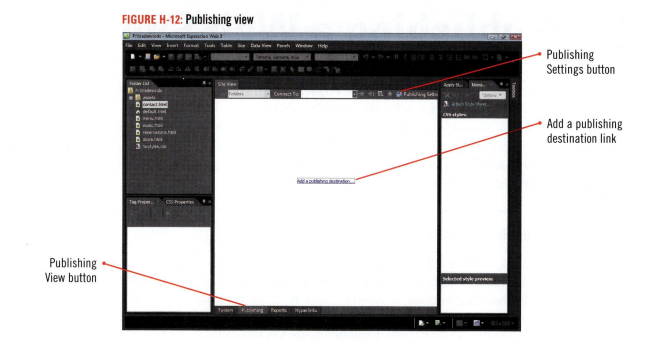

Publishing
Settings button

Add a publishing
destination link

Publishing
View button

FIGURE H-13: Connect to dialog box

FIGURE H-14: Publishing view when connected to publishing destination

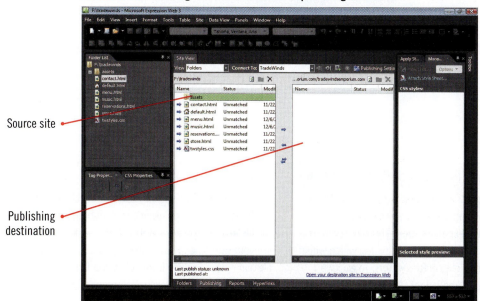

Source site

Publishing
destination

Publishing a Web Site

Once you have set up your publishing destination, publishing your files is simple. Expression Web includes features for publishing your files for the very first time as well as options for updating a site with additional files when necessary. You will want to publish your files whenever you make a change to the design or content of the site. How often you need to publish files depends on how frequently you are adding or editing content. Some sites are updated several times a day, while others may go months without a change.  You are ready to publish the TradeWinds site, so you familiarize yourself with the steps in the publishing process.

DETAILS

To publish your site:

- **First, choose a publishing option**

  Expression Web offers several options for publishing, which appear between the left and right panes in the Publishing view tab, as shown in Figure H-15. The most common option is to **publish files to the destination site**. This makes sense because you are working on files on your computer first and then publishing them to the publishing destination. You can also choose to **get files from the destination site**. This option can be useful if your source files have gotten lost or corrupted, because you can re-create your source site by copying the files from the destination site. However, use extreme caution with this option; copying older files from the publishing destination can cause you to lose any intentional changes you made to source files. Finally, you can choose to **synchronize** the files, meaning that Expression Web will copy whichever version of the file is newer to the opposite site so that you end up with a matching set of the newest version of all files at the end. This option is useful when multiple people are working on a site.

- **Next, publish your site**

  Click the arrow that represents the publishing option you chose. A dialog box will open displaying details of the file transfer and will close when the files have been published.

- **Finally, verify that your site was published**

  When your files are published they appear in the publishing destination, as shown in Figure H-16. The status window also shows the date and time of the last publish and provides a link to the log files, which offer more details on which files were published, as shown in Figure H-17.

Excluding unfinished files from being published

By default, Expression Web posts all changed files to the publishing destination whenever you publish a site, but you can exclude files that you are still working on in Publishing view. This allows you to publish a Web site without including unfinished pages, which would reflect poorly on the site and might confuse visitors. To exclude a particular page from being published, right-click the file name in the left panel of the Publish View, then click Exclude from Publishing on the shortcut menu. An Exclude from Publishing icon appears beside the file in and Expression Web will not include the file when publishing your site. When you are ready to publish the file, right-click the file name, click Exclude from Publishing to remove the icon, and then publish the site again.

FIGURE H-15: Publishing options when connected to publishing destination

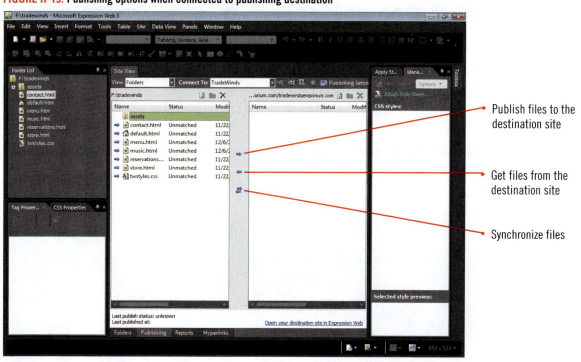

Publish files to the destination site

Get files from the destination site

Synchronize files

FIGURE H-16: Publishing view after publishing files

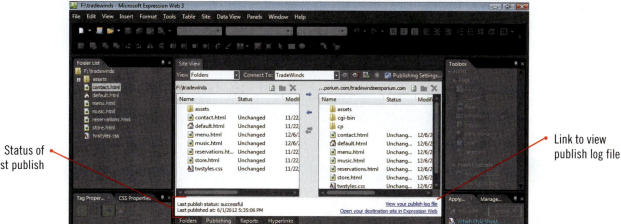

Status of last publish

Link to view publish log file

FIGURE H-17: Publish log file

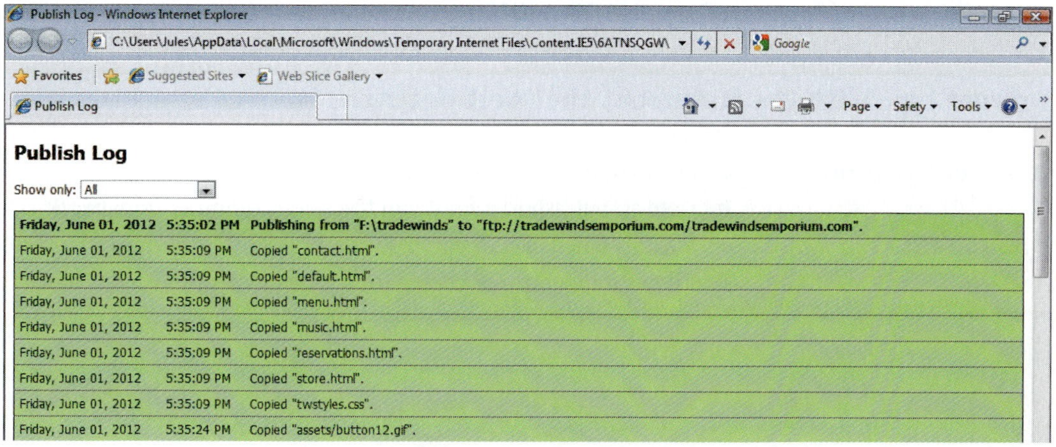

Friday, June 01, 2012	**5:35:02 PM**	**Publishing from "F:\tradewinds" to "ftp://tradewindsemporium.com/tradewindsemporium.com".**
Friday, June 01, 2012	5:35:09 PM	Copied "contact.html".
Friday, June 01, 2012	5:35:09 PM	Copied "default.html".
Friday, June 01, 2012	5:35:09 PM	Copied "menu.html".
Friday, June 01, 2012	5:35:09 PM	Copied "music.html".
Friday, June 01, 2012	5:35:09 PM	Copied "reservations.html".
Friday, June 01, 2012	5:35:09 PM	Copied "store.html".
Friday, June 01, 2012	5:35:09 PM	Copied "twstyles.css".
Friday, June 01, 2012	5:35:24 PM	Copied "assets/button12.gif".

Publish Log

Show only: All

Testing and Publishing Your Web Site

Practice

Concepts Review

For current SAM information including versions and content details, visit SAM Central (http://samcentral.course.com). If you have a SAM user profile, you may have access to hands-on instruction, practice, and assessment of the skills covered in this unit. Since we support various versions of SAM throughout the life of this text, you will want to check with your instructor for instructions and the correct URL/Web site to access those assignments.

Refer to Figure H-18 to answer the following questions.

FIGURE H-18

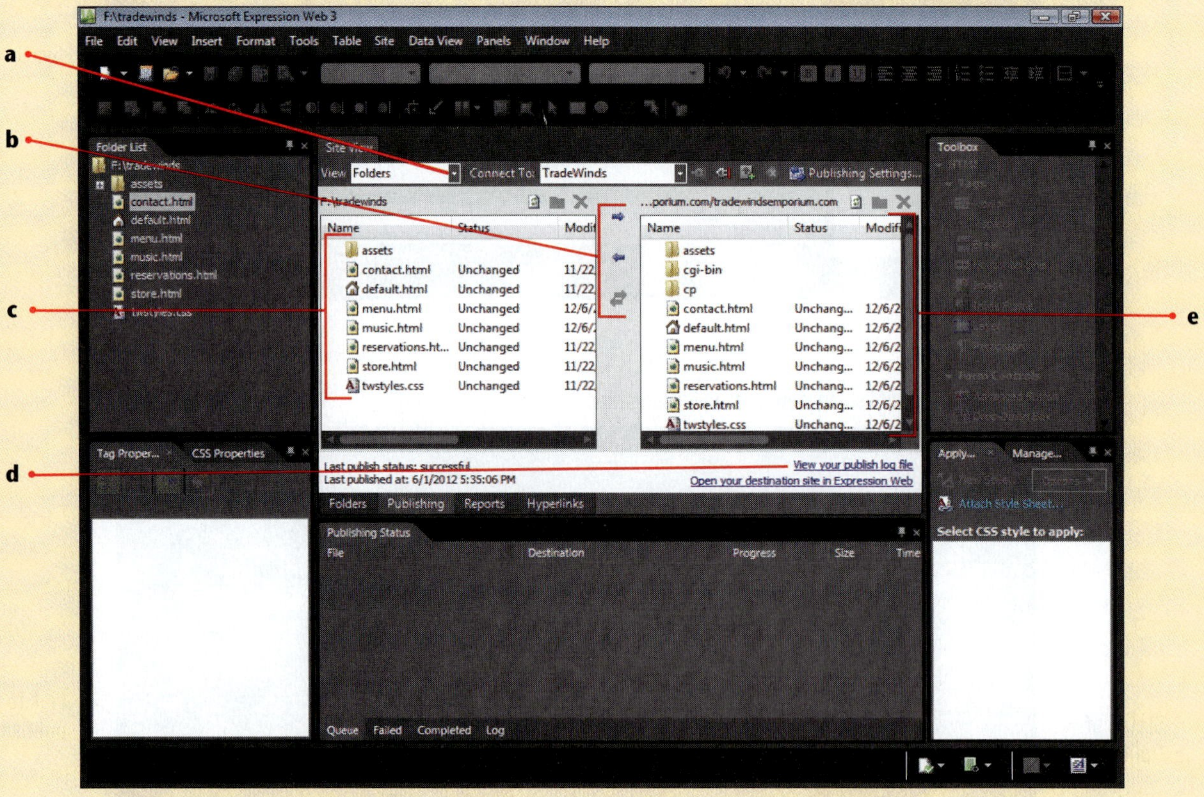

1. **Which element shows the files that are on your computer or network drive?**
2. **Which element shows the files that are on the Web server?**
3. **Which element do you click to see a list of files that were transferred during the last publish?**
4. **Which element do you click to change which files are displayed?**
5. **Which element shows your options for publishing files?**

Match each server type with the statement that best describes it.

6. FrontPage Server Extensions	**a.** Most common server type
7. WebDAV	**b.** Used to publish to a folder on the same computer or network
8. FTP, SFTP and FTPS	**c.** Used in older Web design software to publish and support interactive features
9. File system	**d.** Allows for a group of people to work on a common set of files

Select the best answer from the list of choices.

10. **Which set of accessibility guidelines is used internationally?**
    a. Section 508
    b. WCAG
    c. XHTML 1.0
    d. World Accessibility Forum

11. **Which publishing option is the one most commonly used?**
    a. Publish files to destination site
    b. Get files from destination site
    c. Synchronize
    d. Delete

12. **If you want to copy all the files from your publishing destination onto your computer or disk to replace your source files, which option do you choose in the status area?**
    a. Publish files to destination site
    b. Get files from destination site
    c. Synchronize
    d. Delete

13. **By default, Expression Web publishes:**
    a. All files.
    b. Only changed files.
    c. Only HTML files.
    d. No files.

14. **A company that sells Web server space is known as a:**
    a. File transfer provider.
    b. Data backup provider.
    c. System administrator.
    d. Web hosting provider.

15. **Which of the following should you test before you publish your site?**
    a. Spelling and grammar
    b. Display of site in different browsers
    c. Display of site on different screen resolutions
    d. All of the above

16. **In which view can you easily edit page titles?**
    a. Folders view
    b. Publishing view
    c. Reports view
    d. Hyperlinks view

17. **Which of the following is not an assistive technology used by people with disabilities to access Web sites?**
    a. Screen reading software
    b. Headphones
    c. Adaptive keyboard
    d. Mouth stick

18. **In the Accessibility Checker dialog box, which option would you choose to see a list of serious issues that definitely need to be fixed?**
    a. Show Warnings
    b. Show Manual Checklist
    c. Show Errors
    d. Generate HTML report

Skills Review

1. **Verify hyperlinks.**

   a. Launch Expression Web, then open the careers site.

   b. Click the Reports View button on the Site View tab.

   c. Run the Unverified hyperlinks report, clicking Yes to confirm the process.

   d. Repair any broken links if necessary, then use the Hyperlinks list arrow to return to the Site Summary.

2. **View and edit page titles.**

   a. Click the Hyperlinks View button on the Site View tab.

   b. Click the home page in the Folder List task pane.

   c. Right-click in a blank area of the Site View tab, then click Show Page Titles.

   d. Right-click in a blank area of the Site View tab, then click Show Page Titles to turn off this setting.

   e. In Hyperlinks view, right-click the about page link to the left of the default.html icon in the Site View tab, click Properties, in the Title box type **About Careers Guaranteed** to replace the highlighted text, then click OK.

   f. In Hyperlinks view, right-click the contact page, click Properties, replace the highlighted text in the Title box with **Contact Careers Guaranteed**, then click OK.

   g. In Hyperlinks view, right-click the services page, click Properties, replace the highlighted text in the Title box with **Careers Guaranteed Services**, then click OK.

   h. Right-click in a blank area of the Site View tab, click Show Page Titles, then compare your screen to Figure H-19.

   i. Right-click in a blank area of the Site View tab, then click Show Page Titles to turn off this setting.

3. **Test accessibility.**

   a. Switch to Folders View using a button on the Site View tab.

   b. Click the services page to select it, click Tools on the menu bar, then click Accessibility Reports.

   c. In the Accessibility Checker dialog box, make sure that Selected pages is selected under Check where; that WCAG Priority 1, WCAG Priority 2, and Access Board Section 508 are selected under Check for; and that only Errors and Warnings are selected under Show.

   d. Click Check.

   e. Right-click the first error listed on the report in the Accessibility task pane, then click Learn More.

   f. Click the link to learn more about this error.

   g. Close the browser, then return to Expression Web.

   h. Click the Generate HTML Report button, then print the report.

   i. Close the Accessibility Report.html tab without saving changes, close the Accessibility task pane, close the careers Web site, then exit Expression Web.

FIGURE H-19

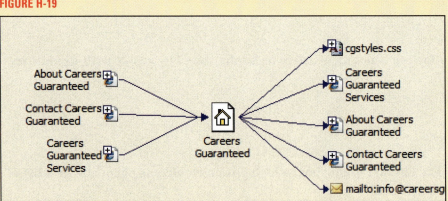

Independent Challenge 1

In this project you continue your work on the ConnectUp Web site. You have a meeting scheduled with Tiffany to show her your progress on the site. You decide to do some testing to make sure the links are working, the pages are titled appropriately, and there are no major accessibility problems.

a. Launch Expression Web, then open the connectup Web site.

b. In the Reports view of the Site View tab, run the Unverified hyperlinks report and verify hyperlinks, as shown in Figure H-20.

c. In the Hyperlinks view of the Site View tab, view the hyperlinks to and from the home page. Show the Page Titles and review the current page titles.

d. In the Hyperlinks view, hide the Page Titles.

e. In the Hyperlinks view, edit the title for the contact page and give it the new title **Contact ConnectUp**.

f. In the Hyperlinks view, edit the title for the faq page and give it the new title **Frequently Asked Questions about ConnectUp**.

g. In the Hyperlinks view, edit the title for the joinup page and give it the new title **JoinUp with ConnectUp**.

h. Select Show Page Titles, then deselect Show Page Titles.

i. Switch to Folders view, select the joinup page, then run an accessibility report on the selected page, checking for WCAG Priority 1, WCAG Priority 2, and Access Board Section 508, and showing Errors and Warnings.

j. Right-click the second error, then click Learn More.

k. Close the browser, then return to Expression Web.

l. Generate an HTML Report, print it, close the Accessibility Report.html tab without saving changes, then close the Accessibility task pane.

m. Close the Web site, then exit Expression Web.

FIGURE H-20

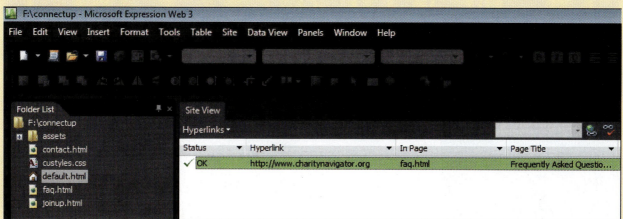

Independent Challenge 2

In this project you continue your work on the Memories Restored Web site. You are ready to prepare for publishing the site, so you decide to verify hyperlinks, review and edit your page titles, and run an accessibility report.

a. Launch Expression Web, then open the memories Web site.

b. Verify any external hyperlinks in the site.

c. Working in Hyperlinks view, review and edit page titles for all pages in the site, as shown in Figure H-21.

d. Run an Accessibility Report on the testimonials page. Generate an HTML Report and print it. Close the Accessibility task pane when you are finished.

Advanced Challenge Exercise

- Run an All Files Report on the memories Web site.
- Press [Print Screen] and paste the image into a word-processing program.
- Add your name at the top of the document and print the document.

e. Close the memories site and exit Expression Web.

FIGURE H-21

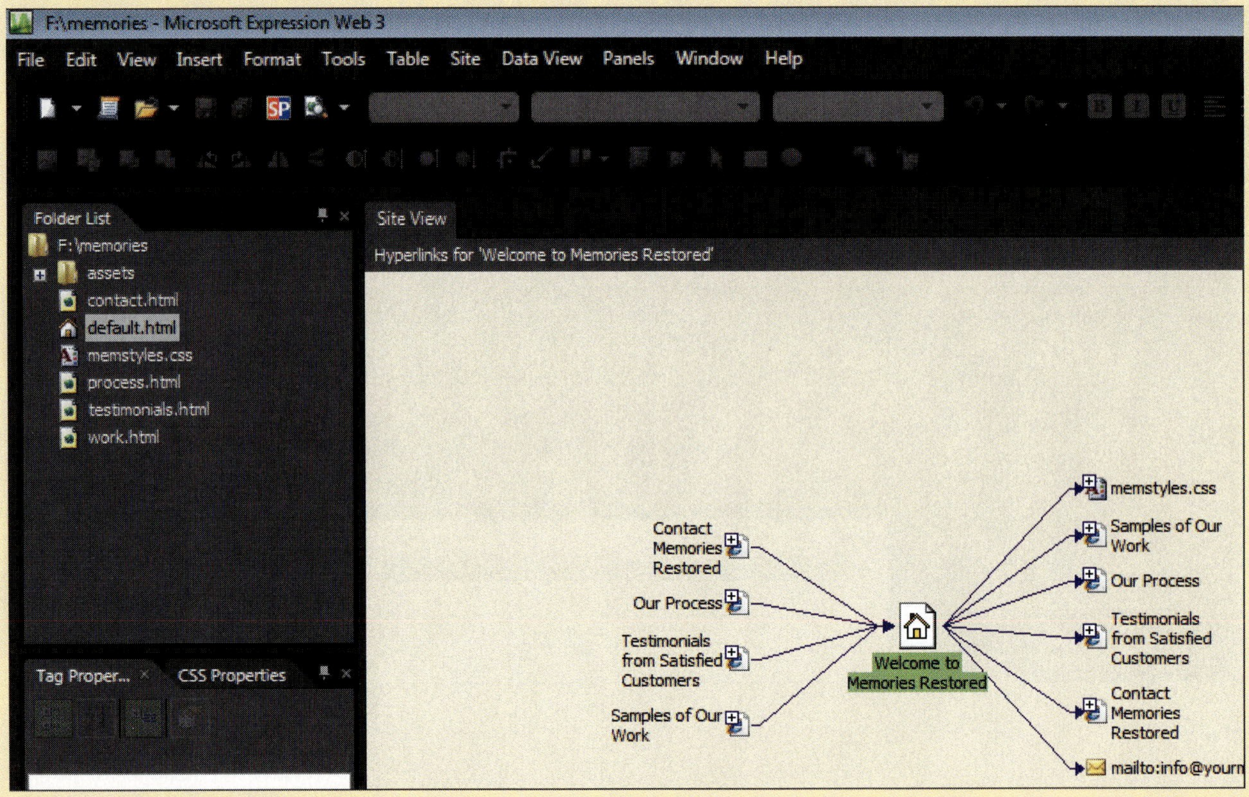

Independent Challenge 3

Note: This Independent Challenge requires an Internet connection.

Technology for All wants you to explore new options for hosting their Web site. They feel that their current Web hosting provider offers poor technical support and is too expensive. They need 75 GB of space, 1000 GB of bandwidth, and a server that has Windows and ASP.NET installed.

a. Using your favorite search engine, research Web hosting providers and find three companies to compare.

b. Visit the companies' Web sites and find the package each company offers that would meet Technology for All's needs.

c. Create a chart comparing the features and costs for each package.

Advanced Challenge Exercise

- Research the Web site for each company to find out how they provide technical support (phone, e-mail, live chat, etc.)
- Research if there are any additional costs for technical support and how quickly customers can expect a response.
- Incorporate this information into your chart.

d. Conclude your report with a recommendation of which company you would choose for hosting and why.

e. Add your name to the document, save it, and print it.

Real Life Independent Challenge

This assignment builds on the personal Web site you have worked on in previous units. You are ready to verify the site's hyperlinks, view and edit page titles, and check for accessibility problems.

a. Proofread your content for spelling and grammatical errors.

b. Verify all hyperlinks in your site. Fix any that are not valid.

c. Review and edit as appropriate all page titles.

d. Run an accessibility report and use the Learn More feature to visit the WCAG Web site for more information.

e. Run a Slow pages report on your site.

f. Test your site in a variety of browsers and screen resolutions.

Visual Workshop

Launch Expression Web, then open the ecotours Web site. Use the appropriate Site view and run the report shown in Figure H-22. When you have finished, press [Print Screen], paste the image into a word-processing program, add your name at the top of the document, print the document, close the word-processing program, then close the Web site and exit Expression Web.

FIGURE H-22

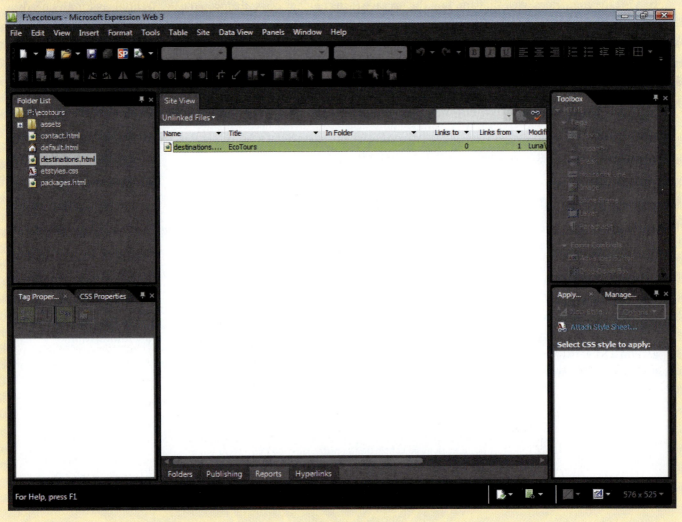

Glossary

Active The state of a link when it has been clicked but the mouse button has not yet been released.

Absolute URL Contains the protocol (such as http://), the domain name (such as centraluniversity.com), and the file path (such as /library/hours.htm) to make up a complete URL; used to create an external link.

Accessible Web site A site usable by all visitors, including people with disabilities or those accessing it with devices such as cell phones.

a:hover The state of a link when a visitor's cursor is pointing to the link.

algorithm A method a search engine uses to decide how search engine results are ranked; the algorithms search engines use are very sophisticated, change frequently, and take into account factors such as the number of times the search term shows up in your content, where the search term occurs on your page, and how many other reputable sites link to your site.

a:link The normal, unvisited state of a link.

Alt text *See* Alternate text.

Alternate text An attribute of the <img> tag that describes the image in words; visitors who use screen reader software hear this text read aloud.

Anchor Another term for a link; also, the name of the HTML element that is used to create a link.

Assets Image, media, sound and other non-HTML Web site files.

Assistive technologies Software or devices that help people with disabilities to perform functions they otherwise would not be able to perform.

Attribute The part of an HTML element that provides additional information about that element.

a:visited The state of a link when it has been clicked in the visitor's browser and is present in the browser's history.

Background-attachment A CSS property that controls whether a background image scrolls with the element's content or stays fixed as the content scrolls over it.

background-repeat A CSS property that controls whether and how a background image repeats across the element.

Bookmark A marker at a specific spot on a Web page that can be used as a destination anchor.

Borders In CSS, a line that that encloses both the padding and content areas.

Browser defaults The built-in styles each Web browser uses to determine the display of HTML elements.

Card sorting A technique in which potential or actual Web site visitors are asked to organize the content from your Web site in a way that makes sense to them.

Cascade The particular order in which style rules are applied to an element.

Cascading Style Sheets (CSS) Rules that describe the presentation and visual design of a Web page, including fonts, colors, and often the layout and positioning of elements on the page.

Class-based style rule A style rule that can be created and applied to any selected content or element.

Code view The view that displays the HTML code that a Web page is written in; useful for writing and revising code, as well as for troubleshooting.

Cognitive disabilities Include learning disabilities, memory impairments, and intellectual impairments.

Common toolbar Provides access to common tasks including creating a new page, saving and opening files, and common text formatting options such as font, font size, bold, and italic.

Content area The innermost box in the CSS box model which contains the text, image, or other content.

Cropping Trimming or removing unwanted parts of a picture.

CSS box model The model on which CSS presentation and layout is based; this model states that every element on a page is a rectangular box with a content area and optional padding, border, and margin areas.

CSS positioning Using CSS to position elements on a Web page.

Declaration The part of a style rule consisting of a property and a value that describes what properties you want to change and how you want to change them.

Definition list HTML element used to list a word or phrase along with its definition or description.

Descendant selectors A selector that defines properties for all instances of an element that occur within a defined container.

Design view The view that displays a page as it will look like when viewed in a browser; most commonly used view when designing pages.

Destination anchor The part of a link that is the file or page that opens when a visitor clicks the link.

Dimensions The height and width of an image, usually measured in pixels; determines how large the image looks on a screen.

Div HTML element consisting of a rectangular area you can position on the page to hold your content, including text and images.

Domain name A name that identifies a particular Web site and is part of that site's URL.

Download time Amount of time it takes a Web page to load into a browser; determined by the file size of the page and its referenced files (including image files), and by the speed of the visitor's Internet connection.

Dynamic Web templates An Expression Web feature that helps maintain a consistent design across all pages in a site.

Editing window Large area under the Common toolbar where most design work is accomplished.

Element In HTML, the combination of an opening tag, content, and a closing tag; elements identify structural parts of an HTML document.

Element-based style rule A rule that redefines the display of an HTML element.

E-mail link A link that opens an e-mail message in the visitor's default e-mail program, with a designated e-mail address already entered in the To line.

External links Links to Web pages or files on a different Web site.

External style sheet A separate file with a .css extension that contains style rules.

Eyedropper tool A tool that allows you to select a color by clicking anywhere on your screen.

File size The physical size of a file, measured in kilobytes (KB); affects how long it takes the picture to display in a visitor's browser.

File system A connection type that allows you to publish a copy of your site to a folder on the same computer or same network.

Fixed page design A design in which the page is the same width on every visitor's computer no matter how large the visitor's screen is.

Folders view Default view in the Web Site tab, which displays a list of files and folders in the site.

Font family A prioritized list of fonts specified in a style rule that allows fonts to be substituted in case the visitor's computer doesn't have a particular font installed.

Footer An area at the bottom of each Web page; usually contains contact information and a copyright statement.

Form An HTML element that allows visitors to send information from a Web site.

FrontPage Server Extensions Files that were used by Microsoft's legacy Web design program, FrontPage, to facilitate publishing and to support interactive Web features.

FTP File Transfer Protocol, the most common method used to transfer files from a source site to a publishing destination.

FTPS A method of transferring files via FTP that is more secure than the FTP method.

Generic font family A font that is displayed if no other fonts in a font family list are available; only three generic font families are consistently understood by browsers and therefore safe to use—serif, sans serif, and monospace.

Get files from the destination site A publishing option that transfers files from a publishing destination to your computer.

GIF Image format best used for images that are drawings, simple graphics, navigation buttons, or that contain large areas of solid color; GIFS can also be animated and can have a transparent background color.

Global navigation Navigation that appears on each page, usually at the top or left side.

Graphics Pictures.

Headings Six different levels of HTML elements that can be used to define text meant to act as a heading or subheading on a Web page.

Hearing disabilities Deafness and hearing loss.

Hex value Abbreviation of hexadecimal code, a numeric value used to define a specific color in CSS rules.

Home page The first page a visitor sees after entering a Web site address in a browser.

Hover state Image state that appears when a visitors points to or hovers over the image.

HTML Acronym for HyperText Markup Language, the language used to create Web pages.

HTML tags Text enclosed in angle brackets that surround pieces of Web page content and describe its structure or meaning.

Hyperlink Text or an image that visitors click to open another Web page, Web site, or file.

Hyperlinks view Illustrates how one file is linked to other files in a site.

IA *See* Information architect.

ID attribute A unique, specific name assigned to an HTML element, often a div, for purposes of applying style rules to the element.

Images Pictures.

Information architect A person who creates structures, navigation systems, and search systems for Web sites; may work as an independent consultant or as part of in-house Web design teams within organizations.

Inheritance A characteristic of style sheets that causes a style applied to an element on the page to also be applied to any elements it contains.

Inline styles Style rules that are placed directly around content similarly to the way HTML tags are placed.

Interactive button Navigation graphic that changes appearance when a visitor interacts with it.

Internal links Links between pages or files within the same Web site.

Internal style sheet A set of style rules enclosed in the head of an HTML document in a <style> tag.

JPEG Image format best used for photographs and other images that contain many different colors, such as detailed artwork.

Keywords An HTML element consisting of a list of terms, separated by commas, that describe the content of a Web site.

Liquid page design A type of design that that shrinks or expands to fit the size of the visitor's screen.

Local navigation Navigation used on large sites that features links related to a subcategory of the site.

Long description An attribute of the img tag that provides a more detailed description of an image than the alternate text.

Margins In the CSS box model, the area that creates space surrounding the other three components (borders, padding, and content).

Markup The use of tags to describe the structure of a document; accounts for the "M" in HTML (HyperText Markup Language).

Menu bar Located under the title bar, includes all Expression Web commands organized into menus such as File and Edit.

Merged panels Panels that occupy the same space and appear one in front of the other.

Monospace font A font with equal space between the characters; an example is the Courier font.

Motor disabilities Includes conditions that may affect the ability to use a standard-issue mouse and/or keyboard to navigate a site.

Named anchor *See* Bookmark.

Navigation bar A set of related navigation links; can be either text or images.

Original state The image state that appears when a page initially opens.

Ordered lists Used to display items where sequence is important; items appear numbered by default.

Padding area In the CSS box model, the area that creates space between the content and the border.

Page layout The placement of content, graphics, and navigation on a Web page.

Panel A small, moveable window in the Expression Web interface that provides access to tools for specific tasks.

Paste Options button Provides options for controlling how much, if any, formatting to include with pasted text.

Pipe A vertical line; the pipe symbol usually shares a keyboard key with the backslash symbol.

Pixel The basic unit of measurement for anything displayed on a computer screen.

PNG Image format created specifically for Web graphics; produces very high quality images with small file sizes but is not well supported by all browsers.

Pressed state The image state that appears while a visitor is clicking an image.

Preview Feature that allows you to view your pages in a Web browser as you are designing them in Expression Web.

Property The part of a style rule declaration that defines which aspect of an element's formatting to change.

Pseudo-class Defines properties for a particular state of an element, such as hover or active.

Public domain Work that is not protected by copyright law and is free to use and copy.

Publish To copy Web pages and related files from a local computer to a Web server so that visitors can view the files.

Publishing destination A folder on a Web server that contains all files for a particular Web site.

Publishing files to destination site A publishing option that publishes files from your computer to a publishing destination.

Publishing source *See* Source site

Publishing view Displays a dual list of files, those in the source site and those on the remote Web site.

Quick tag selector Located just below the tab area; allows you to easily select and edit specific HTML tags on Web page.

Related navigation Set of navigation links that usually appears within the content area and displays links related to that page's content.

Relative URL Describes the location of the file being linked relative to the source file; used for internal links.

Reports view Provides an overview of available Web site reports, including reports of broken hyperlinks, slow pages, recently changed pages, and more.

Resampling Removes extra pixels from an image, changing the dimensions and file size; also decreases file size and download time.

Resizing Changing the height and width attributes in the <img> tag to make an image display differently on the page; the image dimensions themselves don't change and neither does the file size.

Root folder A folder that stores all the files that make up a Web site, including HTLM files, CSS files, and images.

Sample To select a color by clicking on it on the screen with an eyedropper tool.

Sans-serif font A font, such as Arial, that has no strokes at the beginning or end of a character.

Screen reader Software that uses a synthesized voice to read onscreen text aloud for people with vision-related disabilities.

Search engine optimization The process of adjusting a Web site so it ranks higher than competing sites on search engine pages.

Section 508 guidelines Accessibility guidelines issued by the United States government in Section 508 of the Rehabilitation Act.

Select tool *See* eyedropper tool.

Selector The part of a style rule that defines which elements a style should apply to; there are three basic types of selectors—IDs, elements, and classes.

Semantic markup Marking up Web page elements with HTML tags in a meaningful and descriptive way.

Serif font A font, such as Times New Roman, that has visible strokes at the ends of the character.

SFTP A short, boxed area of content on a page that provides additional information about a topic.

Site map A diagram depicting how a Web site's pages are related within the site.

Source anchor The part of a link that is the word, phrase, or image on a Web page that, when clicked, opens another page or file.

Source site The folder on a hard drive, USB drive, or network drive that contains all files for a Web site.

Spam Bulk unsolicited e-mail.

Split view A combination view that displays both a Code pane and a Design pane at once.

Status bar Located along the bottom of the program window, it provides helpful information such as the file size, the page dimensions, and which versions of HTML and CSS Expression Web is using to create your Web page.

Stock photos Photos taken by professional photographers and then offered for sale to Web designers, graphic designers, and others who need images for Web sites, print advertisements, and other projects.

Style *See* Style rule.

Style rule Describes how a particular element or piece of content should be displayed. A style rule has two parts, the selector and the declaration.

Style sheets *See* Cascading Style Sheets

Synchronize A publishing option that copies the newest version of a file to either the source or publishing destination, ensuring that both are up to date.

Table A grid-like container with rows and columns that can be used to display data or to lay out elements on a page.

Target The browser window or frame in which the destination file opens.

Thumbnails Small images, usually linked to larger versions of the same image; used to save space on the page and minimize download time.

Title HTML element that contains the title of a page; the title is not displayed on the page itself but appears in the title bar of the visitor's browser and as the title in a browser's list of favorites or bookmarks if a visitor has added it to that list.

Title bar Appears at the very top of the program window and shows the title of the current Web site (if a site is open) or the current Web page (if only a page is open), the file path of the current site or page enclosed in parentheses, and the name of the program. Buttons for minimizing, resizing, and closing the program window are located on the right side of the title bar.

Unordered lists Used to display items where order is not important; list items appear with bullets beside them by default.

Uptime The time during which servers are running and available.

URL Acronym for Uniform Resource Locator; the address for a Web site, consisting of a domain name, a file name, and sometimes folder names.

Value Options for a property in a style rule.

Visual aids A feature that displays and allows edits to empty or invisible page elements while in Design view.

Visual disabilities Include legal blindness, low vision, and color blindness.

Visual hierarchy Varying the size of text elements in relationship to their importance to help readers quickly scan the page.

WCAG A set of international Web Content Accessibility Guidelines issued by the World Wide Web Consortium; the guidelines are based on research, expert opinion, and observations of people with disabilities using the Web.

WebDav A type of server that allows groups to work on the same files by providing workflow and collaboration features such as file check-in and check-out.

Web browser Software that interprets HTML code and displays the text and images on a Web page.

Web hosting companies Companies that provide server space for a monthly or annual fee.

Web page An HTML document on the World Wide Web.

Web-safe colors Colors that display reliably on all computer monitors that support 256 colors or less; these were more important in the early days of Web design than they are now, since most visitors' monitors now display millions of colors.

Web-safe fonts Fonts likely to be available on Windows, Mac, and Linux-based computer systems.

Web server A computer connected to the Internet that stores Web pages and other Web content and displays it to a Web browser.

Web site A collection of related Web pages, linked together.

Web standards Recommendations for creating Web pages that allow content to be viewed by all browsers and devices.

Windows clipboard A temporary storage area in your computer's memory.

World Wide Web Consortium (W3C) The main standards-setting organization for the World Wide Web.

Wrapping style Dictates how a picture will be positioned relative to its surrounding text.

WYSIWYG An acronym for What You See Is What You Get, meaning that as you're designing, Expression Web displays what your page will look like in a Web browser.

(x) background-position A CSS property that controls where a background image is placed relative to the element's left edge.

XHTML Acronym for eXtensible HyperText Markup Language, a newer version of HTML that has slightly different rules and tags, but still uses the extension .htm or .html.

(y) background-position A CSS property that controls where a background image is placed relative to the element's top edge.

Index

Note: Page numbers in boldface indicate key terms.

A

a:active, **158**

absolute URLs, **55**

accessibility

alternate text, 100, 101

screen readers, 73

testing, 178–179

accessible Web site, **176**

adding

background images, 124–125

borders, 130–131

browsers to Preview list, 8

font families, 132–133

navigation bars to site pages, 156–157

text to images, 106

title, page description, keywords, 32–33

Adobe Flash, 12

a:hover, **158**

algorithm, **177**

a:link, **158**

Allow Blocked Content, 152

alternate text, **100**, 101

anchors, **54**

animation file types (table), 37

Apply Styles panel, 112

ASP.NET, 181

assets, **36**

assistive technologies, **176–177**

attributes, **72–73**

audience of Web sites, profiling, 24–25

audio file types (table), 37

Auto Thumbnail command, 110–111

Auto Thumbnail options, 108–109

AutoHide All Panels, 10

AutoHide button, Toolbox panel, 82

a:visited, **158**

B

background colors

setting, 126–129

transparent GIF option, 152–153

background images, 124–125

background repeat, **124**

background-attachment, **124**

backing up Web sites files, 28

blinking text, 159

bookmarks, creating, **58–59**

borders (CSS), **122**

borders, adding, 130–131

 element, 72

browser defaults, **79**

browser wars, 3

building Web sites, 24

bulleted lists, 78–79

C

.ca (Canada), 34

card sorting, **149**

cascade (style rules), **86**

Cascading Style Sheets (CSS), **2**

adding background images, 124–125

adding font families, 132–133

borders, 130–131

font measurement units, 87

headings, 134–135

layouts, 122–123

padding, margins, 138–139

positioning, 30

setting background color, 126–129, 127

tools available (table), 81

using, 80–81

checking spelling, 14

class-based rule

applying and removing, 88–89

described, **86**

"click here" text, 60

closing files, Web pages, 16–17

Code pane, 10

Code view, **10**

cognitive disabilities, **176–177**

color swatches (fig.), 129

colors

setting background, 126–129

specifying style, 84–85

Common toolbar, **6–7**

Connection Settings dialog box, 180–181

connection types, 180–181

content area (CSS), **122**

contrast, color, 128

copying and pasting content between Web pages, 62–63

copyright issues with images, 99

Corel Paint Shop Pro, 12

creating

  bookmarks, 58–59

  class-based style rules, 86–87

  element-based style rules, 82–83

  e-mail links, 60–61

  external links, 56–57

  folders, 36

  headings, 76–77

  interactive buttons, 150–151

  internal links, 54–55

  link styles, 158–161

  lists, 78–79

  navigation bars, 154–155

  paragraphs, line breaks, 74–75

  thumbnails, 108–109, 110–111

  visual hierarchy, 77

  Web sites, 28–29

crop marks, 105

cropping pictures, 104–105

CSS box model, 122–123

CSS file types, 37

CSS positioning, 30

CSS Properties panel, 10, 85

custom dictionary, 52

D

declarations (CSS), 80–81

default.html, 30

definition lists, 78

deleting Web pages, 36

descendent selectors, 159

Design view, 10

designing

  maintaining consistent graphical style, 109

  page layout, 26–27

  Web sites, 7

destination anchors, 54

dictionary, custom, 52

dimensions, 98

divs

  in CSS layouts, 122

  designing, 30

  page_content, 31

  semantic ids, 136

domain name, 34

download time, 98

dynamic Web page file types, 37

Dynamic Web Templates, 28

E

editing

  hyperlinks, 56

  interactive buttons, 152–153

  pictures, 104–105

  thumbnails, 110

  Web page titles, 174–175

  Web pages, 8

editing window, 6–7

.edu, 34

element-based style rules, 82–83

elements

  described, 72–73

  navigation, 147

e-mail links, creating, 60–61

Expression Studio, 1

Expression Web 3

  capabilities of, 2–3

  exiting, 16–17

  exploring workspace, 6–7

  getting Help, 14–15

  overview of, 1

  program window, 4–5

  starting, 4–5

  templates, 28

  User Guide, 14–15

external links, creating, 54, 56–57

external style sheets (CSS), 80

eyedropper tool

  described, 126

  sampling color using, 126–127

F

file extensions, 30

file formats

  image, 98

  video, 37

file size, 98

File System, 180

files

  excluding from being published, 184

  saving, closing, 16

  synchronizing, 184

  transferring, 180

  Web site types (table), 37

fixed page design, 26

flipping images, 104–105

focus groups, 25

Folder List panel, 36–37

folders, creating and managing, 28, 36–37

Folders view, 38–39

font families, 132–133

fonts

  adding families, 132–133

  choosing style, 84–85

  CSS measurement units, 87

  for navigation buttons, 156

footers, 50

  creating link style, 159

  styling, 136–137

formatting marks, viewing, 74

forms, 12

FrontPage Server Extensions, 180

FTP, 180

FTPS, 180

G

generic font families, 132
get files from the destination site, 184
GIF, 98–99
global navigation, 148–149, 156–157
graphics, 97
 file types (table), 37
 overview of Web, 98–99

H

h1 tags, 12–13
<h1> tags, 72
<h2> tags, 76–77
headings, 12, 73
 creating, 76–77
 styling, 134–135
hearing disabilities, 176–177
Help, getting, 14–15
hex value, 84
hiding panels, 10
home page, 30
hotspots, creating with Pictures
 toolbar, 104
hover state, 150
HTML (Hypertext Markup Language), 2
 creating headings, 76–77
 creating paragraphs, line breaks, 74–75
 structuring content with, 72–73
 with, and without style sheet applied, 3
 and XHTML, 77
.html files, 30, 36
HTML page file types (table), 37
HTML tags, 72–73
hyperlinks
 described, 12
 verifying, 172–173
Hyperlinks view, 38–39, 174–175

I

id attribute, 136
images, 97
 See also graphics, pictures
 adding background, 124–125
 adding text to, 106
 file formats, 98
 moving, 100
 setting Auto Thumbnail options,
  108–109
img tags, 12–13, 100, 102
importing Web pages, 34–35
information architects (IAs), 147
inheritance (of styles), 84
inline styles (CSS), 80
Insert Hyperlink dialog box, 54–57
inserting
 See also adding
 pictures in Web pages, 100–101
interactive buttons
 creating, 150–151
 editing, 152–153
Interactive Buttons dialog box, 150–153
internal links, 54–55
internal style sheets (CSS), 80

J

JavaScript, using multiple style sheets
 with, 89
JPEG, 98–99

K

keywords
 adding to Web sites, 32–33
 designing, 32

L

layouts
 CSS, 122
 CSS positioning, 30–31
 Web page, 24, 26–27
<li> tags, 72, 82
line break element, 73
line breaks, creating, 74–75
linking to bookmarks, 58–59
links, 12
 creating internal, 54–55
 styles, 158–161
 text-only, 50
 verifying, 172–173
 viewing Web site, 38–39
liquid page design, 26
lists
 creating, 78–79
 HTML tags for, 72
local navigation, 148–149
logos, 101
long description, 100

M

maintaining links, 54
Manage Styles panel, 112
managing Web pages, folders, 36–37
margin area (CSS), 122
margins
 setting for images, 106–107
 setting for pages, 138–139
market research, 25
markups, 72
measurements in pixels, inches,
 centimeters, 103
menu bar, 6–7

merged panels, 6–7

Microsoft Expression Web 3. *See* Expression Web 3

Microsoft Expression Web Online command, 14

Microsoft Word text, pasting into Web pages, 48

Modify Style dialog box, 84–85

monospace, **132**

More Colors dialog box, 127

motor disabilities, 176–177

moving images, 100

N

name, domain, **34**

named anchors, creating, **58–59**

naming files, 8, 104

navigation
 overview of, 147–149
 planning Web site, 26–27
 with screen readers, 73
 text-based, 50
 using lists for, 78

navigation bars
 adding to site pages, 156–157
 creating, **154–155**

New dialog box, 30–31

New Style dialog box, 82–83, 87

numbered lists, 78–79

O

Open File dialog box, 9

opening Web pages, 8–9

ordered list element, 73

ordered lists, **78**

.org, 34

original state, **150**

P

<p> tag, 72, 88–89

padding, setting, 138–139

padding area (CSS), **122**

Page Editor Options dialog box, 108–109, 133

page layout, **24**

Page Properties dialog box, 32–33

panels, **6–7**
 CSS tools (table), 81
 working with, 10–11

paragraph element, 73

paragraphs, creating, 74–75

Paste Options button, **48**

pasting
 content between Web pages, 62–63
 text into Web pages, 48–51

photographs
 finding for your site, 99
 See also graphics, images, pictures

Picture Properties dialog box, 106–107, 113

pictures
 See also graphics, images
 editing, 104–105
 inserting in Web pages, 100–101
 resizing, resampling, 102–103
 setting wrapping style, margins, 106–107

Pictures toolbar, using, 104–105

pipes (|), **50**

pixel, **84**, 103

planning
 Web page layout, 26–27
 Web sites, 24–25

PNG, 98

positioning, CSS, **30**

pressed state, **150**

Preview feature, **8**

previewing Web pages in browser, 8–9, 58

Print Page Setup dialog box, 16

printing
 Help topics, 14
 Web pages, 16–17

property (CSS), 80–81

pseudo-class, 158

publish, **2**, 171
 files to the destination site, **184**
 Web sites, 24

publishing destination, setting up, connecting to, **182–183**

publishing source, **38**

Publishing view, 38–39, 182–183

publishing Web sites, 184–185

pull-down menus, 148

Q

quick tag selector bar, 6–7

R

related navigation, 148–149

relative URLs, **55**

renaming
 files, 104
 Web pages, 36

reports
 accessibility, 178–179
 CSS, 81

Reports view, 38–39

resampling, **102–103**

researching Web sites, 24–25

Reset Workspace Layout command, 10

resizing pictures, **102–103**

resolution, screen, 8

rollovers, **150**

root folder, **28**, 29

S

sample, 126

sans-serif, 132

Save Embedded Files dialog box, 100–101, 110

saving

files, 16

pages while working, 32

screen readers, 73

screen resolution, 8

search engine optimization, 177

Section 508 guidelines, 176, 178

Select tool, 126

selectors (CSS), 80–81

semantic div ids, 136

semantic markup, 72

serif, 132

SFTP, 180

Show Code View, 6–7

Show Design View, 6–7

Show Split View, 6–7

site map, 24, 25

Site Summary report, 38–39

sorting, card, 149

source, 38

source anchors, 54

spam, 60, 61

special characters, inserting, 50–51

spell-checking, 14, 52–53

Split view, 10, 74–75

standards, Web, 2, 3

starting Expression Web 3, 4–5

states, link, 158–159

status bar, 6–7

style

maintaining consistent graphical, 109

wrapping, **106**

style rules

applying, 84–85, 88–89

class-based, 86–87

element-based, 82–83

style rules (CSS), **80–81**

style sheets, **2**, 89

styles

automatically generated, 112

border, 130–131

link, 158–161

styling

footers, 136–137

headings, 134–135

thumbnail pictures, 112–113

SuperPreview, testing Web pages using, 182

swatches, setting background color using, 128–129

Symbol dialog box, 50–51

symbols, inserting, 50–51

synchronize, **184**

T

tables, **12**

Tag Properties panel, 10–11

Target Frame dialog box, 56–57

targets (of links), **56**

templates, 28

testing

accessibility, 178–179

Web pages using SuperPreview, 182

Web sites, 24

text

adding to images, 106

alternate, 100, 101

decorator styles (table), 159

pasting into Web pages, 48–51

writing good link, 60

Thesaurus, using, 52–53

thumbnails, **108**

creating, 110–111

setting Auto Thumbnail options, 108–109

styling, 112–113

title bar, **6–7**

titles, **32**

adding to Web sites, 32–33

viewing, editing page, 174–175

toolbars available in Expression Web 3 (table), **7**

traffic analysis, 25

troubleshooting CSS styles, 85

U

undoing actions, 106

unordered list element, 73

unordered lists, **78**

uptime, 181

URL, 34

absolute and relative, 55

ensuring accuracy of, 57

User Guide, 14–15

V

value (CSS), **80–81**

verifying links, **172–173**

verifying Web site publication, 184–185

video file types (table), 37

viewing

formatting marks, 74

Web page elements and visual aids, 12–13

Web page titles, 174–175

views

See also specific view

working with, 10–11

visitor surveys, 25

visual aids, 12

visual disabilities, 176–177

visual hierarchy, 76

W

Wayback Machine, 27

WCAG, 176–177, 178

Web addresses, 34

Web browser, 2

   defaults, 79

   opening Web pages in multiple, 9

   previewing Web pages in, 8–9

Web content

   Allow Blocked Content, 152

   and information architects (IAs), 148

   structuring with HTML, 72–73

Web graphics

   overview of, 98–99

   See also graphics

Web hosting companies, 180–181

Web pages, 2

   adding navigation bars, 156–157

   archived, 27

   copying and pasting content between, 62–63

   creating e-mail links, 60–61

   creating visual hierarchy, 77

   download time, 98

   finding photographs for your, 99

   importing, 34–35

   managing, 36–37

   navigation. *See* navigation

   navigation bars, 154–155

   opening, previewing, 8–9

   pasting text into, 48–51

   planning layout, 26–27

   printing, closing, 16–17

   properties, 32–33

   structuring content with HTML, 72–73

   viewing, editing page titles, 174–175

Web server, 2, 180

Web sites, 2

   accessibility, 176–177

   adding title, page description, keywords, 32–33

   backing up files, 28

   changing views, 38–39

   connection types, 180–181

   development process (fig.), 25

   file types (table), 37

   methods of profiling audience (table), 25

   navigation. *See* navigation

   publishing, 2, 184–185

   researching, planning, 24–25

   search engine optimization, 177

   spell-checking, using Thesaurus, 52–53

   using lists for navigation, 78

Web standards, 2

WebDAV, 180

Web-safe colors, 126

Web-safe fonts, 132

Windows Clipboard, 48

World Wide Web Consortium (W3C), 3

   accessibility guidelines (WCAG), 176–177

wrapping style, 106

WYSIWYG, 2

X

(x) background position, 124

XHTML (Extensible Hypertext Markup Language), 77

Y

(y) background position, 124